THE WASHINGTON COMMUNITY
1800–1828

THE
WASHINGTON
COMMUNITY
1800-1828

James Sterling Young

COLUMBIA UNIVERSITY PRESS

New York and London

This study, prepared under the Graduate Faculties of Columbia University, was selected by a committee of the Faculty of Political Science to receive the annual Bancroft Award established by the Trustees of the University.

In 1967 this book received one of the three Bancroft Prizes of equal rank awarded each year by the Trustees of Columbia University for the most distinguished works in American history in its broadest sense, American diplomacy, and the international relations of the United States.

James Sterling Young is Assistant Professor of Government at Columbia University.

FOR ELEANOR AND MILLICENT

PREFACE

This book is about people in power. The behavior of rulers is the subject of analysis, and the group of rulers who comprised the early Washington community is the unit of analysis.

While group approaches have become a familiar feature of the literature on American national government and politics, it is a striking fact that the contingent of power-holders at Washington has not itself been studied as a group. Analytic studies of the national government conventionally focus upon one or a cluster of subunits within the governing group (Congress, an executive bureau, the congressional party, President-and-Congress, for example) and upon only one type of behavior within the group, namely, problem-solving behavior, chiefly policy-making. A growing body of literature thus affords ever better understanding of certain substructures and certain subsystems of behavior within the governing establishment. But the insights that have been brought to bear upon the parts have not been brought to bear upon the establishment as a functioning whole. What is missing is knowledge about the governing group as entity: legislators, executives, judges, and all who gather round them at the seat of power; their inner life as a group; their special world as a governing fraternity; the lifeways and workways, the outlooks and values, the organizational patterns, that distinguish this unique group in American society. What is lacking, in short, is knowledge of the governmental community at Washington.

This study attempts to supply that lack for a brief but important episode in American national development, the Jeffersonian era. It does so with three purposes in mind. The first of these is to bring the government of the new nation within range of modern understanding about human organization in general and about power and politics at Washington in particular.

One cannot survey the literature on national government and politics in the period from 1787 to the Jacksonian era without noting a profound disparity in knowledge about the kind of national government planned at Philadelphia in 1787 and the kind of government that emerged in actual practice after the Constitution was ratified. The choices the constitutional framers made concerning the organization and uses of national power, and the perceptions, values, and interests which underlay their choices have been subjects of exhaustive inquiry. No such knowledge exists about the group of politicians who assembled soon thereafter to govern at Washington. Their problems as rulers of the new nation and their responses to these problems; their choices as to organizational and operational arrangements at their rendezvous on the Potomac; the perceptions, values, and interests underlying their choices: these matters have never systematically been inquired into. Few indeed of the questions that political scientists ask about the rulers today have been asked about the rulers of the young republic. Still less has understanding of the early governing group been brought abreast of modern insights about organized groups.

In consequence, we do not really know what sort of governing establishment the nation commenced its history with. We know only the sort of government it was meant to have. For it is axiomatic that the acts and choices of the participants have fully as much impact upon the nature of an organization as the acts and choices of those who planned it. It is axiomatic that there exist possibilities of disparity between the paper organization and the operative organization, between the formal structure and the informal structure of an organized group. It is axiomatic that knowledge about a given organization of people begins, not ends, with knowledge of what its charter specifies.

Portraiture of the early governmental institution and its problems is thus the first purpose of this study—portraiture which makes use of current knowledge about human organization and political behavior. The aim is to discover what the patterns of behavior and the structure of power among the rulers were, and the extent to which these accorded with the arrangements prescribed by the Constitution. Of particular interest will be the success of the governing group in developing internal leadership—a normal attribute of organized groups but one which the Constitution, intending a government by "separate and rival interests," neither authorized nor encouraged.

The second purpose of this study is to broach new answers to the question of why the rulers behaved the way they did. A legalistic heritage and a democratic ideology have predisposed American political science to search outside the Washington community for explanations of behavior in that community—legalism looking to the Constitution as a determinative influence, and democratic ideology looking to public opinion and constituency "pressures" as determinative influences upon the conduct of men in office. Only in recent years has attention come to be given to influences having their source in the Washington community itself. And political science has yet to confront squarely the proposition that the governing group at Washington, like virtually all other enduring groups, has an inner life of its own—a special culture which carries with it prescriptions and cues for behavior that may be far more explicit than those originating outside the group, and no less consequential for the conduct of government. This study accepts that proposition. It therefore departs from tradition in political science by exploring the inner life and values of the governmental community in detail. One of the concerns of this book, for example, is the attitudes of the ruling group toward power and politics, and the relationship between these attitudes and the way the members comported themselves in official and extraofficial activities. The aim here is not to supplant prevailing determinisms with new ones. Attention is given also to the Constitution and the constituencies as sources of influence upon the men in office in Jeffersonian times; and no prejudgments are made about the importance of intragovernmental influences relative to extragovernmental influences. The aim, rather, is to provide a more complete portrait of the early governing establishment and a broader comprehension of the influences that played upon its members than customary approaches to government can provide.

The third purpose of this study is to learn something about the strengths and weaknesses of the ruling establishment. In viewing the Washington community of 1800–1828 we observe the government of a new nation with an uncertain destiny. We view the nerve center of a loose and fragile polity which was headed for major systemic changes beginning with the Jacksonian revolution in 1828 and, after another thirty years, disintegration and internecine war. Three queries suggest themselves. First, how serviceable was the Washington community, in the years before Jacksonian democracy, as a system for *representing* the disparate interests of a large and heterogeneous society? Second, how serviceable was that community, thirty years before the fracture of the Union, as a system for *governing* a large and heterogeneous society—for managing the potentially disruptive conflicts that inhered in such a society? Finally, were there, in the Jeffersonian era, unsolved problems or unfulfilled needs of the governmental establishment itself which might have acted as stimuli for future political changes? Like most large questions, these require answers more subjective than scientific. But knowledge about the rulers as a group does provide a necessary basis for informed evaluations of their strengths, weaknesses, and problems as a government.

The objectives of this study are, then, to discover how the pioneer rulers of the nation behaved, why they behaved the way they did, and the consequences of their behavior beyond their place and their time in history. While the approach is novel, the subject interest of this work thus places it clearly with recent trends in political science which move the discipline ever nearer to the rulers and how they rule where they rule. Conventionally and simply described, this is a study in depth of the early governing group which will help in understanding the nature of government and politics at Washington, then and now.

Achieving knowledge of a ruling community over a period of

nearly thirty years is a large research task, for every item of behavior and every event taking place at Washington are potential
data on that community. This work is relieved of what would
otherwise have been an impossible burden by the existence of previously published works on the demography and sociology of the
early capital (*Washington: Village and Capital,* by Constance McL.
Green), on the political history of the Jeffersonian era (excellent
examples are Dangerfield's *The Era of Good Feelings* and the
nine-volume history of the Jefferson and Madison administrations
by Henry Adams), and on public administration (Leonard White,
The Jeffersonians), to which the reader is referred for detailed
knowledge on these subjects. The compass of this work precludes
also an intensive investigation of policy-making. The workways
of the ruling group are by no means ignored; the question of policy
leadership is given considerable attention in this book; and preliminary analyses of congressional voting behavior, heretofore lacking, are provided. But a study which takes the Washington community as its unit of analysis does not serve and cannot serve the
essential purposes of a study which takes policy-making as its
central theme.

Yet, for all the mass of material remaining to be explored, to
bring the whole Washington establishment from 1800 to 1828 within
an analytic framework is not the unrealistic aspiration it may seem
at first glance. For the establishment was then very small, the
whole governing group at Washington comprising fewer personnel in 1801 than the number of legislators in Congress today.
Its inner life is, moreover, extraordinarily well recorded in the
published memoirs and correspondence of the members and in a
rich variety of accounts by visitors from abroad, who were attracted by the score to the new nation and especially to the place
where they might view its rulers at work. But it is the circumstance of the government's location at Washington in 1800—after
a period of wandering—which does most to bring the early ruling
establishment within reach of modern scholarship.

For Washington was more than a capital. It was the company
town of the national government—owned by the government,

occupied by the government, conceived and created by the government to serve exclusively the purposes of government, and good for nothing else but government. Thus, the plans and provisions the rulers made for Washington were projections of the rulers' own ideas and images of government. Thus, the physical arrangement of Washington was the structure of the government expressed in terms of space. Thus was politics its outlook, its intellectual and social life, its very existence. Washington at work was the ruling group at work and Washington at leisure was the ruling group at leisure: for here the rulers not only worked together but also resided together, in a remote and isolated outpost with none but themselves for company. The structure of the Washington community was the structure of the governing group itself; even in the settlement patterns of the community one discerns the chosen social groupings of the rulers. The relations between this community and the hinterland society were the relations, in significant aspects, between the governors and the governed.

The assemblage of the rulers in a community therefore affords unusual possibilities for insights about them as a government, and the sheer variety of situations in which they confronted each other, as members of the same community, exhibits their behavior in its widest possible range. The result is a virtually unique opportunity to study the ruling establishment as an entity. History presents the modern scholar with a governmental establishment in the form of a community. It wants only to be analyzed and interpreted.

Stress needs to be given, in closing, to the fact that it is the research accessibility of the ruling group afforded by their residence at Washington—and this alone—which explains why this study begins with the year 1800. The failure to treat the first decade of national government under the Constitution, when New York and Philadelphia were serving as temporary capitals, conceals no assumption that the move to Washington in 1800 produced any basic change in the behavior and attitudes of the ruling group. On the contrary, the patterns of behavior found at Washington were, so far as I have been able to ascertain, already extant or were emergent in the governing group prior to the move to the Potomac. I do not think it likely, furthermore, that a significantly different institutional entity with a significantly different set of problems would have emerged had the governing politicians chosen to remain indefinitely at Philadelphia or New York. To be sure, greater sensitivity to constituency sentiment might have resulted from permanent residence in a larger, less isolated, preestablished city; but it is improbable that the governing group would have made any significantly different adaptation to the demands of a representative government. The amenities and prestigious associations afforded by a continued residence in New York or Philadelphia might have removed one source—but not the most important source—of the restiveness of the group at Washington. Personal, social, and official rivalries within the governing group might have been less intense in a community which afforded more opportunities for the members to escape each other's company after hours; and the greater accessibility to mercantile interests might have precipitated intragovernmental cleavages differing in emphasis, but no less difficult to resolve, than those within the Washington community. In the main, however, the behavior of the governing group and the political problems associated with it were, as this study hopes to make clear, far too deep-rooted and complex to have been caused by environment alone. No inference to the contrary should be drawn from the title or the approach of this work.

My indebtedness to Professors David B. Truman and Richard E. Neustadt extends far beyond the guidance and helpful suggestions they offered as readers of the manuscript. Their desire to make the idea of this book *work* saved it from the flaggings of my own faith that it could work. Each of them opened new perspectives upon the subject matter which I alone would have missed. Enlightenment, a small ray of which may glimmer in these pages, is my gain from association with them both.

Professors Arthur W. Macmahon and Conrad M. Arensberg set the spark which kindled this work. But for the insights I received from them, political scientist and anthropologist respectively, and but for their encouragement of a graduate student groping for new paths, the experimental essay out of which this book grew would never have been written.

For their constructive criticism and commentary on the manuscript I am deeply grateful to Professors Lawrence H. Chamberlain, James P. Shenton, and Ruth Bunzel. More times than I can count, the insights of my wife, Dr. Virginia Heyer Young, retrieved this work from error and brought me new light.

Grateful acknowledgment also is made of a research fellowship from the Samuel S. Fels Fund and of the generosity of Dr. Elizabeth Young Banner.

I am indebted to William F. Bernhardt of Columbia University Press for the finest of editorial assistance. Marc W. Sawyer checked references, a service for which acknowledgment here can only inadequately express my thanks. I am also indebted to Miss Joann Osborn for the drawings in Figures 2 and 3 of this book. Figure 1, the L'Enfant plan, was made available through the courtesy of the New York Public Library.

The magnitude of my indebtedness to those mentioned above makes it my special obligation not to burden them with responsibility for what follows. That is mine alone.

J.S.Y.

October, 1965
Columbia University

CONTENTS

Contents

TABLES

FIGURES

THE WASHINGTON COMMUNITY
1800–1828

THE COMMUNITY PLAN

Though they seem to be always with man, communities and governments are seldom the creatures of man's inspired intellect. Human needs and discontents will endlessly reshape them and impart to them a variety of design; but most are, in their form, the products of cultural convention and, in their purpose, the creatures of necessity. Rare indeed is it to encounter communities or governments which have originated in a truly creative impulse: unprecedented in form, conceived out of nothing save men's visions, and planned into existence. History is not so lavish with the opportunity to create, and men more often imitate than innovate institutions so intricate as these.

The world's first successful rebellion against colonialism presented such an opportunity to the people of the United States, and politicians were at hand to make creative use of it. From their effort, itself unique in human history, there issued a government that was unique in history. Not so widely appreciated is the fact that this extraordinary creative effort was soon followed by another, equally bold. Its issue was a new community, also unique in human history. This was the community of rulers which the world today knows as "Washington."

Washington was created specifically for the national government, a new community for a new sovereign. As fully as any can be, it was a planned community: planned as the occupant government itself had been planned, and in no less detail; planned but four years after the governmental plan itself had been completed; planned for the same larger purpose of securing the institutions of power against

the influence of historical fortuities; the product of that same revolutionary urge—masquerading, illogically, as a love of order and
form where power was concerned—which had inspired the Constitution of 1787.

Customarily, understanding of the legal entity that is American
national government begins with scrutiny of the governmental plan,
the Constitution. To understand the human entity that emerged as
the government of the new nation, the community plan, conceived
for the site at which the governors were to live and work, may usefully serve as the point of departure. For the community plan, no
less than the Constitution, is a blueprint for the governing establishment. No less than the Constitution, the community plan lays down
principles of organization to be followed by the rulers of the nation.
Both plans prescribe frameworks for action, place the actors, set the
stage for the drama of power.

Equally important, the community plan of 1791 projects—as the
constitutional plan of 1787 does not—an image of the new government as seen by the men who actually ran it. The community plan
for Washington is not only the first unambiguous evidence on record but also, in its way, the most eloquent statement on record
about the kind of government that was envisaged and desired by the
pioneer politicians whose job it was to rule the new nation. While
authorship of the plan technically belongs to Major Pierre Charles
L'Enfant, there is a certain hard justice in the relative obscurity to
which history has consigned this unusual figure.[1] For the real authors of the plan for Washington, in all but the narrow and technical
sense, were the rulers themselves. It was they who commissioned a
plan from L'Enfant. It was they who altered his plan, though in
minor ways only, to render it conformable to their desires: some of
the ornamental features called for in the plan were discarded for
reasons of economy; and the governing politicians greeted with profound disinterest L'Enfant's provisions for a national church to be
placed near the heart of the governmental community. It was they
who approved the plan, thus amended, with their "universal applause," [2] as being eminently suited for a community of republican
rulers. It was they who implemented the plan, even though they saw

fit to dismiss L'Enfant himself. It was the governing politicians of the new republic and the generations of politicians following them at Washington who chose to preserve the L'Enfant plan and to make it, still today, the ground plan of the governmental community. For all practical purposes the plan is thus not L'Enfant's at all. In the broader and more meaningful sense, it is the plan of men who were not artists or engineers, as Major L'Enfant was, but politicians and rulers.

What kind of government was it, then, that these ruling politicians envisaged, desired, and intended when they made the plan for the governmental community on the Potomac?

Picture, thrown down upon a rural landscape like a piece of jigsaw puzzle not yet fitted into place, an odd-shaped mosaic of unconventional design, dotted over with open spaces having the appearance of focal points which are laced together by a busy web of streets—avenues of communication radiating outward to every point of the compass: the blueprint for the governmental community (see Figure 1). The plan at once suggests two dominating objectives on the part of the planners: first, to create a community divided into separate and discrete units; second, to create an accessible community, dependent upon some distinctive kind of interaction with the outlying society.

There is no single center in the ground plan of the governmental community, no one focus of activity, no central place for the assembly of all its members. What catches the eye instead is a system of larger and lesser centers widely dispersed over the terrain, "seemingly connected," as L'Enfant put it,[3] by shared routes of communication. It is clear that the planners intended a community whose members were to work or live not together but apart from each other, segregated into distinct units. Among these units, three major centers vie for dominance. They are separated by a considerable distance, and situated so as to command different aspects, avoiding mutual confrontation. One is assigned to the Congress; one to the President; and one to the Court. President Washington had approved this arrangement as being necessary "to obtain the primary object—i.e., the ground and means" for each govern-

FIGURE I. THE L'ENFANT PLAN
1. President   2. Court   3. Congress

mental function.[4] Major L'Enfant offered this percipient explanation: "The main establishment . . . should be begun at various points equidistant as possible from the center; not merely because [separated] settlements . . . are likely to diffuse an equality of advantages over the whole territory allotted . . . but because each of these settlements by a natural jealousy will most tend to stimulate establishments on each of the opposed extremes."[5]

On the highest elevation in the terrain the plan places the Congress. Only one large structure being planned to accommodate its members and component units, this segment of the community appears to have been conceived as a collective entity, to be engaged in collective work.

A mile and a half away, with a different outlook on the landscape, is the center for the executive branch. Unlike Congress the executive has not been treated as a collective entity. The dominating structure here is to be created not by bringing together component units under one roof but by building a palace, a combined office and residence for the President which is oversized for its solitary occupant. This segment of the community was intended, then, to have a ranking personage, suggesting organization along hierarchical or status lines.

As to the subordinate units of the executive branch, their place in the plan had been the subject of controversy. John Adams, presiding officer of the Senate, felt they should all be located near Congress. President Washington, on the other hand, urged a location adjacent to the executive mansion. His reason for insisting, Washington explained, was that "the daily intercourse which the secretaries of the departments must have with the President, would render a distant situation extremely inconvenient to them, and not much less so would one . . . close to the Capitol; for it was the universal complaint of them all, that, while the legislature was in session [during the government's residence at Philadelphia], they could do little or no business, so much were they interrupted by the individual visits of members, (in office hours,) and by calls for papers."[6] While the plan allows space for some executive departments next to the presidential mansion, it fails clearly to define any place for them in the over-all pattern of the community, leaving the determination in large measure to be worked out by the participants themselves.

Wide promenades or avenues radiate in many directions from each of these two major centers of the community, extending outward to its perimeter and opening directly on to the hinterlands beyond. For the Congress and the President the planners thus prescribed independent and coequal systems of communication with the outlying society. Noteworthy is the fact that this objective has taken priority over any effort to interconnect the two: communication between them is provided by a single route which extends beyond both to the edge of the future city. Not only distance but formality and visibility were apparently considered appropriate for the relations between Congress and the President, access being provided by a broad avenue suitable for communication of a ceremonial nature. "No message to nor from the President is to be made," L'Enfant explained, "without a sort of decorum." [7]

The third element of the triad, the Court, is made distinctive in the plan by its exclusion from these lines of communication. Placed roughly equidistant from the presidential and congressional centers, the site for the Court is provided no avenues to render it accessible to either of its coordinate centers within the community or to the outlying society. In a community in which outside communication is planned to figure so prominently it would seem that this segment is an anomaly.

The plan sets aside no space for the productive use of natural resources, and the dispersion of focal centers over the entire expanse of terrain, with the remaining space taken up by elaborate networks of streets, leaves little room for facilities of production on a scale commensurate with the planned size of the community and the needs of its prospective population. While "laid out on a dimension proportioned to . . . greatness," [8] the community is not, therefore, to be a self-supporting economic unit.

Is its greatness, then, to derive from arms? Clearly not. The sole provision for military protection is to be a naval yard occupying less land area than the grounds of the President's mansion. The plan calls for no battlements, no earthworks, no moats, no enclosing walls, no protecting barriers of any sort. Armed boundaries would be wholly incongruous, indeed incompatible, with the basic design of the community, its perimeter pierced on all sides by the open termini of wide avenues facilitating access directly to the centers of the community. Defensibility has not, therefore, merely been ignored in the plan. The plan specifies an open community, intentionally and peculiarly vulnerable to penetration; its accessibility has been preferred over its defensibility, and at the cost of defensibility. The possession of military strength by this community was evidently a prospect feared more by its planners than its survival was valued—its survival by military might, at least. Military considerations having no importance in the ground plan of the community, it may be assumed also that military personages were not intended to occupy dominant positions among its membership. Furthermore, from its accessibility—indiscriminately to friend and foe—this community was meant to be limited to those activities favorably received and supported by its environing society.

Militarily indefensible and economically unproductive, the community was intended, in short, to be a dependent community, not self-directing, without the means to control its own destiny. The wide-ranging avenues which sweep outward from the interior foci of the community plan thus assume importance as the community's intended lifelines, and suggest that the very survival of the occupant institution was meant to be conditioned upon open and free interaction with the outlying society. They reflect, too, an extraordinary effort to inculcate in the community members a sense of this dependence—to instill in them, as L'Enfant expressed it, "grand and far-distant points of view." [9]

But while the community was intended to be in regular, or at least periodic, communication with the outlying society, the routes of communication provided for the plan have not been integrated into any preexisting system of communication in the society. They stop short at the community's frontier, there unjoined to any incoming routes of passage. The pattern of accessibility that is so distinctive of the community plan thus appears to have been dictated by the intrinsic requirements of the institutional design, and not to have been created in response to the pressures of traffic thrusting toward the community from the exterior. While access was invited, one suspects that it was not widely sought. Could a community so planned survive in isolation? In the extension and in the vitalizing of these lines of communication with the outside society appear to lie a major unplanned area of development for the community, and its own greatest need.

Many of the above precepts of the L'Enfant plan require little translation to become familiar. They are renderings, in a different language, of the constitutional prescriptions for the structure and functions of the national government. The plan for government, like the plan for the governmental community, intends a tripartite segmentation of governing personnel, with legislative, executive, and judicial functions assigned to differently composed and differently organized groups within the government. The failure of the community plan clearly to define a place for the administrative units of the executive branch finds its parallel in the ambiguity of the Constitution itself regarding the place of these units in the scheme of "separation of powers." Constitutional and community plan alike specify a subordinate role for the military. The accessibility to the hinterland society of the presidential and congressional centers in the community plan, each independently, has its obvious analogue in the representative character of the constitutional government, and in the establishment of a chief executive elected independently from the legislature. The reclusive situation assigned to the Court in the community plan accords with the situation prescribed for it in the Constitution, its members being nonelective, intentionally sheltered from popular influence outside the government and from presidential and congressional influence inside the government. The dependence of the community on sustaining responses of support and approbation from its environing society that is intended by the community plan reflects the constitutional principle of government by the consent of the governed.

With extraordinary faithfulness, the community plan for Washington repeats the organizing principles, even the ambiguities, of the constitutional plan for government. The similarities between these two plans suggest, therefore, that the principles and values of the practicing politicians who approved the L'Enfant plan coincided, to a most extraordinary degree, with the principles and values of those who had framed the Constitution.

So far, indeed, did constitutional values pervade the thinking of the power-holders themselves—at least in 1791—that they proposed, by their plan for Washington, to make a legal structure originally devised for the limited purpose of policy-making into a pattern for their own community living at the seat of power. The highly contrived, unconventional compartmentations of personnel called for by the Constitution were to be carried over to the whole community structure of the ruling group. The same roles and relationships, the same institutional checks upon power which the Constitution imposed upon their official activities, the governing group elected to impose upon their extraofficial activities as well, in their corporate existence as a community. Here was more than mere token allegiance to the Constitution. Here was an intention to carry the organizing principles of the Constitution far beyond the purposes for which it had been conceived.

Suggestive though it is, however, the plan for the Washington community, like the constitutional plan for government, remains in essence little more than a statement of the kind of governmental establishment the politicians *intended* to create. The two plans, converging in their implicit values and in their organizing principles, may reveal much, or they may reveal little, about the kind of establishment that actually emerged in early Washington. To what extent did the new ruling establishment conform to the paper establishment planned in 1787 and in 1791? Once settled in their new community beside the Potomac, did the ruling politicians actually have the sustaining responses of citizen interest which the community plan suggests they so vitally needed? Once settled on the terrain, how did the ruling politicians actually organize themselves? To what extent did they share the attitudes of the constitutional framers, share their mistrust of power, carry into their extraofficial relationships the constitutional separations of personnel designed to check power? With what implications for the performance of government, the stability of the governing group, the future course of governmental and political development? What place, in a ruling establishment so planned, was left for the political party?

These are the questions of political significance which arise when the plan for the governmental community is brought under scrutiny.

PART ONE

GOVERNMENT AND CITIZENRY

CHAPTER 1

"GOVERNMENT AT A DISTANCE AND OUT OF SIGHT"

Where will Congress find a resting place? —they have led a kind of vagrant life ever since 1774, when they first met to oppose Great-Britain. Every place they have taken to reside in has been made too hot to hold them; either the enemy would not let them stay, or people made a clamour because they were too far north or too far south, and oblige them to remove. . . . We pity the poor congress-men, thus kicked and cuffed about from post to pillar—where can they find a home? [1]

Until 1800, the common governing organization of the American states was an itinerant body. Including the Stamp Act Congress of 1765, it had met at eight towns in four states, a place of reassembly having to be agreed upon, tediously, by each Congress before its adjournment. In Revolutionary times the prospect or eventuation of military action in the vicinity had kept Congress on the move between Philadelphia, Baltimore, Lancaster, and York. Following the cessation of hostilities the meeting place shifted between Philadelphia, Princeton, Annapolis, Trenton, and New York. During these years of itinerancy the government had no authority to control its working environment and depended for protection, provisioning, and physical facilities on the resources of the host community. Usually the members of the government did not enjoy exclusive use of the buildings where official business was conducted, sharing quarters and offices with the state or local government, as at Philadelphia, or squeezed into the faculty room of a college, as at Princeton's Nassau Hall.

The presence of the national body was often uninvited and not always enthusiastically welcomed. In Philadelphia, the community most frequently favored as a meeting place, the government was put to rout by its own troops. In June, 1783, the Pennsylvania statehouse and the Congress convened within were besieged by a mutinous band of Revolutionary militia agitating for overdue pay. Forced to rely for its security on the state authorities, Congress dispatched a delegation to the Executive Council of Pennsylvania upstairs with a request to disperse the mob, only to have them report back that no "exertions were to be looked for from [the Council] except in case of further outrage and actual violence." "Doubt[ing] what measure of outrage would produce this effect," [2] Congress secretly adjourned to reconvene at Princeton two days later— "insulted by the soldiery which it commanded, unsupported by the citizenry in whose name it governed." [3]

The experience at Philadelphia was taken as a lesson for the future, and it served to crystallize the idea that the national government could achieve neither viability nor respectability until it enjoyed freedom from dependence upon state structures. Upon collecting themselves at Princeton, Congress appointed a committee "to consider what jurisdiction may be proper for Congress in the place of its permanent residence," and the panel concluded without dissent that it "ought to enjoy an exclusive jurisdiction." [4] From this time until the objective was realized, it was never seriously disputed that the government ought to have a home and to wield sole authority over the environs; and when Congress at last reached its permanent abode in Washington, that body showed how dearly it prized its freedom from local interference by refusing the District's citizenry the right of formal participation in not only national but also state government.[5] "The indispensable necessity of complete authority at the seat of government, carries its own evidence with it," wrote the author of *The Federalist*, No. 43. "Without it, not only the public authority might be insulted and its proceedings interrupted with impunity; but a dependence of the members of the general government on the State comprehending the seat of government, for protection in the exercise of their duty, might bring on the national councils an imputation of awe or influence, equally dishonorable to the government and dissatisfactory to the other members of the Confederacy."

Although "muteability of place had dishonored the Federal Government," as one convention delegate put it,[6] no decisive commitment to put an end to its itinerant status was made until a more impressive institution of government had been cast by the Constitutional Convention of 1787. The provision for a distinctively governmental community was then made part of the new government plan, which assigned to Congress in Article I, Section 8 of the Constitution the authority

To exercise exclusive legislation in all cases whatsoever over such district (not exceeding ten miles square) as may, by cession of particular States and the acceptance of Congress, become the seat of Government of the United States, and to exercise like authority over all places purchased by the consent of the Legislature of the State in which the same shall be, for the erection of forts, magazines, arsenals, drydocks, and other needful buildings.[7]

While agreement was easily gained on the desirability of a national capital under national jurisdiction, the matter of where to place it, which the Constitution-writers left for Congress to decide, precipitated a long and bitter debate. Barraged ever since 1782 with competitive solicitations from scores of towns, Congress found itself stalemated by intransigent home-town loyalties among its members and was unable to produce a firm majority favoring any one community.[8] An itinerant government—then caricatured in the press as a kind of Trojan horse, concealing the public officials "with their books, papers, etc." [9]—had begun to seem a permanent prospect when Congress finally, in 1790, delegated the choice of a capital site, within a general geographic area, to President Washington.[10]

Of the many considerations which congressmen had urged as paramount in locating the capital—scenic attraction, for example, access to the ocean, military defensibility, hospitality of the inhabitants, climatic advantages—there was only one principle of sufficiently general acceptability to prove useful in organizing majority support for the residence bill of July, 1790. This was the principle that the capital ought to be located at the center of the new nation.

By this was not meant any vital center: a place of flourishing commerce; an urban concentration; a center of high culture, of religion or learning; a place of historic significance; a crossroads of communication. In a representative body on a question arousing the most intense parochial loyalties, the "center" of the nation could be agreeably defined only as an abstract, theoretical center such as the cartographer, the surveyor, or the demographer would construct. Southern congressmen whose region was thus favored made calculations of the midpoint along the north-south axis of the United States, and it was to this principle of spatial centrality that the members committed themselves when they voted to limit the President's choice to a 105-mile stretch of shoreline along the Potomac River "between the mouths of the Eastern Branch [Anacostia River] and the Connogocheague." [11]

The room it left for further maneuvering was no doubt a factor in the passage of the residence bill. It was emphasized that "we are not confined by the bill to a particular spot on the Potomac, but may fix upon a spot as far north as the gentleman from Connecticut wishes"; [12] and the fact that Philadelphia was designated as the temporary capital until 1800 consoled Pennsylvania delegates with the opportunity thus provided for inveigling the government, once there, to remain. Even with these ambiguities the measure passed by a bare margin of two votes in the Senate and three in the House,[13] and then only as part of a political bargain, consummated at Thomas Jefferson's dinner table, between northern Hamiltonians who opposed the Potomac site and southerners who opposed Hamilton's assumption bill. "It was observed," Jefferson reported of his repast, "that this pill [the assumption bill] would be particularly bitter to the Southern states, and that *some concomitant measure should be adopted to sweeten it a little to them.* There had before been a proposition to fix the Seat of Government . . . on the Potomac; and it was thought that . . . this might, as an anodyne, calm in some degree the ferment which might be excited by the other measure alone. So two of the Potomac members (White and Lee but White with a revulsion of stomach almost convulsive) agreed to change their votes, and Hamilton undertook to carry the other point." [14]

The tenuousness of Congress' commitment to a national capital on the Potomac was to manifest itself repeatedly throughout the history of Washington up to the secession of the southern states.

After a two-week reconnaissance of the area during the following October, President Washington decided to locate the federal district at the southernmost extreme of the designated territory. Although the federal district included both Georgetown in Maryland and Alexandria in Virginia, it was soon made clear that neither town would become the capital. Instead the federal city was to be raised on the largely untenanted expanse lying between them on the east bank of the Potomac: the capital was to be, as the national government had originally been, created where nothing was before. That the decision to create an entirely new city for the government was one man's alone seems of minor importance, so precisely consistent was it with the principle accepted in Congress of situating the capital without reference to any preexisting focus of activity, and so fitting to the newness of the government itself. It was, perhaps, an eminently republican choice, this decision of the government to evict itself from the vital centers of national life at the very outset of national history.

At the time, however, the expectation was that the seat of government would itself become the vital center of national life. Throughout the debates on the establishment of a national capital the confidence was widely voiced that the national government, wherever it located, would attract enough wealth, commerce, and population to make the future capital a hub of American enterprise and culture—a Paris in the Île-de-France or, to use the image favored by the leaders, the Rome of the New World.[15]

Confident further that the influx of population and wealth to the governmental seat could be exploited to make the building of the capital a self-financing operation, the President did not request, and Congress did not appropriate, money for this purpose. The President was merely "authorized and requested to accept grants of money."[16] The scheme for financing the capital was, in its essentials, simple. Using funds already promised by Maryland and Virginia, the government would secretly purchase an excess of land on the capital site at a cheap price; and then, having revealed the intention to establish the capital there, would sell the unneeded portions on the open market at a greatly inflated price. The resulting profit would be used to pay administrative costs and for the construction of public buildings, roadways, bridges, parks and other embellishments. The creation of the capital city was thus to be a venture in land speculation, the critical factor in its success being the inflationary effect on land values of heavy citizen demand for locations at the seat of power. The lack of historical precedent for building a governmental center *ex nihil* did not, apparently, generate any misgivings about the bold enterprise. The location of the government in a wilderness did nothing to diminish faith in its drawing power. And the evidence of the congressional debates that the presence of the government was indeed much sought after seemed to justify making the whole undertaking a test of the government's ability to arouse the support and interest of its citizens.

President Washington himself managed the project in its initial phases, and it was not until after the land for the capital had been secured from the farmer-owners that he utilized the administrative apparatus provided by Congress, a three-man commission. He engaged secret agents to negotiate, ostensibly as private buyers, for the land on which the federal town was to be raised.[17] When the local landowners got wind of the intention to locate the capital there, he laid a false scent by creating the impression that the capital was to be built along the Anacostia River instead of the Potomac, ordering surveying operations to begin in that sector.[18] After negotiations through the secret agents had sufficiently matured, the President revealed the government's interest in the site, appeared personally to confront the owners, and, appealing to their sense of patriotism, struck a final bargain. The government paid £25 ($66.50) an acre for land that was afterwards reported to the President at a prevailing market price of £5. It agreed also to sacrifice almost half the net proceeds received from land sales by promising to turn back to the original owners half of the lots not used for official purposes, which they could then sell in a competitive market with the government.[19]

Soundings were taken of the Potomac and the Anacostia so that their suitability for commercial navigation could be advertised. The future city was given the name of the national hero; Jenkins Hill was renamed Capitoline Hill; and Goose Creek, meandering through the center of the future city, officially became the Tiber. The grand design projected for the capital was made public, printers were engaged, and promotional literature was circulated over the land.

Thus prepared for, the first auction of lots was held in October, 1791, on the site, with the President, Thomas Jefferson, and James Madison attending as onlookers.[20] Of ten thousand lots in government hands only thirty-five were sold, four of them bought by the commissioners in order to keep bidding prices up to a profitable level. Actual cash receipts, representing down payments, amounted to only two thousand dollars from a total land holding valued at more than one and a half million dollars. All the lots sold were in the vicinity of the projected President's house, a prestigious location, and none at commercial sites along the river. The sale was closed prematurely on the second day because of the lack of bidders.

Bad weather, the printer's failure to supply copies of Major L'Enfant's grand design for the city in time for the auction, and subversive rumors attributed to northern opponents of the site were held responsible for the poor showing. Yet with the second sale, a year later, came little improvement.[21]

Painstaking efforts were made to stimulate buyer interest at the third public auction in 1793. The capital witnessed its first parade as President Washington and his commissioners, accompanied by two brass bands, the Virginia Volunteer Artillery, and colorfully bedecked Masons filed eastward through the woods of President's Square, forded the Tiber on a felled tree trunk and "a few large stones," and mounted Capitol Hill. After fervent invocations and flamboyant rituals the cornerstone of the Capitol was laid while salvos and fanfares echoed in the stillness of the countryside. A barbecue and "every abundance of other recreation" followed. The President himself then led off the auction by stepping forward to purchase four lots.[22] Few others followed his example, however. This sale fared even worse than the previous two,[23] and it became clear that the primary demand for land in the capital had at once originated and ended with that of the government for its own use.

The President promptly suspended public auctions altogether and directed the commissioners to conduct future sales privately, a stratagem which avoided the humiliation of repeated demonstrations of citizen apathy but which brought land transactions virtually to a standstill.[24] Owing to defaults by previous purchasers the commissioners had almost as many lots on their hands in 1793, at the time of the third auction, as they had started with at the beginning.[25] Over the entire decade between the first land sale and the arrival of the government in 1800 less than one tenth of the lots held by the government were sold at public auction, including those bought by purchasers who later defaulted.[26]

The low volume of land sales, since they were the principal source of funds for building the capital, instantly threatened the whole project with failure. Although the selling price of the lots was nineteen to sixty-three times higher than the cost to the government, the commissioners were seeking loans before the foundations of the first public building had been completed. From 1793 onward they went steadily into debt and by 1796 lots were so unmarketable that reputable creditors refused to accept them even as collateral for loans. Desperate for buyers, the commissioners lost their discrimination. On little more than a promise to lend them money and buy their lots, they passed title to large blocks of land to a syndicate of speculators. "We should, without this contract, have been almost still," they reported to an approving President. But it turned out that the syndicate had insufficient capital either to make the promised loan or to pay for the lots, and the commissioners incurred the disgrace and the impossible financial burden of having to buy back the lots they had given away, in order to regain title.[27] Government aid was the only way out of bankruptcy, and President Washington took this last resort in 1796. To have asked Congress for a direct appropriation would have bared the magnitude of the failure, and its probable result would have been the abandonment of the Potomac site altogether. His communications with Congress on the subject were masterfully adroit. Low volume of sales was attributed to the commissioners' prudence in conserving the government's land treasure; inability to obtain loans was attributed to lack of congressional authority for offering government-owned lots as collateral; and if Congress would give such authority—with the effect of pledging repayment of prospective loans—the legislators could rest assured that real estate values would appreciate sufficiently after the government moved to Washington for future proceeds to cover the cost of the indebtedness.[28]

Congress granted his request, unable to make a better judgment as to what the future held, apparently unaware that the commissioners had been offering government-owned lots as collateral as early as 1792 without the benefit of congressional authority, and not knowing that Congress' guarantee of repayment—and not public lots—was the only collateral that would satisfy creditors.[29]

One can only guess whether their abortive efforts to recruit a citizen proprietorship for the capital caused the leaders to doubt that much-vaunted theory of the *The Federalist* which esteemed it an element of strength for the national government to be freed from dependency upon the states and based directly upon the people—"the fountain of all authority." For it was states, not citizens, that were revealed to have a proprietary interest in the national establishment, and it was states that came to the rescue when the entire project was threatened with collapse. Maryland and Virginia, no doubt fearing the loss of the capital, finally provided the loans which would allow work to continue on the public buildings.[30]

Lack of buyers and lack of money were by no means the only symptoms of a meager public response to the new governmental establishment. The trickle of newcomers was insufficient even to supply labor needs for the three public buildings which had been commenced by 1800—the executive mansion, the Treasury, and one wing of the Capitol—let alone for clearing the land. The commissioners turned to Europe in a futile effort to recruit skilled labor. For unskilled labor they resorted to hiring slaves from nearby plantation owners. Street-clearing was virtually abandoned after a few swaths of trees had been topped; and work on the President's house had to be halted before it was half finished so that the workers could make the Capitol habitable in time for Congress' arrival.[31]

Private enterprise had been counted upon for housing construction, and the commissioners had neither plans nor funds to provide the government personnel with places to live. But private enterprise had produced, by one report, only four new houses and one tavern in the five years following the first land sale; and the commissioners, under pressure from the President to reside in the city they were supposed to be promoting, begged off on the ground that "no decent houses" were to be had.[32] To stimulate private construction they suspended their original ban against frame and single-story dwellings—only to witness a mushrooming of workers' shantytowns, one such appearing on the very grounds of the executive mansion. They lowered the price of lots to purchasers who would build on them and, alternatively, required owners to build before they could resell their lots—only to produce a welter of jerry-built houses which, being too expensive for resident laborers, remained unoccupied and fell victim to vandals and the elements.[33] When the government arrived in 1800, only 109 "permanent" structures (brick or stone) stood in all of Washington, to house the 500 families already residing there and an additional 300 civilian members of the government, many of them with families of their own. The commissioners then reported 372 dwellings as "habitable," but, as a cabinet officer noted, "most of them [are] small miserable huts." [34]

Commerce, instead of increasing, waned. After years of growth, business at the port of Georgetown fell off steadily from the time the location of the new capital was announced, and in 1796 the value of exports was only half what it had been in 1791.[35] Three of the four commercial enterprises which came to Washington had closed their doors within a decade, a brewery alone surviving.[36]

Blight, not prosperity, was everywhere evident as the time approached for the arrival of the government. The new capital was, to a shocked congressman, "both melancholy and ludicrous . . . a city in ruins." [37] The only entire block of buildings in the town was falling to pieces, having been seized for debt on the verge of completion. A luxurious structure, intended as the grand prize in a money-raising lottery that had failed, was made prominent in its half-finished and abandoned state by a large crimson sign reading HOTEL. Near it, abandoned by the commissioners for lack of funds, were mosquito-breeding excavations for a city canal.[38] Greenleaf's Point, the largest single cluster of buildings in the city, presented "the appearance of a considerable town, which had been destroyed by some unusual calamity. There are fifty or sixty spacious houses, five or six of them inhabited by . . . vagrants, and a few more by decent looking people; but there are no fences, gardens, nor the least appearance of business." [39] In the commercial sector along the Anacostia's banks, Albert Gallatin found "a very large but perfectly empty warehouse, and a wharf graced by not a single vessel." [40] On Rock Creek lay the ruins of a bridge intended to provide Washington with outside communication via a post road. Supported by an arch of thirteen stones inscribed for the original states, this symbol of the Union had collapsed because of its experimental and untested design.[41]

Optimists attributed the debacle to the physical absence of the government, and nourished their hopes on the belief that the arrival of the governmental contingent in 1800 would change the capital's fortunes. "There appears to be a confident expectation that this place will soon exceed any in the world," observed a cabinet official; "Mr. Thornton, one of the Commissioners, spoke of a population of 160,000 as a matter of course in a few years." [42]

But the governmental presence failed throughout the Jeffersonian era, and failed utterly, to attract the commerce, the wealth, and the population that were needed to make the capital prosper. The dismal history of land sales from 1791 to 1800 repeated itself after 1800. Contrary to every hope, two auctions held a year after the government arrived failed to yield enough proceeds to repay the first installment on the commissioners' indebtedness, even though they sold some of the land below cost.[43]

Hopes for a great university to grace the capital faded when Congress refused financial assistance, and plans to raise private money by lottery ended with the incarceration of the lottery operator.[44]

All measures to attract commerce were unavailing. Renewed
efforts to build a canal giving Washington access to the growing
markets and rich resources of the Ohio Valley ended in a virtually
total loss for local stockholders in the venture and in Washington's
acquisition of an eyesore and an open sewer.[45] Competition for
commerce led Georgetown citizens to invest in costly dredging of
the Potomac which instead clogged the channel and cut off Alexandria from its upriver traffic. Alexandria citizens built a bridge across
the Potomac which created a navigational obstruction to commercial shipping that Washingtonians were trying to attract from
downriver.[46] Shortage of money led local banks to issue floods of
scrip not covered by specie reserve and the commissioners to issue
"slips of paper signed by the mayor and bearing a face value of anything from a penny to a dollar." The brief blaze of prosperity that
ensued from these measures, and from increased government expenditures on the Washington Navy Yard during the War of 1812,
fizzled as quickly as it flared, ending in the further impoverishment
of the local economy. To the problems of scarce investment capital
and the burdens of repairing the destruction wreaked by the British
raiders were added the blights of numerous merchant bankruptcies,
the collapse of four of the thirteen local banks, and a drastic reduc-
tion in consumer purchasing power.[47] Congress, instead of coming to
the rescue, talked of abandoning Washington forever.[48] Sentiment
favoring a change of capital came close to prevailing in 1814, and
uncertainty about the government's permanence further tarnished
Washington's reputation as a place of business.

In consequence, there was "not a single great mercantile house"
in the District of Columbia, observed a foreign dignitary in 1811–
12;[49] "no trade of any kind" (1828);[50] a "total absence of all sights,
sounds, or smells of commerce" (1832).[51] "The greatest and most
respectable business that is done in Washington," read a handbook
for newcomers in 1829, "is keeping boarding-houses."[52]

The presence of power proved as weak an attraction for population as for commerce. Dreams of a city of "160,000 in a few years"
were dashed against the reality of a village of less than 10,000 whites
after twenty years of government residence.[53] The nation grew

faster than the nation's seat of government. With the 1800 influx of government personnel discounted, the District of Columbia's population growth lagged 12 percentage points behind the national rate to 1830, and from 115 to more than 300 percentage points behind the growth rate of the nation's four principal urban counties.[54]

The better part of Washington's population increase, moreover, was not of a sort to enhance the ruling establishment. For it was not, by and large, the people of substance or of political purpose whom the government attracted to Washington: planters and financiers; men of accomplishment in trade or business; educated persons; spokesmen for citizen interests in search of political influence; newsmen in search of stories. The press galleries of the Capitol were empty in the Jeffersonian era except for a local newspaper publisher or two, who doubled as reporters for the official record; and press conferences were unknown. No national associations made the government's headquarters their headquarters, and few came on errands to Washington. Resident lobbyists, in the modern definition of the term, there were none. Far more in evidence than citizens, among the delegations who visited early Washington, were Indians, come to present grievances or to pay respects to the white father. Outsiders eager to assist and manipulate the operations of government were conspicuous by their absence; the drama of national politics in early Washington was played without this supporting cast of characters whom big government and a complex industrial society have since attracted to the residence of power.

Rather, the ruling establishment acted as magnet for society's idle and society's unwanted: people sick in mind or body, imagining conspiracies against them, imploring help, or bent upon revenge; pleaders for pardons and reprieves; small-time confidence men; needy pamphlet-writers, selling their talents for calumny for the price of a public printing contract; "a class of swaggering sycophants . . . forc[ing] themselves into the presence of distinguished and well-bred people." [55] Most conspicuously of all it was the indigent who migrated to Washington—"the straggling vagabond beggars, which the seat of government draws together," [56] their hopes fastened on a merciful sovereign, a bountiful treasury, and public jobs. The government had jobs for but a handful, no bountiful treasury, and no authority for philanthropy; and there were no industries to employ the new arrivals. Stranded penniless, they stayed on in the wilderness capital to survive, many of them, on handouts, or by petty thievery, or by servitude: "The people are poor, and live like fishes, by eating each other." [57] In 1802, only 233 males in a local population of approximately four thousand owned personal and real property having a value, separately or combined, of one hundred dollars or more.[58] In 1803, census takers could classify only one sixth, roughly, of the white residents as to occupation: 363 laborers and mechanics; 86 merchants and hostelers; 22 professional persons; and 15 "gentlemen." [59] Washington grew old and tired while it was still new: funds sorely needed for community betterment went instead into jails, an asylum for the insane, orphanages and schools for pauper children, a workhouse for the "safeguarding of vagrants." Poor relief claimed 42 percent of the town's revenue as early as 1802, and the unconscionable burden of caring for the poor prompted the town fathers to ask the government in 1820 for authority to keep indigents from entering the boundaries. When Congress refused, what was probably America's first soup kitchen was set up on Capitol Hill.[60]

The disillusionment was complete. The seat of government had become, instead of the national emporium, the nation's poorhouse, a travesty upon power itself.

To what may this fiasco be attributed? Why was the public response to the national government as a social presence so markedly different from the public response to the Constitution when it had been presented for ratification? Poor location and bad publicity obviously contributed. Clearly, too, mismanagement and miscalculation by those responsible for planning and building the capital were factors. Their ineptitude was so great and their miscalculations so enormous, indeed, as to raise the question of how deeply motivated these men were to make the seat of government the vital center of the nation. Would men wholly committed to the ideal of a flourishing metropolis for the governmental residence have isolated the government from all the established centers of national life, chosen a wilderness for its site, and placed it beside a river dubiously navigable where it was not wholly impassable because of rapids and falls? Would they then have staked the success of the venture upon the willingness of citizens to migrate in force to this wilderness and to pay for the privilege of residing near the politicians of the nation? Would they have required citizens even to travel to the spot in order to buy their plots, instead of making them purchasable in the towns where the people lived—at local post offices, for example? Would they have failed to use the most obvious source of funds for making the capital a showplace—the public treasury?

It could be that the rulers, in staking the success of the venture upon a favorable mass response, were utterly blind to the possibility that a free citizenry may also be a politically indifferent citizenry. It could be, too, that they entertained a colossally distorted notion of their own importance in the public eye. But it would be less surprising, in explanation of their "ineptitude" in making a capital, to find some measure of ambivalence concerning the objective itself: to find, among men of republican sentiments, something less than a wholehearted dedication to the task of centering the life of the nation around the seat of national government.

It is doubtful, however, that the most unambivalent commitment and the most expert management on their part would have significantly altered the course of events that made such a dismal travesty of their magnificent visions. The failure to attract population, wealth, commerce, and all the embellishments of high culture to the seat of government would appear to stem from deeper causes than poor location, difficult logistics, bad publicity, and bad management. Fundamentally, it would appear that the government itself was an institution of too little significance to attract population and wealth to its residence.

For the government of Jeffersonian times was not, by any candid view, one of the important institutions in American society— important as a social presence or important in its impact upon the everyday lives of the citizens. It was, for one thing, too new, an unfamiliar social presence in a society whose ways of living and whose organization of affairs had developed over a century without any national governmental institution whatever: a society of preeminently provincial attachments. Even those who came to Washington as elected persons must have found the places of power dubiously rewarding, for they resigned in extraordinarily high numbers to continue their office-holding careers elsewhere than in Washington.[61] And if the seats of power themselves held so little attraction, what incentive was there for ordinary citizens and free men to pay for places below the throne?

The early government was also a small institution, small almost beyond modern imagination. In 1802, the twelfth year of its existence under the Constitution, the entire task force of national government—army, navy, marines, and all the civil establishments abroad and in the continental United States—numbered considerably fewer persons than the federal employees now engaged in Indian affairs, or in apprehending federal criminals (see Table 1). Less than three thousand nonuniformed personnel were affiliated with the institution: one (federal) public servant for every 1,914 citizens, as against one for every sixty-two today. Still less impressive was the size of its headquarters contingent on the Potomac (see Table 2). The official members of the governmental community, two years after they arrived in Washington, numbered 291—roughly one-fifth the size of a single army battalion, including a bureaucracy not as numerous as Congress. Twenty-seven years later, at the end of the Jeffersonian era, the headquarters establishment had barely more than doubled in size. Of this increase, 40 percent was due to an increase in the number of legislators and 41 percent to an increase in the civil staff of the Treasury Department and General Post Office. The whole comprised a mere 625 men in 1829, from the lowliest clerk, messenger, and page boy to the President, members of Congress, and Supreme Court justices. Some establishment for the government of a nation; some government to inspire a mass trek to Washington!

Small size indicated slightness of function. Two months of the year spent in Washington were sufficient for the Supreme Court to perform its business. Congress ordinarily worked only after the harvest season and before spring planting. There was no Chief Execu-

TABLE I

THE GOVERNMENTAL ESTABLISHMENT, 1802 [a]

		Percent of total	Percent of nonuniformed total
Fighting establishment [b]			
Nonuniformed personnel:			
War Department, Washington	19		
War Department, field	74		
Navy Department, Washington	11		
Navy Department, field	13		
Uniformed personnel:			
Army	3,350		
Navy	2,488		
Marine Corps	524 6,479	70.1	4.1
Revenue-producing functions			
Treasury Department, Washington	89		
Collectors of revenue	1,223		
Deputy postmasters	947		
Land offices	8 2,267	24.6	78.9
Leadership			
Congress [c]	152		
Supreme Court	7		
Presidency [d]	2 161	1.7	5.6
Foreign relations			
State Department, Washington	9		
Ministers and legations	10		
Consulates	63		
Treaty commissioners and agents	34 116	1.3	4.0
Social control and law enforcement			
Attorney General, Washington	1		
District judges	36		
District attorneys	24		
Marshals	24		
Clerks	18 103	1.1	3.6
Citizen benefits and nonrevenue services			
Lighthouses, navigation	40		
Pension administration	38 78	0.8	2.7
Miscellaneous			
U.S. Mint	13		
Purveyor of public supplies	4		
Territorial administration			
(civil employees)	15		
Commissioner of Patents	1 33	0.4	1.1
Total, all personnel	9,237	100.0	100.0
Total, nonuniformed personnel	2,875		

Source: Civil and Military List of February 17, 1802, *ASP*, Misc. Ser., I, 260–319. Exceptions noted below.
[a] Many personnel were not limited to a single function, and the categories

tive and no cabinet at the seat of government for almost three months of each year, usually; and the government of the nation was entrusted largely to the chief clerks of departments during the summer season.

What government business there was was not, most of it, of a sort to attract any widespread, sustained citizen interest. As a task force, the early government was an organization principally of warriors and revenue collectors. Approximately 95 percent of its manpower was assigned to military functions and to the production of revenue, with more than four times as many personnel engaged in servicing the national treasury as were assigned to all other civil functions of government, foreign and domestic. How attenuated were its functions as an instrument of social control is indicated by the fact that there were more people making the law than enforcing it, Congress outnumbering the whole law enforcement establishment including marshals, district attorneys, and federal courts. As a provider of services and benefits to citizens, the national government was insignificant, unless one counts the postal service, which was then looked upon, and actually was, a profit-making enterprise of the Treasury Department.[62] And a government could not be very

---

used in the table are intended merely to indicate the major assignments of the governmental personnel. The postal service is treated as a revenue function because it was part of the Treasury Department, because it was generally considered to be a revenue activity, and because it did in fact yield profits which were turned into the general funds of the Treasury. See White, *The Jeffersonians*, pp. 302–3.

[b] The figure for uniformed Army personnel is the number authorized by statute. (2 Stat. 132.) The Marine Corps figure represents less than the actual statutory authorization; it is the number actually on duty in 1803, the nearest year for which exact information is available. As for the uniformed Navy personnel, the Civil and Military List enumerates only commissioned officers and midshipmen. The number of noncommissioned personnel has been estimated on the basis of operational crew complements for 4 frigates of 44 guns (291-man crew each), 1 frigate of 36 guns (234-man crew), 2 frigates of 32 guns (162-man crew each), 1 small frigate of 32 guns (147-man crew), 1 schooner of 12 guns (80-man crew), and skeleton crews for 4 additional vessels laid up and partially dismantled in the Washington Navy Yard (280 men). (See *ASP*, Naval Affairs, I, 77, 83, 111, 119.)

[c] Includes the Vice President and all clerks and ancillary personnel, as well as Senators and Representatives.

[d] The President and his personal secretary, who was paid out of the appropriation for the maintenance of the executive mansion in an amount at the President's discretion.

TABLE 2

THE HEADQUARTERS ESTABLISHMENT AT WASHINGTON IN 1802 AND 1829[a]

	1802		*1829*	
Executive branch				
Presidency	2		2	
Treasury Department and General Post Office	89		226	
War Department	19		34	
Navy Department	11		23	
State Department, including Patent Office	10		32	
Attorney General's Office	1	132	1	318
Legislative branch				
Vice President	1		1	
Senators	32		48	
Representatives	106		225	
Ancillary personnel (clerks, officers, librarian)	13	152	25	299
Judicial branch				
Supreme Court justices	6		7	
Clerk	1	7	1	8
Total		291		625

Sources: For 1802, the Civil and Military List of February 17, 1802, *ASP*, Misc. Ser., I, 260–319; for 1829, *A Register of Officers and Agents, Civil, Military, and Naval in the Service of the United States, on the 30th of September, 1829.*

[a] The table above does not include personnel employed at the Washington Navy Yard, nor a small number of federal employees appointed to serve the District of Columbia and not part of the headquarters establishment, e.g., local post office personnel, district attorney and marshals, customs officers, and judges.

much more than a debating society which had, at its headquarters, a Congress larger than its administrative apparatus.

Almost all of the things that republican governments do which affect the everyday lives and fortunes of their citizens, and therefore engage their interest, were in Jeffersonian times *not* done by the national government. The administration of justice, the maintenance of law and order, the arbitration of disputes, the chartering and supervision of business enterprise, road building and the maintenance of transportation systems, the schooling of the young, the care of the indigent, even residual control over the bulk of the military forces—these functions fell principally within the province of state and local governments to the extent that any governmental bodies performed them. An institution whose involvement in the in-

ternal life of the nation was limited largely to the collection and delivery of letters could hardly have been expected to be much in the
citizens' consciousness, let alone to attract many to Washington.
"The links of connection formed by Congress, whatever may be
their effects in giving union to the country in its collisions with foreign powers," a British diplomat at Washington observed in 1811–
12, "are too little felt in the ordinary concerns of life to vie in any
considerable degree with the near and more powerful influence produced by the operations of the local government[s]." [63] In 1823 a
Representative observed "that this Government, if put to the test
. . . is by no means calculated to endure, as a Government for the
management of the internal concerns of this country . . . [be-
cause] it is a government not having a common feeling and a common interest with the governed." [64] To the truth of these observations the vast, unpeopled spaces and the unfinished public structures
of Washington in the Jeffersonian era bore eloquent testimony.

Small wonder, then, that the public response to government as a
social presence was so very different from the public response to the
Constitution when it was presented for ratification in 1787–88. Small
wonder that a people already on the move westward did not turn
east to the place where politicians congregated. Small wonder that
the invitation to gather round an institution so new and unfamiliar,
so slight in size and so meager in its business, so inessential to the
achievement of individual life goals, received little reply but from
society's idle and its rejected. The failure of the efforts to make a
flourishing capital was no more, and no less, than a failure to create
an important center of activity around an institution of secondary
social importance at best. The failure of people to come to Washington was not so much the work of inept management as it was the
people's judgment upon the significance of national government itself.

As cogently as the causes of this failure, its consequences compel
attention, namely, the isolation of the governors from the governed.

"Monks in a monastery," the rulers at Washington called themselves.[65] It may have been hyperbole with respect to their behavior, but it was realistic with respect to the situation of a governing

group consigned to sylvan solitude. Theirs was the lot of governing a society which they could neither see clearly nor know well except in the fragments of it that were their own home constituencies. They did not even know the shape of the new entity called the nation in 1800, in so basic a matter as precisely where its frontiers lay; they had no inventory of national facts upon which to draw except what the tax revenues and the decennial census revealed about the state of the country.[66] They had no observers and listeners among their own people as they had in the capitals of Europe. To remind them of what and whom they were governing, nothing representative of American life was visible in their surroundings. They failed to encounter, when they were governing, those critically important surrogates of the popular will that bother but also aid and inform the men in office today—the citizen delegates trooping to the capital full of opinions to air and demands to press, the quasi-official cadres of reporters, lobbyists, pollsters, professional party politicians, bringing the officeholders' constituencies within talking distance and providing clues to the public mood. For almost all exchanges of intelligence with the outside world they were dependent upon mail that was not only slow in arriving but was also subject to compromise by prying eyes.[67] They were a governing group who could not know, in the War of 1812, for a whole month after the fact whether the nation was at peace or war. Necessarily they governed in uncertainty if not in ignorance about their standing with their constituents, save as they made their hazardous journeys home once each year in spring thaws or summer heat.

One wonders what feelings Alexander Hamilton might have experienced if he had witnessed early Washington and recalled his words in *The Federalist*, No. 27: "A government continually at a distance and out of sight can hardly be expected to interest the sensations of the people." Intended as an epitaph for the old Confederation, no better phrase describes national government throughout the Jeffersonian era than government "at a distance and out of sight." Put in a wilderness, beyond the horizons and off the pathways of a busied citizenry, the government had won release from the captivity of the states, but at the cost of being marooned. It had acquired a citizen constituency, only to be shunned by citizens. Rulers had won a place in the new nation, but only to become pariahs, quarantined in the countryside.

The modern image of Washington as a vital center and of government as the target for citizen demands of every sort ill prepares us for the image of a sequestered and secluded governmental community that emerges from the record of 1800–1828. Perhaps it is due to a tendency to project this modern image upon the past that the isolation of the early government has received no more than perfunctory notice in studies of early political history. But whatever the reason for the omission, a realistic perception of government in the young republic requires it to be corrected. Remoteness of the rulers from the citizenry and remoteness of the citizenry from the rulers is a circumstance not to be taken lightly in assessing any national polity, and it is particularly ominous in a new nation which is constituted a representative republic. Discovery of that circumstance in the early republic opens new perspectives upon its government, its politics, and its evolution as a political system.

If the failure of the governmental community to attract citizens either as residents or as bearers of political demands was, indeed, a significant measure of citizen interest in national government, then the political quiescence of the country that generally characterized the Jeffersonian era appears in a rather different light from that familiarly presented in history texts. The comparatively low "temperature" of national politics and its relative decorum before the Jacksonian era may have testified not so much to the skill of a ruling Republican oligarchy as to a generalized or residual indifference among citizens toward national government itself. Negligibility of public response to the presence and the work of the early government was in any case the equivalent, in operational terms, of public apathy toward government.

One wonders, therefore, whether eliciting the interest and attachment of a free people was not a more fundamental problem for the newly established government than the problem of deciding policy for a free people. To observers of emerging nations today the problem of building citizen interest and support for a new governmental establishment is not unfamiliar. Neither was it unfamiliar to Alexander Hamilton when he wrote pessimistically, in *The Federalist*, No. 27, about the capacity of "government at a distance and out of sight" to "interest the sensations of the people."

> The more citizens are accustomed to meet with [government] in the common occurrences of their political life, the more it is familiarized to their sight and to their feelings, the further it enters into those objects which touch the most sensible chords and put in motion the most active springs of the human heart [he observed], the greater will be the probability that it will conciliate the respect and attachment of the community. . . . The more it circulates through those channels and currents in which the passions of mankind naturally flow, the less will it require the aid of the violent and perilous expedients of compulsion.

One can thus detect, in the isolation of the governmental community and the citizen indifference which gave rise to it, a major operational problem for the rulers of the new nation and a major dilemma for a representative government founded on the doctrine of popular sovereignty: How to "interest the sensations of the people" and "avoid the violent and perilous expedients of compulsion"? The Jeffersonian era dramatized rather than solved this problem of a distant and isolated government. But the Jeffersonians were succeeded by a new breed of rulers, riding to power on that very surge of popular interest so conspicuously lacking in earlier government. Is there, then, a new significance to be discerned in the Jacksonian revolution?—in the development of that lively interaction between government and citizenry which marked the end of the Jeffersonian era, began the era of Andrew Jackson, and ultimately made Washington the "crowded pinnacle of democracy"? While Jacksonian democracy lies beyond the scope of this study, discovery of an isolated governing group does suggest the wisdom of reexamining this "revolution" in government-citizenry relationships for its functional significance in solving the problem of government at a distance and out of sight.

Not only institutional needs but also the interests of the power-holders would seem to have dictated efforts to arouse citizen interest in men and policies at Washington. Isolation of the ruling establish-

ment further suggests, therefore, the wisdom of searching the inner
life and politics of the Jeffersonian governmental community for possible sources of the Jacksonian impulse. Perhaps we ought to look
inside the Washington community of 1800–1828, not solely outside
it in the constituencies, for initiatives in developing those techniques
and institutions for arousing popular interest that were the trade-
mark of the Jacksonian movement. Perhaps we ought to reconsider,
in the historical context of the era ending with the victory of the
Jacksonians, that pervasive and eminently democratic precept which
instructs us to ignore "the principal politicians strutting across the
stage in Washington"—to quote a recent student of American
politics—and to look "out into the country . . . among the people
themselves" for the "real drama" and the prime moving force of national politics.[68]

Isolation of the governmental community opens new perspectives
not only upon political developments following the Jeffersonian
era but also upon policy-making at Washington during the Jeffersonian era. Awareness of the manipulative aspects of modern lobbying, aided and abetted by hallowed democratic doctrine, tends to
nourish a widespread belief that the policy choices of the men in
government are determined by influences having their source outside the governmental establishment itself. The determining influence of extrinsic factors is, indeed, a major premise of large segments of the literature on American government, while intragovernmental influences upon the political behavior of men in office
have tended to be either ignored altogether or relegated to minor
significance. Such an explanatory framework does not consistently
capture the reality of policy-making even under modern conditions
of intense citizen pressures and sophisticated lobbying techniques. It
positively distorts the reality of policy-making in the environment
of 1800–1828. If, as scholars take increasing pains to point out,
policy-makers in modern government still have considerable latitude
of choice, the isolated circumstances of the early governing group
must have afforded a freedom of choice as nearly uninhibited as any
representative government could have. For the Jeffersonian period,
therefore, we must abandon prevailing notions about why the men

in government perform the way they do. Isolation of the governmental community downgrades the significance of public opinion and citizen pressure as influences upon policy-making, and it sharply upgrades the significance of intragovernmental influences on the political behavior of men in government. In a period when government was conducted as nearly in a vacuum as it ever has been, the internal organization and the internal culture of the governmental community assume paramount significance as influences upon governmental performance.

For all these reasons, then, knowledge about the inner life of the governmental community at Washington becomes imperative for understanding the political system of the new nation. It is to that subject that our attention now turns. If the public did not respond according to plan, did the politicians of the Washington community? Freed from distracting influences, isolated beside the Potomac, virtually unwatched by the citizenry, did they establish a society and a group culture quite different from that envisaged by the Constitution and the community plan? These are the questions of political significance which Part Two will attempt to answer.

PART TWO

THE RULING ESTABLISHMENT

CHAPTER 2

"THE NATIONAL BANTLING"

Almost no one, it seemed, could find anything flattering to say about the capital in the Jeffersonian years. To travelers and diplomats from abroad, the showcase of the new nation was a gigantic monument to pretension, the confirming evidence that the Americans had attempted something beyond their capacities. "Voilà un Capitol sans Ciceron; voici le Tibre sans Rome," said one visitor, and recited Thomas Moore's famous gibe about "This embryo capital, where Fancy sees/ Squares in morasses, obelisks in trees." [1] Among Americans, also, the capital became a butt for jokes, and poking fun at Washington became something of a national pastime. "The national bantling" it was dubbed, the benighted and ungainly offspring of the nation. "The Federal city is in reality neither town nor village," crowed a Philadelphia editor; "it may be compared to a country seat where state sportsmen may run horses and fight cocks; kill time under cover and shoot Public Service flying. . . . There sits the President . . . like a pelican in the wilderness, or a sparrow upon the housetop." [2]

And to those whom ambition and desire for service brought to Washington, it became "this city which so many are willing to come to and all [are] so anxious to leave." [3] For the utter desolation that public disinterest had made of their environment was not the least of those "splendid torments" that Jefferson called the political vocation: Washington was an ever-present reminder to the men in power of the low esteem in which power was held.

The stage for the national drama was a vast construction site "bearing the marks of partial labour and general desertion." [4] Two unfinished stark white citadels towered above the terrain from hill-tops on opposite shores of a dismal swamp, more like ruins amid the fallen fragments of their own stone than new and rising edifices. Where monuments had been planned, brush piles moldered and rubbish heaps accumulated. Where majestic avenues were to sweep, swaths of tree stumps stood, rough quarried stones marking the intersections. Where houses were to be, barren hillocks, stripped of vegetation, rose like desert islands amid a sea of bogs and marshes.

Cows grazed on future plazas and bullfrogs chorused on the mall. Wildlife overran the premises. "Antoine killed a brownish snake, two feet long, in the house, at the foot of the staircase," reads the diary of the Secretary of State; "the heat of the weather almost unremitted, with myriads of flies, bugs, and vermin of all filths, adds to the discomforts, if not to the anxieties of this occupation." [5] Hogs rooted in the refuse that was discarded in the roadways and it was not until 1820 that scavengers were hired to clean it away.[6] Epidemics of fever were chronic, abetted by "several immense excavations of brick yards always full of green stagnant water . . . and numerous dead carcasses left to putrify," and by the sluggish Tiber which fed mosquito-infested marshes.[7]

Except for poverty's children, subsisting in windowless shacks in the copses and in the heatless chambers of an unfinished hotel, population was not much in evidence. "One might take a ride of several hours within the precincts without meeting with a single individual to disturb one's meditation." [8] "There was a stillness and vacuity over the whole place." [9] "In the very heart of the city . . . not a sound is to be heard" by day,[10] and, by night, only the sounds of idleness emanated from the little house-rows dotting the woods around: baying dogs, squalling cats, parlor music, and domestic feuds—"yelling of savages in the wilderness would be as much if not more entertaining," a Treasury auditor wrote of summer evenings along executives' row.[11] "Every thing here seems in a dead calm," observed a newly arrived congressman; "an absolute supineness overwhelms all." [12]

To this Rome, with its Tiber and its Capitoline, few roads led. The bridge across the Potomac that was the capital's main link to

the west was fired during the British occupation in 1814, simultaneously by the enemy on the Washington side and a zealous American
corporal on the Virginia side.[13] To the east communication was restricted largely to the Bladensburg Road, which had its terminus in
Georgetown. Members sometimes had difficulty finding their way
to the capital. The President's wife once got lost in the woods en
route from Baltimore, "wandered two hours without finding . . .
the path," and at last came upon a vagabond whom she engaged as a
guide "to extricate us out of our difficulty." [14]

It was almost as difficult to find one's way inside the capital as into
it. There were no sidewalks or lamps to guide one by night, no signs
as guides by day, and roads meandered into cow trails. A group of
congressmen returning from a dinner party near what is now called
Haines Point got lost and spent until daybreak in their carriage
weaving through bogs and gullies in search of Capitol Hill, only a
mile away.[15] Houses were so far between and so few of the streets
had been laid out that the inhabitants found it necessary to identify
their place of residence in directories not by house number nor street
but by the public building nearest them—"a few paces from the Capitol," "near the President's house," "west of the War Office," "opposite the Treasury." As late as 1817 a cabinet officer gave for his
address in the *Congressional Directory* the "high ground north of
Pennsylvania Avenue." And even in 1832 this intended thoroughfare was yet so undeveloped that the new Treasury building then
erected was later discovered to have been placed athwart it, pre-
empting the President's vista eastward to Capitol Hill and necessitating a permanent detour of traffic between the Capitol and the
White House.[16] When Anthony Trollope spoofed Washington in
1862 he was realistically describing the city in the Jeffersonian era,

where a man may lose himself . . . not as one loses oneself in London
between Shoreditch and Russell Square, but as one does so in the deserts
of the Holy Land, between Emmaus and Arimathea. In the first place no
one knows where the places are, or is unsure of their existence, and then
between their presumed localities the country is wild, trackless, unbridged,
uninhabited and desolate. . . . Tucking your trousers up to your knees,
you will wade through bogs, you will lose yourself among rude hillocks,
you will be out of the reach of humanity.[17]

Paved streets were unknown and roads were few, dust bowls in dry weather and morasses when it rained. To venture forth upon them was to risk life, limb, and vehicle. Diplomats in full regalia, paying state visits, would find themselves marooned outside the executive mansion in their magnificent equipages, mired in the red mud of Pennsylvania Avenue "to the axletree. . . . It was necessary to leave the carriage, which had to be dragged out and scraped to remove the mud and slush which stuck to it like glue." [18] "It was a mercy that we all got home with whole bones," wrote a cabinet officer upon returning from an evening visit; "our carriage . . . was overset, the harness broken . . . and at the Treasury Office corner we were obliged to get out of the carriage in the mud. I called out the guard of the Treasury Office and borrowed a lantern." [19] Made dangerous by the condition of the roads and arduous by the unprecedented "distances to be traversed in the ordinary intercourse of society," [20] the communication that is necessary for even a rudimentary social life was no mean logistical problem for the members of the early governmental community. "The house Mr. G[allatin] has taken is next door to the Madisons' and three miles distant from us. I regret this circumstance, as it will prevent that intimate intercourse which I wished to enjoy." [21]

Against this desolate landscape the halls of government stood as Henry Adams was to see them decades later, "unfinished. . . . white Greek temples in the abandoned gravel-pits of a deserted Syrian city." [22] To the men who occupied them they brought no reassurance of dignity and little comfort. Those most charitably inclined likened them to "the splendid ruins of Roman grandeur." [23]

Commanding the terrain from the tallest hill, the Capitol was built to be seen. But failure to erect the central portion, connecting the Senate and House wings, made it an architectural monstrosity—twin boxes of white stone on a shrubless heath of hard-packed stone dust, the void between them bridged by a covered boardwalk resembling the construction sheds that dotted the grounds. The Senate wing boasted an elegant semicircular auditorium furnished with chairs of red morocco leather to serve for debates and, on its periphery, a lounge with couches arranged about two massive fireplaces where Senators could escape from chilling drafts while remaining within earshot of the floor proceedings. But behind the showy façade shoddy workmanship and poor design soon became apparent. Part of the ceiling fell in 1803, narrowly missing the Vice President's chair and necessitating an adjournment.[24] Columns supporting the gallery split open and were wrapped with white muslin to conceal the defects.[25] Printed notices warned spectators in the balcony "not to place their feet on the board in the front of the gallery, *as the dirt from them falls upon Senators' heads*." [26] The House chamber had a glass-domed ceiling which leaked so badly that pools of water were left on the floor after heavy rains.[27] Hot-air furnaces installed beneath the floor emanated heat to a degree that was "noxious and insupportable, and it has affected me to fainting," a Representative complained; "I have at length prevailed on the Speaker to forbid our subterranean fires. The effect produced by them is that upon an oyster baked in a Dutch oven." [28] The acoustics were, as Woodrow Wilson found them half a century later,[29] abominable. Whispered confidences resounded in the far corners of the chamber while shouts to a person ten feet distant were absorbed in a well of silence: "It must have been long since perceived, by every gentleman in the House," declared a Representative from the floor, "that the splendid hall in which they were assembled was perfectly unfit for the purpose of legislation, and that it was impossible in its present state, either to hear or be heard; they were consequently under the necessity of voting on questions which they could not understand, much less the reasons offered for or against them." [30]

Too cavernous for a home, too shabby for a palace, the executive mansion made its occupant "an object of ridicule with some and of pity with others." [31] Abigail Adams found only six of its thirty rooms plastered and "not a single apartment finished . . . the principal stairs . . . not up . . . not the least fence, yard, or other convenience without, and the great unfinished audience-room I make a drying-room of, to hang the clothes in." [32] Eight years elapsed before the staircase to the second floor was built. The ceiling in the audience chamber collapsed before the room was sufficiently finished to be used, and when the room was first opened for entertaining in the administration of John Quincy Adams it was still partially unplastered.[33] Not even the exterior of the building had been finished when the British burned it in 1814. The roof "leaked in such a manner as materially to injure the ceilings and furniture," reads an official report from 1809, and the timbers of the building, less than twenty years old, "are in a state of considerable decay." [34]

For years the grounds remained cluttered with workmen's shanties, privies, stagnant pools of water in basins once used for mixing mortar, "ruins of old brick-kilns, and the remains of brick yards and stone-cutters' sheds," "so that, in a dark night [according to a visitor in 1806] instead of finding your way to the house, you may, perchance, fall into a pit, or stumble over a heap of rubbish." Guests, after negotiating hazards in the yard, had to ascend to the mansion by rough board steps almost a full story aboveground.[35] "When I perceive the President's circumvallation unfinished, his garden in gullies and the room[s] of his house unplastered," a resident wrote in 1810, "I ask—can these disgusting scenes to strangers be pleasing to the citizens?" [36] "This parsimony destroys every sentiment of pleasure that arises in the mind, in viewing the residence of the president of a nation," commented a foreign visitor, "and is a disgrace to the country." [37]

To the worse than Spartan comfortlessness of the surroundings was added the unnerving monotony of politics unrelieved by diversion. "Il nous ne manque ici," wrote a Senator to a European acquaintance, "que maisons, caves, cuisines, hommes instruits, femmes aimables et autres petites bagatelles de cette espèce, pour que notre ville soit parfaite . . . c'est la ville du monde où on peut le mieux vivre—dans l'avenir." [38] There were only two places of public amusement in the capital, one of them a racetrack where "persons of all descriptions . . . collected together . . . shouting, betting, drinking, quarrelling and fighting"; [39] the other a theater "most astonishingly dirty and void of decoration," [40] where boys of the town gained admittance by lifting loose boards and crawling through the floor.[41] "One must love the drama very much," commented a Treasury official, "to consent to pass three hours amidst tobacco smoke, whiskey breaths, and other stenches, mixed up with the effluvia of stables, and miasmas of the canal, which the theatre is exactly placed and constructed to receive." [42]

With only such escape as these facilities afforded, and having little other society except shopkeepers and laborers, the members of government were necessarily thrown upon each other in leisure hours as well as at work. Thus their social life, rather than affording them relief from politics, became itself another arena of politics. Who was and who was not invited to a tea, a dinner, or a reception, who accepted and who declined, who was and who was not calling upon whom, became matters pregnant with political significance. "General Jackson has not visited Mr. Crawford," President Adams noted of his successor, but their "ladies have interchanged visits . . . [and it appears that they] will effectually knit the coalition." [43] Like it or not, party-going and party-giving tended to become obligatory, essential to the maintenance of one's political position. "Washington . . . is the only place in the Union where people consider it necessary to be agreeable,—where pleasing . . . becomes a sort of business"; [44] one was "obliged to go to other peoples parties, sick or well, for fear of giving offence." [45] The social round, so far from providing relaxation for the members, became itself a chore: "Such a party could give me no pleasure," commented a hostess, "but I hope it did others." [46]

Unable to get away from each other except by solitary walks into the woods or along the Potomac's banks to hunt, fish, or swim, "brutalized and stupefied . . . from hearing nothing but politics from morning to night and from continual confinement," [47] the members staged an eager retreat from the capital as soon as the public business could be disposed of each year. Thus, as the public structures dominated the landscape and as politics dominated society, so even the rhythm of Washington life became the rhythm of governmental activity itself. Once, in the autumn, with the arrival of the public persons from the hinterlands, the community came alive, and reverted to dormancy as they returned to their homes and constituencies in the springtime, leaving a ghost town behind: houses boarded up, the halls of Congress silent and empty, the

White House deserted, the foreign legations closed. "The winter campaign is over—the tents are struck and the different parties are leaving the field—Congress has adjourned. . . . A universal dullness pervades." [48]

Such was power's home in a nation wedded to the doctrine of the sovereignty of the people: a pleasureless outpost in the wilds and wastes, manned for only part of the year, abandoned for the rest.

~~{ CHAPTER 3 }~~

SELF-IMAGE: "SPLENDID TORMENT"

If the stage was primitive and the set shabby, the actors were, on the whole, an uneasy and disenchanted lot. A second characteristic of the Washington community, no less distinctive than the bleakness of its physical setting, was the pronounced antipathy of the governing group toward their community, their disparaging perceptions of their vocation, and their restiveness in their role as power-holders.

That Washington was made a laughingstock in the public press and by the foreign diplomats might have been expected to arouse some sense of civic loyalty in the rulers, or at least to put them on the defensive about the primitive capital. Instead they adopted, with a unanimity of sentiment rarely displayed on any other subject, the derogatory attitudes of outsiders toward Washington. The "insiders" were, in fact, foremost among the detractors of the governmental community. Hardly an aspect of the outpost on the Potomac was spared their scorn. The climate was intolerable. The place was a menace to health, pervaded with "contaminated vapour" which brought on all manner of "agues and other complaints." [1] Washington was a "desert city," an "abomination of desolation." [2] The public buildings were either pretentious to the point of bad taste or "large naked ugly buildings" surrounded with fences "unfit for a decent barnyard." [3] Ridicule was lavished upon Washington's lack of "industry, society, or business" and the "heartless amusements and vapid pleasures" offered by its meager facilities.[4] The cuisine was atrocious—"hog and hominy grits" and "not even any fruit fit for hogs to eat." [5] The residential accommodations were "narrow uncomfortable lodgings in this most uncomfortable and expensive place in the whole world." [6] Washington society was a "golgotha of numbskulls," "vice and intemperance" pervading its lower orders and "extravagance in the manners and habits" of its upper ranks.[7]

All the rulers seemed to find something repellent about the place of power. "A hateful place," an executive official described it.[8] "I left Washington," recalled a retired congressman, "with the feelings of a man quitting Tadmor in the Wilderness, 'where creeping things had possession of the palace, and foxes looked out of the windows,' and sought refuge in home." [9] Washington was "this abode of splendid misery, of shabby splendor," in the view of a southern Representative.[10] The experience of Washington, a New Englander wrote home, "has produced in me nothing but absolute loathing and disgust." [11]

And yet the governing members, for all their complaints, never made any serious effort to have the causes of them corrected. Over a period of twenty years the government spent less money for the improvement of its headquarters than it spent each year for the President's salary alone. Fifteen thousand dollars of public funds spent in two decades to improve the capital suggests little inclination among the rulers to remedy the faults of which they so incessantly complained.[12]

For the members not only adopted the disparaging attitudes of outsiders toward the capital. They in fact considered themselves to be outsiders there, mere sojourners at the seat of power. Except for the civil staff of the executive departments who made their year-round residence in the capital, Washington was not "our" community in the eyes of the governing politicians; it was "theirs"—the townspeople's. Virtually every effort by the local citizens to implicate them in local improvements was rebuffed. When the mayor asked Congress to share the town's staggering financial burden for poor relief, Congress considered the problem the town's, not its own, and refused even to permit the town officials to ban the paupers whom the presence of Congress was attracting to Washington. When the townspeople asked Congress for financial aid to build streets and sidewalks, for lamps to light them, for sanitation, for a canal, for commercial facilities, for schools, they were brushed aside and cold in effect to tax themselves.[13] Not even the humiliation of Washington's occupation by the British in the War of 1812 brought any marked change in the governing group's antipathy toward the place of power. Quite the contrary: when Congress returned in 1814 to find the public buildings in ruins, the members, so far from committing themselves to rebuild the capital, and with it the national prestige, rather undertook to debate the desirability of keeping the capital in Washington. The House came within nine votes of deciding to abandon Washington altogether.[14] The Senate hesitated for three and a half months, deciding to stay after local bankers volunteered a loan to pay the costs of restoring the government buildings.[15]

The governing politicians' perception of themselves as outsiders in Washington and their adoption of the outsiders' disparaging attitudes toward the capital—their avoidance of identification with the place of power—is very much in conformity with the sentiments they expressed about politics, the political vocation, and about power-holding itself.

Expressions of enthusiasm for what they did at Washington were as rare as expressions of satisfaction with the place. The thankless-ness, the indignity, and the meanness of the political vocation are such recurrent themes of comment in the community record, and the drumfire of self-censure was so constant an accompaniment to the work of governing, as to convey the impression of a community at war with itself.

No one acknowledged either taste or talent for politics. The members professed themselves to be misfits in a vocation reprobated as "a species of *mania*," [16] "an unprofitable way of life." [17] The political vocation was "at war with my natural taste, feelings, and wishes," said one prominent power-holder.[18] "As to political honors," wrote another, "it may be evidence of a poor spirit, but I have not a nerve in my system that responds to their call." [19]

Nothing enjoyable was associated with politics in their commentaries on life and work in Washington. The experience of power was commonly portrayed as a kind of mental agony. "It is impossible to conceive the comfortlessness and desolation of feeling," reflected a former legislator, "the solitariness and depression of spirits . . . the constant tension . . . in which [my] two years were passed" in Washington.[20] The political discipline "brutalized and stupefied"; [21] power dehumanized the man. "I have compared myself," wrote John Adams of his experience in the Presidency,

> to an animal I have seen take hold of the end of a cord with his teeth and be drawn slowly up by pullies through a storm of squibs, crackers, and rockets, flaming and blazing round him every moment; and though the scorching flames made him groan and moan and roar, he would not let go his hold till he had reached the ceiling of a lofty theatre, where he hung some time . . . and at last descended through another storm of burning powder.[22]

To be a politician was to lose one's freedom, to be "delivered into the hands of others." [23] It was to lose one's privacy, to be made naked to one's enemies, the object of "perpetual and malignant watchfulness with which I am observed in my open day and my secret night, with the deliberate purpose of exposing me to public obloquy or public ridicule." [24] "A politician should have the hide of a rhinoceros, to bear the thrusts of folly, ignorance and meanness. . . . The fact is that every man, in a high public station, must become fire-proof and bullet-proof, in his own defense. . . . My skin is too thin for the business," protested a long-time server in government.[25]

A political career also meant financial ruin, the rulers constantly reminded themselves. Politics was a vocation pursued at the cost of "abandonment of our professions or occupations, and the consequent derangement of our private affairs." [26] It was a game played "at a certain loss of money [and] a very *un*certain gain in reputation," [27] in which men "barter their hopes of an independent and peaceful old age, for the temporary possession of . . . a bauble" and where the highest prize to be won—the Presidency—was but a "feast for eight years, and a famine for the residue of life." [28]

To be in public life was to shut oneself off from normal society. "When I look to the ineffable pleasures of my family society, I become more and more disgusted with the jealousies, the hatred, the

rancourous and malignant passions of this scene. . . . Worn down
here with pursuits in which I take no delight . . . I pant for that
society, where all is peace and harmony." [29] Politics was reviled, by
those who did not bring their families "to live on the plentiful
things of this *abounding* metropolis," [30] for estranging them from
their wives and children—and no less reviled by those who did
bring their families to Washington for causing them to be "thrown
. . . upon ourselves for all the pleasures, which intimate and confidential society affords. . . . The peculiar nature of Washington society makes it so." [31] The community life of the politicians was said
to be "destitute of those strong and tender ties with which affection
and friendship bind." The "ceremonious intercourse of strangers"
replaced "the confidential intercourse of congenial minds and kindred feelings." [32]

The rulers saw their society as the antithesis of desirable human
relations. Politics kept men at a distance: "I do not know how it is,
but I cannot get into these men," wrote a Senator of his colleagues;
"there is a kind of guarded distance on their parts that seems to pre-
clude sociability. I believe I had best be guarded too." [33] Politics
turned friends against each other: "Men, who have been intimate all
their lives, cross the street to avoid meeting, and turn their heads
another way, lest they should be obliged to touch their hats." [34]
Power-holding subordinated personal relationships to considerations
of utility and expediency: "In Congress my intercourse with [other]
members . . . was regulated by party rather than by personal
friendship. The latter we had few and limited opportunities to cultivate." [35] Politics was combat, likened to gladiatorship "scarcely
less dangerous, (he would not say cruel,) than those [displays] that
contributed to the amusement of ancient Rome"; "sarcasm and ridicule were the sword and the lance." [36]

As compensation for the personal deprivations that were said to
go with membership in the Washington community, satisfaction in
work done was felt to offer slight returns. What, the rulers asked
themselves, were the rewards for "passing five months of ceaseless
occupation and discomfort" in Washington each year,[37] for "the
privations which members . . . submit to—privations . . . from

the loss of the society of family and friends, to that of life itself" ? [88] Honor? "I have seen enough of political honors," Jefferson once wrote, "to know they are but splendid torments; and however one might be disposed to render services on which many of their fellow citizens might set a value, yet when as many would deprecate them as a public calamity, one may well entertain a modest doubt of their real importance and feel the impulse of duty to be very weak." [39]

Renown? "He did not believe," declared a member of the House, "that any man was entirely prepared to commence life in the service of his country, who was not perfectly prepared to end it without a murmur, whenever, and in whatever way it might be necessary —possibly in exile, probably in disgrace, and certainly in obscurity." [40]

Prestige and popular acclaim? Not so in the eyes of the power-holders. George Washington, the President with greatest prestige in the nation before the Civil War, "got into one of those passions when he cannot command himself," reported a witness: saying that "he had never repented but once the having slipped the moment of resigning his office, and that was every moment since [he had taken it], that by God he had rather be in his grave than in his present situation. That he had rather be on his farm than to be made emperor of the world, and yet that they were charging him with wanting to be a king." [41] "I will give you another fact," related a lesser light to legislative colleagues after returning from a visit to his constituency. "There were several persons together at a neighbor's house; the neighbor wishing to mark some of his hogs [for slaughter], examined the almanac to find when the dog days would expire, and when he could not find them, swore that Congress had destroyed all the dog days, and that myself was the instigator; for which I should never come here again." [42] "We are on the way to becoming," suggested one of the politicians, "the only degraded caste in this society." [43]

Guiding the national destiny? But how could the national destiny be guided when the ship of state might be a ship of fools—"he found himself . . . committing an unpardonable error, in presenting arguments to this body," declared a Representative; "the ear of this House . . . is sealed against truth and reason" [44]—a ship on an ocean "into tempest wrought, To waft a feather, or to drown a fly"? [45] "Sir, as I was returning the other evening from the capitol, I saw what has been a rare sight here this winter—the sun . . . and I ask[ed] myself if . . . I was not the most foolish of men to be struggling and scuffling here in this heated and impure atmosphere, where the play is not worth the candle." [46]

If nothing good was seen in the vocation of politics, badness was thought to pervade it. The "ambition of individuals," as one veteran of the community put it, "is the main spring of the great political machine which we call The Government." [47] And political ambition was "that canker" [48] that brought out all the worst of human traits: "jealousies . . . hatred . . . rancourous and malignant passions"; [49] "lying, abusing, quarreling, and almost fighting for a little short-lived distinction"; [50] "crimination and recrimination, denunciation and retort, violence, abuse, and clamor." [51]

Power made men unscrupulous. Among men in power, "ambition swallows up . . . principle," [52] and "stratagem and intrigue" were the way of life.[53] The possession of power was seen to unleash men's aggressive instincts, and power-seeking was associated with antisocial behavior. Power-seekers "delighted to mangle honest sensibility, devour reputation, and hunt down talents and independence." [54] Politics—the pursuit of power—was such a vocation that encouraged one man to "rise upon the ruin" of another's reputation; [55] the way to get ahead was not by proving one's own merit but by destroying others. In the fraternity of power-holders one could not "get honors but by being rolled in the dirt, and rolling others there." [56] And no less to be trusted, no less unethical than the successful man in power, was the loser in power—for "misery loves company," as one congressman reminded his listeners, and those who were thwarted would, "Samson-like, endeavor to crush their opponents beneath the general wreck their own conduct has produced." [57]

Power tended to corrupt integrity, and parted men from their

honor. The view of power-holding as essentially a degrading experience was eloquently expressed by an aging member of Jefferson's
social circle at Washington, at the close of the Jeffersonian era:

One drama is just finished, the curtain has dropped, the actors have left
the stage . . . disappointed, exhausted, worn out, retiring with broken
fortunes and broken constitutions and hearts rankling with barbed arrows.
Another drama is preparing. New characters, in all the freshness and
vigour of unexhausted strength, with the exhilaration of hopes undaunted
by fear, of spirits intoxicated with success, with the aspirations of towering ambition are coming on the self-same stage . . . . they in their turn
will drink the cup of honor to the bottom and find its dregs nauseous and
bitter.[58]

One therefore expected the worst of fellow politicians in the
community. The society of rulers was where "characters are torn to
pieces," [59] where "the most pure and honorable motives were ever
liable to misrepresentation," where "honest opposition . . . would
be attributed to . . . base, low, and contemptible" designs, and
where "little souls, bursting with malignity, would be constantly
scattering their filth and their venom round." [60] In a community of
power-holders, members felt themselves unable to speak with
candor; dissimulation was all but necessary in self-defense: "I abhor
duplicity. But a politician is bound to act cautiously, and not less to
be on his guard in conversation with his opponents." [61] Power-
holders were unreliable, and every colleague in the community was
potentially an enemy. "So disgusted [am I] . . . with political men
and political life—nay with mankind itself, that I wish I could shut
myself up for life and have nothing more to do, with any one but
my wife and children. I look around—and exclaim where is there
one man I can trust! and I feel there is not one!" [62] Politicians of
the governmental community saw themselves surrounded with
"falsehood, deceit, treachery"—"surrounded by enemies and spies,
catching and perverting every word which falls from my lips, or
flows from my pen, and inventing where facts fail them." [63]

In brief, the politicians of the early governmental community saw
themselves in a cosmos of evil and immorality. "The public history
of all countries . . . is but a sort of mask," one official mused; "the interior working of the machinery must be foul." [64] The center of

power was "this sink of . . . corruption," [65] a place of "iniquity and defilement," [66] the scene of "a thousand corrupt cabals." [67] For "the possession of power," in the words of one participant, "was of all known causes the greatest promoter of corruption." [68]

It is difficult to imagine a community which entertained a more unflattering, disdainful, indeed abhorrent, image of itself. To read the participants' commentaries on life and work in early Washington and forget that this was a political center would almost compel the conclusion that one confronts a community in the throes of disintegration—virtually devoid of civic pride among its leading members, scorned as a place to live, deprecated for the rewards it offered, anathematized for its way of life; a community pervaded with mistrust one man of another, riven by animosities and dissension, its members never at peace with themselves or with each other and professing a deep aversion to the work they carried on there.

To appreciate that this was a governmental community makes such a self-image more understandable, to be sure. For the premises of power are rarely places of tranquillity or trust between men. That the members' commentaries mirrored, in some degree, the realities of life and work in Washington is beyond question. Public life was no bed of roses. The extraordinarily high number of resignations from the early Congress alone suggests the degree of the politicians' dissatisfaction with public life in the capital. From 1797 to 1829 (5th through 20th Congresses) more Senators resigned than failed to be reelected by their state legislatures. On the average, 17.9 percent of the Senate membership resigned every two years, almost six times the biennial turnover in the modern Senate due to resignation. Among Representatives, an average of 5.8 percent resigned in each Congress, about twice the percentage of resignations in the modern House.[69] Investigation of the careers of the 229 legislators who resigned from 1797 to 1829 reveals, moreover, that more than two thirds of them subsequently held public offices elsewhere than in Washington, and almost half of them had other public jobs outside of Washington within one year following their resignations.[70] It was not, therefore, from the political vocation that the members tended to resign, but rather from the Washington community.[71]

The pecuniary rewards for public service, too, were indeed meager, and long service at Washington, with the neglect of lands and family fortunes it entailed, often brought financial ruin.[72] Only one Jeffersonian President, John Quincy Adams, left the chief magistracy without severe financial embarrassment. James Monroe lived six years in "abject penury and distress" after leaving the White House and died "in wretchedness and beggary." [73] Dolley Madison saved herself from poverty only by a persistent and ultimately successful campaign to sell her deceased husband's papers to Congress. At the very hour of Thomas Jefferson's death, a subscription for the relief of the former President was being solicited in the halls of Congress, among a crowd of legislators and citizens gathered to celebrate Independence Day. And when, after a reading of the Declaration of Independence, friends passed round the hat on behalf of its author, "not more than four or five" contributions were received.[74] Nor was it any fantasy that instructed the pioneer politicians of the governmental community to expect public ingratitude for their services. This is the report of a visitor to Monticello not long after Jefferson's death:

I beheld nothing but ruin and change, rotting terraces, broken cabins, the lawn, ploughed up and cattle wandering among Italian mouldering vases, and the place seemed the true representative of the fallen fortunes of the great man and his family. He died in want, almost his last words were that if he lived much longer a negro hut must be his dwelling. His family scattered and living upon the charity of the world, and to complete the picture the simple plain granite stone that marks his resting place defaced and broken . . . and all his estate even the dust of his body the possession of a stranger. . . . I could not but exclaim, what is human greatness.[75]

That there was an element of political necessity, or of expediency, in the propagation of a disparaging self-image by the members of the governmental community should likewise be recognized. Confronting a citizenry predisposed to suspicion of political power, the men in power stood, conceivably, to gain political advantages by their own self-denial, and by emphasizing the hardships of public life while leaving the rewards of power-holding unacknowledged. It was perhaps impolitic, too, for the dominant political party to depart from its public commitment to "republican simplicity" by using taxpayer money to enable themselves "to live in ease and affluence—to contract habits and tastes above the intelligent part of [our] constituents, and inconsistent with the plain republican manners of [the] country." [76] Such was the degree of citizen indignation when legislators voted themselves a pay increase in 1816 that almost two thirds of them failed to return to Capitol Hill after the next election, even though they had hastily repealed the compensation law in the meantime.[77]

It would be less than understanding, however, to dismiss the views of the governing group on life and work in Washington as political posturing, or, on the other hand, to see in them nothing more than objective portraiture. To appreciate the bias of their self-image and the genuineness of their censorious attitudes, it is necessary only to recognize that the power-holders did not, in their own outlook, escape a culturally ingrained predisposition to view political power and politics as essentially evil.

For what is most striking about the politicians' self-image is its similarity to the image of politicians and political power that prevailed outside the governmental community as well, in the society at large. Thus the rulers, like the people they ruled, tended to view power in moral terms. If Americans in general saw power as tending to corrupt, no less did the power-holders themselves perceive that "the possession of power . . . was of all known causes the greatest promoter of corruption." If the pursuit of power was socially disparaged as a vocation, no less so was power-seeking disparaged within the governing group, and the officeholders self-perceived as a "degraded caste." [78] If it was the popular belief that politicians were not to be trusted, that "in questions of power then let no more be heard of confidence in man," [79] no more were the rulers at Washington inclined to trust each other. If it was an American culture trait to perceive politicians as unprincipled men, no less did the power-holders themselves perceive integrity corrupted in their own colleagues. If, in the popular view, the motives of politicians were suspect, no less were the politicians disposed to question the motives of each other, and if their acts "be within the possible reach of imputation, [to] ascribe them to bad rather than to good intentions." [80]

It appears, then, that the politicians in government projected upon themselves what was essentially the outsiders' image—the cultural stereotype—of politicians and power. It appears, in other words, that we confront a community of power-holders who shared, to a significant degree, the antipower outlook and values of their culture.

If this be so, far deeper sources of restiveness among the rulers are discerned than the physical hardships of their life in the primitive capital, or the meagerness of their material rewards, or the normal vocational insecurity of officeholders. To the degree that the governors did carry into office the negative values of their culture toward political power, their roles as power-holders must have subjected them, in addition to the intergroup conflicts always encountered in the task of governing, to an inner, "moral" conflict as well. To sense the evil of power as acutely as many members of the early governmental community did does not conduce to a tranquil spirit in the possessor of power. It is not unlikely, therefore, that one source of the restiveness that pervaded the governing fraternity was a nagging doubt about the moral legitimacy of the trade they plied there, and a compelling need to justify themselves as power-holders—not only to the outside public, but also to each other and in their own minds' eye.

Certainly the historical context and their community environment could only have nourished the ambivalence about power-holding that the American antipathy toward power may have planted in them. For the pioneer politicians at Washington had few of the circumstantial justifications or rationalizations for power-holding that have helped resolve the moral question for their modern successors. Governors of a nation but recently born in revolt against government, they lacked the social acceptance that a long institutional tradition has brought to officeholders in the modern state. Denied the opportunity to perform a wide range of citizen services, they were denied the rationale of contributing significantly to the public weal. Tangible signs of public prestige and popular interest to quiet their qualms were wholly lacking for power-holders isolated in a community barren of wealth and abundant with poverty. To rationalize and justify power-holding, the sense of performing needed roles as managers of a large organizational empire was not theirs to savor, nor the sense of being "in demand" that is conveyed by the regiments of reporters and the crowds of citizen petitioners who converge upon the rulers today. Power could scarcely have been its own justification in the Jeffersonian era, or have avoided being a questionable pursuit in the eyes of those who engaged in it.

Ambivalence about power among men in power jars one's expectations: a Macchiavellian image of those who rule is, after all, much more congenial to the democratic mind. And an uneasy conscience among powerful men is an idea so very alien to the modern understanding of why politicians in government behave the way they do that to suggest it at all is to appear naïve or at best Shakespearean in one's approach toward men in power. But then it has rarely been the effort of American scholars to view politics and power through the eyes of the rulers themselves; and the attempt to grasp what it meant to hold power, to comprehend the human experience involved, has been least among the concerns of historians of the Jeffersonian era. To make this inquiry is to conclude that the experience of power, at that time and that place in history, was indeed "splendid misery." It is to surmise that one element in the "splendid torment" of rulership was the psychic stress of men who, even as they indulged the urge to power, could not easily turn aside their democratic conscience that instructed them of power's evil.

The antipower values to which they subscribed carry important implications for the social and political behavior of the ruling group at their rendezvous on the Potomac. It will be helpful to state those implications before proceeding to the third distinctive characteristic of the ruling establishment—its social organization.

One conclusion drawn from the members' commentaries on life and work at Washington is that the republican-democratic values of the larger culture were incorporated, reinforced, and sanctioned in the specifically political culture of the governmental community. It is therefore a fair inference that behavioral conformity to republican-democratic norms was sanctioned within the governing group independently of any citizen pressures or legal strictures conducing to democratic behavior on their part. "Republican-democratic norms" may, to be sure, condone a wide latitude of conduct, not all of it exemplary. Precisely what outer limits they prescribed for the behavior of the power-holders need not concern us so much for the present. What is important is the strong likelihood that these norms were included in the "rules of the game" which would govern not only the public conduct of the rulers but also their behavior *in camera*, at the secluded outpost on the Potomac. Among men who conspicuously shared the attitudes of their culture concerning power, behavior offensive to republican-democratic precepts would be improbable for moral as well as political reasons. One would therefore not expect to find in the early governmental community, despite its isolation and the relative freedom of behavior this afforded its members, modes of conduct markedly deviant from those that would be tolerated in the more open governmental environment of later times.

Nor would one expect to find a politically or a socially cohesive community, despite the negligibility of conflicting outside pressures upon the ruling establishment. The shared attitudes in the community toward power and politicians would seem, in and of themselves, to have made conflict and dissension intrinsic to the governing society. They would seem to have posed an enduring threat, even where other factors did not, to the stability of social and political ties within the community: insinuating into the relationships between the power-holders themselves the culturally derived suspicion of power-holders; inhibiting the development of trustful relationships among them; affording a ready rationale for asserting one's independence, for keeping one's "distance," and for resisting the leadership initiatives of others in the community. Antipower attitudes would presumably pose special impediments to the stability of relationships that were defined as "political"—that is, relationships which connoted power-seeking. One would expect the political party tie, for example, to be an especially unstable relationship in the governmental community. Reasoning from the power-holders' attitudes toward politics and power alone, and ignoring for the moment any other factors productive of intraparty cleavage, one could predict a weak sense of party loyalty and considerable difficulties in achieving party cohesion. In a community whose members tended to see themselves surrounded by unscrupulous men, the implicit moral prescription for behavior was not accommodation or cooperation with other power-holders but rather avoidance of dependence upon them. In a social environment perceived as corrupting, a regime of assertive, inner-directed, righteous individualism was called for.[81]

Thus the opprobrious attitudes of the ruling group toward power and politicians prefigure a community in which the maintenance of collaborative relationships in general and party solidarity in particular would be problematic, quite apart from any policy disagreements or conflicts of interest among the members.

It follows, third, that the antipower values of the community would also inhibit the development of leadership and followership roles within the ruling group, and would attach special liabilities to those who were perceived as power figures or figures of authority. For example, both a moral and a tactical advantage would presumably inhere in the role of citizen representative which would not inhere in the role of Chief Executive, to the degree that he was perceived as a power figure. And in cases of conflict between President and Congress one would venture to speculate that the advantage would lie with the contenders whose power claims were adumbrated by their roles as spokesmen for the people. Narrow limits for *de facto* leadership in a community lacking well-articulated leadership and followership roles are therefore indicated.

The same values which foreshadow difficulties for leadership and avoidance of strong identification with political parties suggest also that the members would be attracted toward behaviors and personal associations which were sanctioned—as political parties and party discipline were not—by the Constitution, established law, custom, or by unambiguous popular approbation. Behavior and associations so sanctioned would presumably have a twofold value. In a community given to making scapegoats of power-seekers, they would tend to confer immunity from reproach; at the same time, they would tend to give a needed sense of righteousness to men eager to escape their own stereotype of politicians. Marked predisposition toward constitutional orthodoxy in their community behaviors and associations is the forecast, then, for a ruling group acculturated to mistrust of rulers.

One would infer, finally, the presence of psychological stimuli within the governing fraternity to reach out for the attention and approbation of those they governed. What better balm was there for the democratic conscience of the rulers than popular applause? What happier way to reconcile their mistrust of power as Americans and their urge to power as men than to play the king by popular demand? A compelling need for affirmative and enthusiastic citizen responses, and ultimately an urge to contrive ways of eliciting such responses, are forecast for a governing group in search of a rationale for ruling.

These behavioral tendencies inferred from the antipower outlook of the governing group might usefully be kept in mind as we turn next to explore the patterns of association among them. It will be helpful, too, to keep in mind the ultimate question which is raised by the discovery that the governing politicians themselves regarded power as evil, power-seeking as corrupting, and politicians as unprincipled. To what degree was their image of power and politicians compatible with the practical demands of rulership in a government of "separated institutions sharing powers"?[82]

CHAPTER 4

ORGANIZATION: SEPARATE
SOCIETIES FOR
SEPARATE BRANCHES

Desolate in surrounding, derogatory in self-image, the governmental community was also distinctive for the extraordinary manner in which the personnel chose to situate themselves in Washington—the social formations into which they deployed on the terrain. The settlement pattern of a community is, in a sense, the signature that its social organization inscribes upon the landscape, defining the groups of major importance in the life of the community and suggesting the relationships among them. In the case of the early Washington community that signature is very clear.

The members did not, in their residential arrangements, disperse uniformly or at random over the wide tract of the intended city. Nor did they draw together at any single place. The governmental community rather inscribed itself upon the terrain as a series of distinct subcommunities, separated by a considerable distance, with stretches of empty land between them. Each was clustered around one of the widely separated public buildings; each was a self-contained social and economic entity. The personnel of the governmental community segregated themselves, in short, into distinct groups, and formed a society of "we's" and "they's." References to this unusual social configuration abound in the descriptions recorded by residents and by visitors to the early capital.

Washington is not like one village but like several little villages thrown together with a small space between them.[1]

There is perhaps no city in the world of the same population, in which the distances to be traversed in the ordinary intercourse of society are so large. The most glaring want in Washington is that of compactness and consistency. The houses are scattered in straggling groups.[2]

The plan marked out for this metropolis of the empire, is gigantic, and the public buildings, whether in progress or design, bear all the stamp of grandeur. How many centuries shall pass away ere the clusters of little villages, now scattered over this plain, shall assume the form and magnificence of an imperial city? [3]

In consequence of the gigantic scale on which Washington is planned, and the different interests which influence the population, its inhabitants (including Georgetown) are separated into four distinct little towns, distant from each other about a mile. Thus we have Georgetown in the west . . . the town immediately around the President's house (extending towards the Capitol) . . . that around the Capitol . . . and the buildings at the Navy-Yard, which lies on the east branch. . . . There is also a little group of houses at the junction of the two branches of the Potomac.[4]

From data gathered in an 1801 survey, listing the location of houses completed and under construction in the capital, it is possible to reconstruct the settlement pattern of the early governmental community with reasonable accuracy (see Figure 2). These data confirm descriptive accounts in revealing a pattern of residential segregation, with houses concentrated near the public buildings, each concentration comprised in turn of still smaller neighborhood groups. Excluding Georgetown, the three major residential clusters were, first, the settlement on the northwest side of the Tiber River in the vicinity of the executive mansion on "President's Hill"; sec-

NOTE TO FIG. 2: "An enumeration of the houses in the City of Washington, made November, 1801" (ASP, Misc. Ser., I, 256–67) lists in tabular form the number of buildings in each city block which were completed in May, 1800, and completed and under construction in 1801. The use of tracing paper overlaid on an early city land map made it possible to identify the houses spatially from this tabular enumeration, and thus to elicit the settlement pattern pictured in Figure 2. For purposes of clarity, only those houses completed in May, 1800, are included in the diagram. The inclusion of houses completed and under construction in 1801 would in no way have altered the configurations pictured in Figure 2, but would merely have increased their density. The stream and river courses pictured in Figure 2, and the boundary lines of the reservations on which the public buildings stood, are diagrammatic rather than cartographically precise, having necessarily been derived from topographical and other maps of different scale.

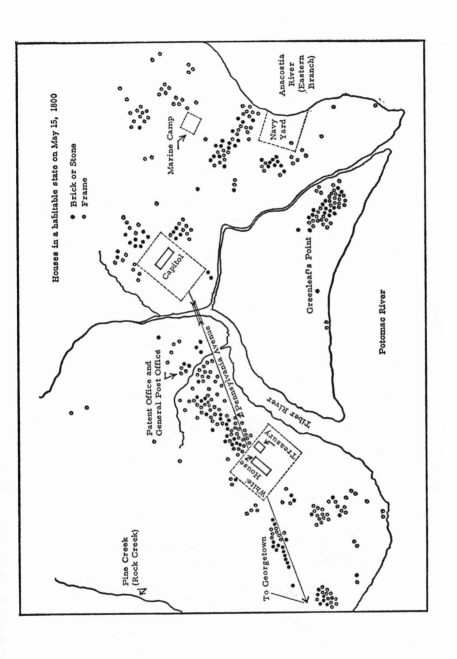

Houses in a habitable state on May 15, 1800

● Brick or Stone
○ Frame

Pine Creek
(Rock Creek)

Patent Office and
General Post Office

Pennsylvania Avenue

Capitol

Marine Camp

Navy Yard

Anacostia
River
(Eastern
Branch)

Greenleaf's Point

White House

Treasury

Tiber River

To Georgetown

Potomac River

ond, the less numerous groups of dwellings on the opposite side of the Tiber, clustered about the Capitol on "Capitol Hill"—sometimes called simply "the Hill"; and third, "the Navy Yard," a settlement fringing the Navy Yard on the Anacostia bluffs. Within these settlements smaller neighborhood clusters, established on high ground, were identified in local parlance by special names, such as "Crow Hill," "English Hill," "Twenty-Building Hill." The lowlands between were generally uninhabited during the first two decades; in the terminal years of the Jeffersonian era, "Swampoodle," "Foggy Bottom," "Hell's Bottom," and "Frogtown" made their appearance on the terrain and in the local vocabulary. Far from being a transitory phenomenon, due simply to the newness of the capital, the configuration of communities-within-a-community was endemic to the governmental establishment, persisting well into the second half of the century.[5]

Members of the different branches of government chose to situate themselves close by the respective centers of power with which they were affiliated, seeking their primary associations in extra-official life among their fellow branch members (see Figure 3).

Despite its relative civilization, old Georgetown attracted few members of government as residents, and most of those who stayed there moved as soon as they could find quarters in Washington,

Note to Fig. 3: Places of residence are located by vicinity or neighborhood lived in. More precise locations cannot be rendered in the diagram because of graphic considerations and because of the vagueness of most addresses listed in the *Congressional Directories* (e.g., "near Attorney General Wirt's," "near the General Post Office").

Information about legislators' residences was derived exclusively from the *Congressional Directory* for 1807. While the tendency was for legislators to disperse more widely from Capitol Hill with the passing years, a check of the *Directory* for 1828 reveals that the large majority was still then residing on or in the near vicinity of the Hill.

A longer time period (1800–1828) and more varied sources had to be used for identifying executive residences because the *Congressional Directories* did not begin listing these until late in the Jeffersonian era, and even then they listed comparatively few. Descriptive accounts, letters, diaries, and published histories of early Washington—too numerous to cite here—furnished much information about residential locations of high-level executives for the period 1800–1828; these were supplemented by the use of the *Congressional Directory* for 1828, which lists, with sufficient precision to warrant their inclusion in the above diagram, the residences of thirty-six executives, excluding those living in Georgetown.

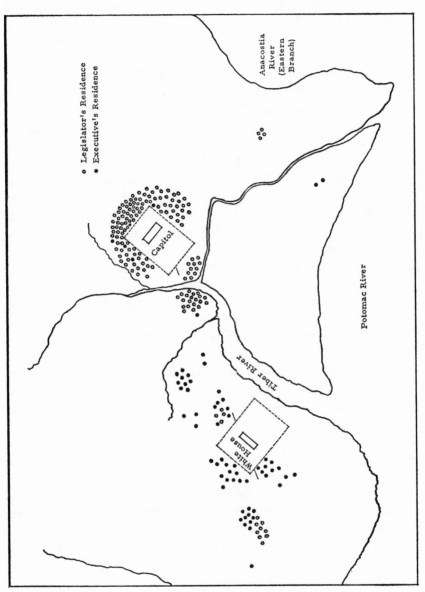

FIGURE 3. RESIDENTIAL DISTRIBUTION OF
LEGISLATORS AND EXECUTIVES

nearer to their places of work. Lacking any public buildings and losing its river trade, Georgetown became a satellite village of the executive community across Rock Creek, supplying consumer goods and services.[6]

At the opposite end of the city, about five miles from Georgetown, near the Capitol but separated from it by a dense swamp, was the village of the armed forces. Symbolized by a monument honoring American casualties in the Tripolitan War (Congress had refused space for the monument in its own territory on Capitol Hill), the settlement here ranged about the Navy Yard and the barracks for a detachment of Marines, who served as nightwatchmen for the public buildings and, with their band, as entertainers at official ceremonies and social functions.[7] As the intended commercial sector of the capital, the settlement never prospered. It was described in 1800 as comprising "half a dozen houses"—exclusive of shacks—"a very large but perfectly empty warehouse, and a wharf graced by not a single vessel."[8] In 1806, "tippling shops, and houses of rendezvous for sailors and their doxies, with a number of the lowest order of traders, constitute what is called the navy-yard";[9] and ten or fifteen years later an observer reported that "there are not many good houses in the quarter of the Navy-Yard, and . . . a great portion of its inhabitants are people dependent on the establishment for support. . . . Seamen, there are none . . . for the simple reason that there is no commerce."[10] Commercialization failing, the environs became the site of the congressional burying ground, a poorhouse, and a penitentiary with an arsenal "near, much too near" it, thus associating by coresidence the men and matériel of war with the dead, the indigent, and the incorrigible.[11] The settlement was generally shunned by civilian members of the government as a place to live, and high-ranking military and naval officers also forsook it eventually to take up residence in the executive sector.

The chief centers of activity were the village community of the executives and the village community of the legislators, lying "one mile and a half and seventeen perches" apart as the crow flies, on the "great heath" bisected by the River Tiber.[12]

Senators and Representatives lived in the shadow of the Capitol itself, most of them in knots of dwellings but a moment's walk from their place of meeting. All but ten legislators resided on Capitol Hill in 1801, and only three in the executive quarter across the Tiber.[13] With the passing years, residence off the Hill found favor among larger numbers of legislators; a small group established themselves near the Patent Office and another, as shown in Figure 3, at the foot of Capitol Hill near the Tiber bridge. The latter was still the largest single grouping of legislative residences away from the Hill in 1828. The large majority of lawmakers continued, throughout the three decades following 1800, to live close by the Capitol, and few sought the different associations of life on the executive side of the Tiber, from which withdrawal was easily accomplished on the excuse of convenience.[14]

The knolltop settlement of legislators was a complete and self-contained village community from beginning to end of the Jeffersonian era. Neither work nor diversion, nor consumer needs, nor religious needs required them to set foot outside it. Eight boarding-houses, a tailor, a shoemaker, a washerwoman, a grocery store, and an oyster house served the congressional settlement in 1801.[15] Within three years a notary, an ironmonger, a saddle maker, several more tailors and bootmakers, a liquor store, bookstores, stables, bakery, and taverns had been added.[16] In twenty years' time the settlement had increased to more than two thousand people and the Capitol was nearly surrounded by brick houses "three stories high, and decent, without being in the least elegant," where the lawmakers lodged during the session.[17] An itinerant barber served the community, shuttling between the scattered villages of the capital on horseback, and a nearby bathhouse catered to congressional clientele. Legislators with families could send their children to school on the Hill. The members had their own congressional library and their own post office, dispatching and receiving mail—which was distributed on the floor of the Senate and the House daily—without leaving the Hill. Page boys, doorkeepers, sergeants-at-arms, and other ancillary personnel for Congress were supplied from the permanent population of Capitol Hill—mainly the boardinghouse proprietors and their families.

Village religious services were provided each Sunday, with the Hall of Representatives serving as the church and visiting ministers as preachers. The vanity and corruption of power were favored themes, although the congregation could not have needed such preachments less, and the sermon was often lost in a hum of conversation as members gossiped and opened their mail, passed out during the service. Music, "as little in union with devotional feelings, as the place," was supplied by the Marine Band.[18]

For diversion, members had only to walk down to the Tiber for good fishing and duck-shooting or step into the woods immediately east of the Capitol for a morning's hunt before Congress convened at eleven or twelve o'clock. There was in addition the Congressional Dancing Assembly, meeting regularly in one of the taverns on the Hill.[19] Public lectures were occasionally to be heard in the Hall of Representatives, when the House might adjourn to offer the podium to an important constituent or an interesting personality who happened to be passing through Washington. So thoroughly was the community life of the congressional contingent centered upon itself that their work activities, the daily debates, became one of the principal diversions for legislative society. Senate and House chambers were the settlement's theaters, the galleries serving as the "lounging place of both sexes, where acquaintance is as easily made as at public amusements." [20] Here, the women with their needlepoint, wives and guests of the members were wont to spend the better part of weekday afternoons chatting with friends and taking measure of the actors on the stage below. Major debates and contests for oratorical preeminence were played to a packed house in a carnival atmosphere, supplies of popcorn and candy being dispatched from the floor to the galleries in slings affixed to fishing poles.[21]

But the President never appeared, except for inauguration and on the day of adjournment; and other executives were rarely to be seen. "A sort of fastidious delicacy [is] observed on this subject, which, in effect, prevents the Secretaries from attending the debates even as auditors." [22] The unwritten rule against executive trespassing on the Hill was mutually advantageous, a legislator explained to a bemused Englishman:

No one, unless he were of cast-iron, could possibly stand the badger-
ing to which an official man would be exposed . . . [and] if our men in
office were called upon, like your ministers, to answer, viva voce, questions put by members . . . the issue in every case would probably be an
impeachment, or such a torrent of invectives as no man could bear up
against. . . . [Besides] I do not see, considering all things, and especially
the horror which my countrymen have for any thing like undue influence on the freedom of debate, how it would be possible to admit men
holding [executive] offices into our legislatures.[23]

Even legislators who received executive appointments made it a
practice to dissociate themselves from congressional society by moving off the Hill into the executive quarter.

A mile and a half away, across the natural moat that was the
Tiber, stood the President's house, at the heart of the executive
community. The Treasury flanked it on the east, occupying a modest brick building that was completed in John Adams' administration and destroyed by fire in Jackson's. On the west side the War,
Navy, and State departments shared a building "sunk to the eaves in
a hollow" that had been excavated so that the building might not
rise higher than the Treasury on the other side.[24] Anticipating their
statutory autonomy, the General Post Office and the Patent Office
separated themselves physically from their parent departments—
Treasury and State respectively—occupying neighboring nondescript houses and later an abandoned hotel on the outer fringes of
the executive settlement, equidistant from the White House and the
Capitol. There was no Justice Department, and the Attorney General's office was wherever his house was, he having not even a clerk
during the Jeffersonian era.

Cabinet officers tended to select residences near the executive
mansion. While members of the executive branch did not cluster, in
their residential arrangements, so closely around the public buildings
in their own village as legislators did around the Capitol, avoidance
of the Hill was clearly the rule. A few executives tolerated life in
the congressional community briefly, but only one, Secretary of the
Treasury Gallatin, is known to have resided for any length of time
on Capitol Hill.

No less than legislators on their hilltop, executives lived a life apart, provided with all the necessities within their own village. A produce market was doing business in the President's front yard in 1800–1802.[25] Nearby, also within easy reach of executive residences, a wide variety of goods and services was available, from well-diggers to cabinetmakers, from blacksmiths to banks, from apothecary shops to a library. The wine sellers and seamstresses and milliners of Georgetown supplied the more prestigious needs of executive society. While legislators were attending the Sunday sermon in the Capitol, members of the executive branch observed the sabbath with services held in a corridor of the Treasury building or at the offices of the War, Navy, and State departments.[26] The children of the executive community did not have to mingle with congressmen's offspring, since each settlement was provided with schools.[27] As the debates in the Capitol furnished the principal spectator sport for the Capitol Hill community, executives had their own commercial theater and a racetrack.[28] To match the Congressional Dancing Assembly, an executive assembly met in a local tavern "once a week between Christmas Day and Ash Wednesday, to which all the respectable ladies were invited." [29] Segregated by residence, separate in economic life, in education, in religion, and in their diversions, congressional and executive residents kept apart even in death, each community having its own burying ground.[30]

At the first sitting of Congress in the new capital, after the members were welcomed with an address from President Adams, "usage required," a Representative wrote, "that the answer should be presented in a personal attendance of the whole house at the presidential mansion. But how could this be done? The only access was by a road long and circuitous to avoid the swamp . . . and the mud very deep. Fortunately a recruit of hackney coaches from Baltimore, by their seasonable arrival, enabled us to proceed in fine style, preceded by the sergeant-at-arms with the mace, on horseback." [31] At the next sitting of Congress a new precedent was established which remained unbroken until Woodrow Wilson's administration. The use of couriers was substituted for personal confrontations between President and Congress, "the circumstance under which we find ourselves at this place," President Jefferson explained, "rendering inconvenient the mode heretofore practiced." [32]

"The circumstance under which we find ourselves at this place" was the separation of the congressional and executive communities by a mile-wide wilderness of viny thickets and virtually uninhabited moors,

wet, marshy ground covered with weeds and wancopins, where sportsmen shot ortolan, where cattle formed paths in zigzag courses, where negroes hunted stray cows with tinkling bells about their necks, and where fishermen often took their spoil, especially at full tide.[33]

"Figure to yourself," wrote a congressman in 1807 after having fallen from his horse midway between the White House and the Capitol, "a man almost bruised to death, on a dark, cold night, in the heart of the capital of the United States, out of sight or hearing of human habitation, and you will have a tolerably exact idea of my situation." [34]

Plans never materialized, before 1832, to bridge this watery wasteland by a grand thoroughfare joining the congressional and executive establishments. In 1801 shanties and brickyards standing above the water line in the path of Pennsylvania Avenue were removed and a swath was cut through the morass. A footpath of shards from stonecutters' waste was begun from the congressional side and a flagstone walk from the executive side, but the project was abandoned before the two ever came close to joining.[35] President Jefferson had a double row of poplars planted along the route, with the ludicrous result of giving congressmen, at their end, an uninterrupted vista to the ramshackle stables of the Treasury building, and executives, at their end, a sight line straight to Congress' back door —the executive exposure of the Capitol being its rear, the main entrance facing east.[36] With that, efforts at improvement apparently ceased, and Pennsylvania Avenue remained a desolate country road, where "every turn of your wagon wheel . . . is attended with danger." [37] Flash floods and spring tides made the avenue impassable altogether, necessitating either a long detour via highland roads or a trip by packet boat running between Georgetown, Greenleaf's Point (near the Navy Yard), and Alexandria to effect communication between the marooned communities at either end of the avenue.[38] Fair-weather communication was provided by hackney coaches and by a scheduled stage plying between Georgetown and

Capitol Hill, with an intermediate stop at President's Square—three hours the round trip. Twice daily the "Royal George" approached and departed Capitol Hill "in a halo of dust . . . pitch[ing] like a ship in a seaway, among the holes and ruts of this national highway," with a small cargo of commuting congressmen perched precariously on its lofty open-air seats.[39]

The failure to improve the central section of the capital thus both dramatized and encouraged the social separation between executives and legislators, putting between them in their respective communities a no man's land bridged only by a causeway inconvenient and hazardous to traverse. Such an arrangement was evidently considered not unsatisfactory on either side of the Tiber. Neither the executive nor the congressional community desired communication strongly enough, at least, to facilitate it by committing funds for the purpose: that was left to the politicians of the Jacksonian era.

The place intended for the Supreme Court on the north shore of the Tiber swamp remained unoccupied and undeveloped. Probably the expense of clearing the area, covered with brambles where it was not sunk in bogs, was considered unwarranted by the small size of the court establishment and the small volume of business handled by the judges during their brief stay in Washington each year. The Court made itself inconspicuous and served justice in the basement of the Capitol. "It is by no means a large or handsome apartment; and the lowness of the ceiling, and the circumstance of its being under ground, give a certain cellar-like aspect, which . . . tends to create . . . the impression of justice being done in a corner . . . while the business of legislation is carried on with . . . pride, pomp, and circumstance." [40] The proceedings of the Court attracted, on the whole, only slight attention in the capital except when lawyers of wide repute were arguing cases, and "the moment they sat down, the whole audience arose, and broke up, as if the court had adjourn'd." [41]

As to residential arrangements, the justices lived in the style of the brotherhood they felt themselves to be, all rooming and taking meals at a common table in the same lodginghouse on Capitol Hill. "The Judges here live with perfect harmony . . . in the most frank and unaffected intimacy," wrote Justice Story. "We are all united as one. . . . We moot every question as we proceed, and . . . conferences at our lodgings often come to a very quick, and, I trust, a very accurate opinion, in a few hours." [42] Not until 1845, apparently, did the judicial fraternity break up, with four justices going to live in one house and three in another.[43]

The justices of the Supreme Court can have only a minor place in a study of the governmental community during the Jeffersonian era, despite the important legal precedents established by the Marshall court and despite their dramatic but brief clashes with Congress and the President in the Chase impeachment and the Burr trial. In the sociological sense the justices were barely members of the Washington community, spending only two months of the year, usually, at the capital. The unanimity of their case decisions provides little food for political analysis, beyond the observation that their single-mindedness on policy questions conformed to the fraternal character of their life style; and the justices were too secretive about their activities in their boardinghouse to afford insights about the group *in camera*. Moreover, they lived such a reclusive existence that the community record does little more than note their presence in the capital. They rarely received guests and they rarely ventured out of their lodgings after hours except to make obligatory appearances at official functions and to pay an annual courtesy call, en bloc, at the executive mansion. Just how reclusive their existence was is suggested by the fact that Justice Paterson traveled a full day in a stagecoach with Thomas Jefferson, neither man aware of the other's identity. Only after the journey's end did the Justice learn that his fellow traveler was the Secretary of State during his first term on the Court and the man who may even have been Vice President or President at the time of their encounter.[44] Justice Story perhaps spoke for the group when he wrote: "I scarcely go to any places of pleasure or fashion . . . [and] have separated myself from all political meetings and associations. . . . since I am no longer a political man." [45]

If the citizenry failed to give the expected response to the new governmental establishment on the Potomac, then, the politicians in the establishment did respond according to plan. The settlement pattern of early Washington clearly reveals a community structure paralleling the constitutional structure of government itself. The "separation of powers" became a separation of persons, and each of the branches of government became a self-contained, segregated social system within the larger governmental establishment. Legislators with legislators, executives with executives, judges with judges, the members gathered together in their extraofficial as well as in their official activities, and in their community associations deepened, rather than bridged, the group cleavages prescribed by the Constitution.

Why did the rulers make this highly contrived, unconventional legal structure into their community structure at Washington? That it was a matter of choice with them seems clear enough. Nothing, surely, compelled them to organize their community in such a fashion—neither the Constitution of 1787 nor even the community plan of 1791. Why, then, did they forego the opportunity to evade, in their social organization, the constitutional barriers to interbranch mingling?

Social distance between executives and legislators was partially induced, no doubt, by the spatial separation of the executive offices and the Capitol and by the understandable desire of the members, given the condition of the roads, to reside conveniently to their places of work. But considerations of convenience do not account for the very pronounced social segregation between Supreme Court justices and legislators, both residing and working on Capitol Hill. It was, moreover, by the rulers' own choice that more distant residences from their places of work were not made convenient: they lacked neither authority nor means to create a system of streets and to develop the central section of the capital, where executives and legislators could both have resided close to the Capitol and the executive offices.

As another contributing factor, the work groups into which the Constitution separated the members offered, perhaps, the most explicit guides for organizational behavior in a new, unfamiliar, and exclusively governmental community. Economic roles in a system of production and distribution, which shape the social structure of "normal" communities, were lacking. To offset the influence of constitutionally prescribed work relationships, personal familiarity among the rulers and shared experiences as a group were at a minimum in a community composed largely of transients and drawn from a variety of provincial cultures. Persistent or intense policy demands by outside groups were lacking, to generate different organizational imperatives within the governing group. All these circumstances presumably gave greater scope than would otherwise have been the case to the influence of the constitutional structure upon the community structure of the power-holders. For executives, too, social segregation may have been partially induced by status considerations, since they, as appointed persons, were lower in social precedence than elected persons. Segregation may have had the advantage also of discouraging congressional interference with their work, a subject of executive complaint before the move to Washington. And, in the case of the Supreme Court, the maintenance of social distance vis-à-vis members of the "political" branches accorded with both the recognized proprieties of judicial conduct and, presumably, the interest of the judiciary in maintaining its own independence.

But a key factor contributing to social segregation by branch affiliation is suggested by the consistency between such behavior and community attitudes about power and politicians. In the absence of any extrinsic forces compelling the rulers to segregate in community life, patterned avoidance between executives, legislators, and judges indicates that they felt a stronger sense of identification with their constitutional roles than with other more partisan roles they may have had in the community. Social segregation on the basis of branch affiliation suggests, in other words, that the rulers generally considered themselves executives, legislators, or judges first, and politicians or party members second. Such a preference for nonpartisan, constitutionally sanctioned roles fully accords with, and tends to confirm the authenticity of, the members' disparaging image of politicians. Their decided preference for associating with fellow branch members in extraofficial life is also precisely the sort of social behavior that was foreshadowed by the attitudes they held concerning power. Power-holders acculturated to antipower values would, it was predicted, be attracted toward behaviors and associations which were sanctioned by the Constitution. By subdividing into separate societies of executives, legislators, and judges, the rulers could not have more literally translated constitutional principles of organization into social realities nor afforded themselves greater security from reproach in this aspect of their community life at Washington. When one sees, moreover, the remarkable consistency between the organizational precepts of the Constitution of 1787 and the community plan of 1791, on the one hand, and, on the other hand, the actual community structure of the governing politicians from 1800 to 1828, one must presume a consistency also in the attitudes from which these principles of organization originally derived, namely, attitudes of mistrust toward political power.

Whatever the underlying causes, here was a community of power-holders who preferred and who sanctioned, in their extraofficial life, a structural configuration that had been designed explicitly to check power. Here was a community of rulers who chose, among all the alternatives of social organization open to them, precisely the one most prejudicial to their capacity to rule.

Even the casual student of American political institutions knows what object the Constitution's framers had in mind when they contrived the governmental structure that the officeholders made into their community structure at Washington. The purpose of these "inventions of prudence," as Madison described the arrangements commonly called "separation of powers," was to divide the power to govern the nation among "rival interests." [46] Not content with an array of devices to ensure that men with conflicting interests would be recruited into the government in the first place, the framers meant also to create contending interests within the governing establishment itself. Their strategy was to separate the governors into three distinct groups—executives, legislators, judges—making each group largely dependent upon the acquiescence of the others in order to achieve fulfillment of its own policy objectives, yet denying each the legal means of compelling that acquiescence from the others. Under such a system of "separated institutions sharing powers," [47] to dominate one branch of government does not ordinarily suffice to ensure dominance over public policy. Effective rulership tends to require what the Constitution clearly intends to discourage, namely, that a party or faction disperse its members or its influence across the branches of government.

Superficially, at least, the Republican party of 1801–28 came near to achieving this objective. Though it failed to dominate the Supreme Court, Jefferson's party commanded a majority in Congress as well as the top positions in the executive branch through almost all of the first twenty-eight years of the nineteenth century. Clearly, then, the party ties to bridge the constitutional gulf between Congress and the executive branch were there. Clearly, too, the governing politicians had the opportunity to reflect these ties in their social organization. Had they done so—had they organized their community around parties instead of around branches of government—it seems almost certain that the resulting reinforcement and regularity of association between executive and legislative party members would have contributed greatly to the effectiveness of the party as *governing* group. The power interests of the governing politicians would seem, in other words, to have dictated a social organization which reinforced and sanctioned that type of association—the political party—promising maximum power to its members in a legal system of separated power groups.

But rulers imbued with antipower values responded to constitutional directives rather than power needs. And in so responding they did not merely forego an opportunity to enhance their capacity for rulership. They positively aggravated the intragovernmental cleavages of interest and personnel by which the Constitution's framers had sought to make rulership difficult. Between men who needed to collaborate in order to rule the nation, their community structure institutionalized avoidance. So far from promoting common interests and collaboration, they created communication problems between the Hill and the executive establishment of a sort hardly envisaged by the most zealous advocate of Montesquieu's doctrines. Men whom the Constitution merely separated into different work groups separated themselves into different societies and made different branch affiliations into different community allegiances. To the problems of achieving concurrence between different policy-making establishments they would add the untold problems of achieving concurrence and coordination between participants in different social systems, each with its own set of values, each with different ways of working and different ways of living.

The structure and values of the governing community thus tended to ensure the integrity of a constitutional structure of "separated institutions sharing powers." But with what effect upon the capacity of the ruling establishment to do its job as a government? The extraordinary marriage of community structure to constitutional structure, and the values of the governing group which sustained it, raise second thoughts about the framers' "prudence" in contriving an organizational scheme intended to "supply . . . by opposite and rival interests, the defect of better motives" among the rulers of the nation.[48] How could a governing establishment pregnant with such sources of conflict within itself be capable of resolving conflicts outside itself, in the society at large? How could a governing community cleaved within itself keep a new and still fragile nation also from cleaving asunder?

How, then, to make the two ruling establishments—Congress on the Hill and the executive community on the other side of the Tiber —act as one? If by the political party, how to keep the party together in the face of a Constitution, a community ground plan, a social structure, and a complex of values among the governors themselves which sanctioned separateness? Where to find the leaders for such a task? How could the power-holders resolve the seeming incompatibility between their own attitudes toward power-seeking and the functional requirements of a workable government? How to muster the will to rule when the spirit was lacking? These were the dilemmas of governing among rulers who modeled their own community structure after the constitutional structure of government, and who adopted the American image of power and politicians as their own. These were the dilemmas of ruling a people that meant to be tough to rule.

Two paramount problems, then, faced the pioneer politicians of the new nation, both of them having large implications for the viability of the polity itself. One was the isolation of the governors from the governed and the citizen indifference which gave rise to it—the problem of "government at a distance and out of sight." The other was how to exercise effective command over separate institutions of power, and thus ensure effective government of the nation.

The first of these problems, we have seen, was not solved during the Jeffersonian era. How nearly was the second solved? And could it be solved without also solving the first? Would it be possible to sustain effective political command *inside* the governmental community in the absence of affirmative and enthusiastic responses from citizens *outside* the community? A study of the inner life and the inner organization of the congressional community on Capitol Hill, in the chapters following, will bring nearer the answers to these questions.

PART THREE

CAPITOL HILL

⸺⁕{ CHAPTER 5 }⁕⸺

COMMUNITY AND SOCIETY

Outwardly, and in certain aspects of its inner life, the Hill resembled nothing so much as an early New England community.[1] The ground plan was similar: instead of the church on the village green with houses huddled round, the Capitol on its plaza, encircled by lodginghouses. The Capitol, like the village church, was the community center, gathering place for Sunday worship and political meetings. No other public building than a meetinghouse being provided in the settlement, the modest, look-alike houses clustered around it suggested a congregational, equalitarian society as unmistakably as the President's mansion, the town houses, and the nondescript shacks of the executive community bespoke hierarchy and status differences. As in the town-meeting villages of New England, it was the collectivity of individuals in the congressional community that made the binding decisions, with the ultimate authority vested not in particular social roles but in a numerical entity, the majority of those voting.

The intensity of the social exposure that was the lot of the New England villager, the experience of living constantly under the eye and in the presence of one's peers, was even more the lot of the legislator on Capitol Hill. Self-sufficient on their summit, the lawmakers lived the winter wholly in each other's company save as they might venture across the wastes of the Tiber to the executive quarter. They worked together, daily assembled in the noisy auditoriums of the Capitol, with no offices but their desks on the floor itself. They lived together in the same lodginghouses. They took their meals together around the same boardinghouse tables. Privacy was no more to be found during leisure than at work, not even privacy when they retired; in their lodginghouses "they lay two in a room, even the Senators." [2]

Here, however, the resemblance ends. For life on the Hill imposed upon a crowd of citizen delegates a communal discipline fit for Calvinists or monks. It threw together, under conditions of social intimacy not easily endured even by men long disciplined to it, a group which utterly lacked binding ties of the sort that reinforced, rationalized, and made tolerable the intensely communal life of the New England villagers. Common membership in the legislative institution they had, and common subjection to the ordeal of election: these were binding ties of sufficient strength, apparently, to draw them into a society apart from executives. Career officeholders they were, too. More than four fifths of the members of one Congress had government experience before coming to Washington (see Table 3), and of 439 Senators and Representatives whose ca-

TABLE 3

PREVIOUS GOVERNMENT SERVICE OF
MEMBERS OF THE 13TH CONGRESS,
1813-1815 [a]

Government experience	Senators (N = 36)	Represent- atives (N = 174)	Percent of total mem- bership (N = 210).
All categories	35	139	82.9
Federal	5	6	5.2
Executive	5	6	5.2
Judiciary	0	0	
State	32	124	74.3
Legislative	30	115	69.0
Executive	9	16	11.4
Judiciary	6	18	11.4
Local	3	36	18.6

Source: Biographical sketches appearing in the *Biographical Directory of the American Congress* and the *Dictionary of American Biography*.
[a] Previous government service means service prior to becoming members of Congress irrespective of when or which chamber of Congress the members first entered.

Since many members had previous service in more than one institution of government (e.g., in both the state legislature and the state judiciary), no two of the above job categories are mutually exclusive.

reers have been investigated more than two thirds continued their political careers in other public jobs after leaving the congressional community.[3] But the stability of group membership, the social sameness, the habituation of the members to each other, and the fraternal feelings that usually distinguish congregational communities were conspicuous by their absence in the community on Capitol Hill.

Instead of a stable community membership, one finds a society of transients. Almost none of the members acquired homes in the capital or established year-round residence there.[4] They merely wintered in Washington, spending more time each year with constituents than with each other. Each new Congress, moreover, brought a host of new faces to the community, drastically reconstituting its membership every two years. For the first four decades of national government between one third and two thirds of the congressional community left every two years not to return (see Table 4). New faces appeared and familiar ones departed with considerably greater frequency than in today's Congress: on the average, the biennial turnover was 41.5 percent of the total membership, as compared with 15.8 percent turnover from the 78th to the 79th Congress and 22.4 percent from the 79th to the 80th Congress.[5] While there were a few for whom the Hill was more than a way station in the pursuit of a career, a man's affiliation with the congressional community tended to be brief.[6] Roughly two thirds of the Representatives on the roster of the 13th Congress, for example, did not serve for more than two terms, and two thirds of the Senators failed to serve more than one term—quite a few of them resigning before they completed even that (see Table 5).

Thus, for all the forced social intimacy of their community life, the rulers on Capitol Hill were largely strangers to each other. "We never remain long enough together to become personally acquainted." [7] "There are many individuals in this House whom I do not know, for I have never met them in the House or out of it." [8] "Friendships . . . we had few and limited opportunities to cultivate," recalled another legislator, and those "were soon broken by our subsequent separation in different and often far-distant states." [9]

TABLE 4

BIENNIAL TURNOVER IN CONGRESS

Congress	Percent of total membership failing to return
1st to 2d	39.6
2d to 3d (Washington) [a]	35.9
3d to 4th	47.8
4th to 5th (John Adams)	42.5
5th to 6th	42.7
6th to 7th (Jefferson)	52.0
7th to 8th	39.6
8th to 9th (Jefferson)	33.4
9th to 10th	32.4
10th to 11th (Madison)	43.7
11th to 12th	37.9
12th to 13th (Madison)	47.4
13th to 14th	49.4
14th to 15th (Monroe)	63.1 [b]
15th to 16th	48.1
16th to 17th (Monroe)	46.5
17th to 18th	33.3
18th to 19th (John Quincy Adams)	40.1
19th to 20th	37.4
20th to 21st (Jackson)	40.8
21st to 22d	38.9

Source: Personnel rosters for each Congress appearing in the *Biographical Directory of the American Congress*.
[a] Parentheses enclose the names of the Presidents elected with these Congresses.
[b] This unusually high turnover apparently resulted from widespread citizen indignation against a Congress which had voted a pay increase for itself.

Not only was the cast of characters constantly changing but it embraced a most improbable variety of men and interests. Here was none of the social homogeneity that ordinarily characterizes communities organized on congregational and equalitarian principles, and that seems essential to peaceful coexistence between men thrown into such intensive interaction.

No English person who has not travelled over half the world, can form an idea of such differences among men forming one assembly for the same purpose, and speaking the same language . . . [forming] a society singularly compounded of the largest variety of elements . . . all . . . mixed up together in daily intercourse, like the higher circle of a little village.[10]

There was, needless to say, the political sectarianism of their different constituency ties, sharpened by the legislators' self-appointed
roles as "advocates, retained expressly to support the particular views
of particular parties" among their electorates at home.[11] There were
differences in occupational background, although lawyers predom-
inated in the same proportion as in the modern House of Representatives (see Table 6). The congressional community mixed together
men widely apart in age, and many sat as equals at work and at
board beside colleagues young enough to have been their sons.[12] The
land-rich were mingled with the money-rich, and both with the in-
affluent. A variety of ethnic strains represented a nation which had
been populated by transatlantic migration—Dutch, French, Scotch,
English, Irish, "brought together out of law-courts, sugar-fields, merchants' stores, mountain-farms, forests and prairies." [13]

Most conspicuous of all were the behavioral contrasts associated
with the various regions of the country from which the members
came, where they spent the better part of each year, and to which
they acknowledged their deepest loyalties. To speak of "regional
differences" in the new nation is to put too mildly the gulf that separated men from North and South, from the seaboard and from the
mountains and the frontiers of the West. For in the Jeffersonian era
men from different regions were men from different cultures, with

TABLE 5

LENGTH OF CONTINUOUS SERVICE OF MEMBERS OF THE 13TH CONGRESS, 1813–1815[a]

	REPRESENTATIVES		SENATORS	
	Number	Percent	Number	Percent
1–2 years	65	37.4	6	16.7
3–4 years	47	27.0	5	13.9
5–6 years	24	13.8	13	36.1
7–8 years	15	8.6	2	5.6
9–10 years	3	1.7	2	5.6
11 years or more	20	11.5	8	22.1
	174	100.0	36	100.0

Source: Biographical sketches of the members of the 13th Congress
appearing in the *Biographical Directory of the American Congress*.
[a] The table includes all continuous service of which service in
the 13th Congress was a part.

TABLE 6

CIVIL OCCUPATIONS OF LEGISLATORS, 9TH AND 13TH CONGRESSES [a]

	Senators		Represent-atives		Percent of total mem-bership (N = 338)	
Professions						
Law	42		142		54.4 [b]	
Other	6	48	34	176	11.8	66.2
Agriculture		9		48		16.9
Trade, commerce, finance		3		45		14.2
Other occupations		1		8		2.7
		61		277		100.0

Source: Biographical sketches appearing in the *Biographical Directory of the American Congress* and the *Dictionary of American Biography*.

[a] The table excludes 64 members whose civil occupations could not be ascertained. A small number of members who served in one chamber in the 9th Congress and the other chamber in the 13th Congress are counted twice.

[b] The proportion of lawyers increased by 13.2 percentage points from the 9th to the 13th Congress, while the proportion of farmers and planters dropped by 8.7 percentage points.

different ways of speaking and acting and thinking, with differing standards of behavior, even with differing concepts of right and wrong.[14] There were those from the plantation culture and the courthouse politics of the southeast—mercurial, proficient at oratory and duels, "ready to construe contradiction into insult" [15] and "great aristocrats in their . . . habits, if not in their politics." [16] The products of an almost totally different culture and life experience were the New Englanders, cultural aliens in the slaveholding southland. Austere, moralistic, inner-directed, they "keep to their lodgings," [17] "an unmixed people . . . and used only to see neighbors like themselves." [18] From the homesteader culture of the frontier came David Crockett and cultural kinsmen—brash, boastful, elemental types, "accustomed to speak at barbecues and electioneering canvassings," [19] at home in Washington's woods but not in its society. Upon them all the new American nationality sat lightly. "We come from every stage of civilisation, fresh from the people, and bring with us the manners and tastes of [our] different regions. We never remain long enough together to . . . acquire, by much intercourse, that uniform system of . . . deportment, without which crowded societies could not get on for a moment." [20] The distinct provincial cultures that more than a century of prenational existence had nurtured on American soil and that primitive means of communication after nationhood still preserved from contact, Capitol Hill brought together. Power made a community of cultural strangers. And power, shared, was hardly a thing to bind strangers together.

To achieve political accord among men of such disparate interests and different acculturation would not have been an easy task even under the most auspicious circumstances. For those gathered to govern on Capitol Hill in the Jeffersonian era, the circumstances were anything but auspicious.

To the political cleavages inherent in any representative assembly were added the deeper social tensions that are generated when men of widely diverging beliefs and behaviors are thrust upon each other in everyday living. Close-quarters living gave rise to personal animus even between "men whose natural interests and stand in society are in many respects similar. . . . The more I know of [two New England Senators] the more I am impressed with the idea how unsuited they are ever to co-operate," commented a fellow lodger; "never were two substances more completely adapted to make each other explode." [21] As social intimacy bared the depth of their behavioral differences, tolerance among men from different regions was strained to the breaking point. Political coexistence with the South and the frontier states was hard enough for New Englanders to accept. Social coexistence was insufferable with slaveholders "accustomed to speak in the tone of masters" and with frontiersmen having "a license of tongue incident to a wild and uncultivated state of society. With men of such states of mind and temperament," a Massachusetts delegate protested, "men educated in . . . New England . . . could have little pleasure in intercourse, less in controversy, and of course no sympathy." [22] Close scrutiny of their New England neighbors in power could convince southerners, in their turn, that there was "not one [who] possesses the slightest tie of common interest or of common feeling with us," [23] planters and gentlemen cast among men "who raised 'beef and pork, and butter and cheese, and potatoes and cabbages'" and carried on "a paltry trade in potash and codfish."[24] Cultural antipathies, crowded barracks, poor rations, and separation from families left at home combined to make tempers wear thin as the winters wore on, leading to sporadic eruptions of violence. In a sudden affray at the table in Miss Shields's boardinghouse, Randolph, "pouring out a glass of wine, dashed it in Alston's face. Alston sent a decanter at his head in return, and these and similar missiles continued to fly to and fro, until there was much destruction of glass ware."[25] The chambers of the Capitol themselves witnessed more than one scuffle, and, though it was not yet the custom for legislators to arm themselves when legislating, pistols at twenty paces cracked more than once in the woods outside the Capitol.[26]

To those who would seek political agreement in an atmosphere of social tensions, the rules of proceeding in Congress offered no aid at all. On the contrary, contentiousness was encouraged by Senate and House rules which gave higher precedence to raising questions than to deciding them and which guaranteed almost total freedom from restraint to the idiosyncratic protagonist.

The Americans, observed an astonished Britisher, have taken "the principle of democracy . . . [and] applied [it] to a legislative body."[27] It was not given to some to initiate action and to others to respond. Any legislator had "the privilege of bringing forward, at any moment, such measures as suit his fancy";[28] and any other legislator could postpone action on them indefinitely by the simple expedient of talking. There was no Rules Committee of the House to control the legislative proposals that got to the floor, and no other body served that function. Not even a mild cloture rule such as that in today's Senate existed in either chamber. Garrulity was the rule, and orations of two or three days' length were not uncommon. There was "a universal tolerance of long speeches,"[29] curtailed by "no coughing—no cheering—no hear! hear!—none of those indefinable, but significant sounds, which are so irresistibly efficacious in modifying the debates in the House of Commons."[30] No limits were placed on the number of times a member might speak on the same bill. There were no rules requiring a member's remarks to be germane to the issue, and "no attempt is ever made to restrict the range of argument or declamation, within the limits even of remote connexion with the subject of debate." [31]

Leadership, power to stop or control debate, was nowhere evident. There were no seniority leaders, seniority not being recognized as a basis for rank or prerogative either socially or politically on Capitol Hill.[32] There were no elective or formally recognized party leaders such as are found in the modern Congress:* "absolutely no persons holding the station of what are called, in England, Leaders. . . . Persons of ability and address do, of course, acquire a certain degree of unsteady influence . . . but this never appears to entitle them to the character of leading men. The bare insinuation of such pretensions, indeed, would inevitably lead to the downfall of the man so designated." [33]

With permissiveness of the rules and lack of formally recognized leadership went no spirit of cooperation, conciliation, or deference to the opinions of others. On the contrary, individuation of behavior and opinion was approved and valued, while following the lead of others was scorned as a sign either of weakness of character or of ulterior motives for personal gain. To accommodate was to compromise one's principles. To "disdain the idea of relying . . . [on] any man or set of men" was doctrine; [34] and manifestoes of personal independence so suffused the legislative liturgy that the stenographer reported them in paraphrase for the official record: "He had, he said, a right to his opinion. . . . He held himself responsible for it to no man . . . but at his own will and pleasure. . . . I will express my opinion on this and every other subject, without restraint." [35] Men who agreed on an issue felt constrained to adduce different reasons for arriving at their opinions: "The actual practice is to acknowledge no . . . guidance; each member taking good care . . . to let [others] . . . see that he is independent." [36] As speaker after speaker would arise to put his own personal stamp on the measure in question and to expound his individual reasons for support or opposition, the logic, the reasons, the motives behind

* The question of informal leadership will be taken up in Chapter 6.

their opinions became themselves the subject of controversy. Debate would veer in unexpected directions; amendments would accumulate; involvement in the conflict would widen and deepen; agreement would fade, and firm majorities might go to pieces.

The number of amendments had now become very great, and the accumulation of obstacles was increasing with every speech. I was assured, —and from the tenor of the debate, I have no doubt it was so,—that a majority was decidedly in favour of the . . . [measure], but minor discrepancies of opinion were found to be irreconcilable. . . . The result was that . . . no money was granted at all, and the matter left for farther debate in another Congress.[37]

Legislators "are not yet sufficiently aware of the necessity of accommodation & mutual sacrifice of opinion for conducting a numerous assembly," President Jefferson complained. In a policy-making body which required some degree of collaboration to accomplish anything,

the object of the members . . . seemed to be merely to thwart, by every means, the wishes of their political antagonists, and to wear one another out by persevering opposition. . . . every man who has had to transact real business, must have found that even [when all sides are in agreement] . . . there must generally be some compromise—some mutual concession,—something of what is familiarly called "giving and taking," in order to smooth away the difficulties incident to the very nature of our being, and the boundless complication in our interests. But [here] a deliberative body come to discuss a question in a spirit of avowed misunderstanding, without the smallest wish to agree.[38]

"Political hostilities are waged with great vigour," commented another observer, "yet both in attack and defence there is evidently an entire want both of discipline and organization. There is no concert, no division of duties, no compromise of opinion. . . . Any general system of effective co-operation is impossible."[39]

The result was a scene of confusion daily on the floor of House and Senate that bore no resemblance to the deliberative processes of either the town meeting or the parliamentary assemblies of the Old World. Congress at work was Hyde Park set down in the lobby of a busy hotel—hortatory outcry in milling throngs, all wearing hats as if just arrived or on the verge of departure, variously attired in

the fashions of faraway places. Comings and goings were continual
—to the rostrum to see the clerk, to the anterooms to meet friends,
to the Speaker's chair in a sudden surge to hear the results of a vote,
to the firesides for hasty caucuses and strategy-planning sessions.
Some gave audience to the speaker of the moment; some sat at their
desks reading or catching up on correspondence; some stood chatting with lady friends, invited on the floor; others dozed, feet
propped high. Page boys weaved through the crowd, "little Mercu-
ries" bearing messages, pitchers of water for parched throats, bun-
dles of documents, calling out members' names, distributing mail
just arrived on the stagecoach. Quills scratched, bond crackled as
knuckles rapped the sand off wet ink, countless newspapers rustled.
Desk drawers banged, feet shuffled in a sea of documents strewn on
the floor. Bird dogs fresh from the hunt bounded in with their masters, yapping accompaniment to contenders for attention, contenders for power.[40] Some government! "Babeltown," a legislator called
it.[41]

Instability of membership; the constant circulation of short-time
servers through the community; cultural, political, temperamental,
occupational, ethnic, and age disparities between the members, inflamed into personal animosities by close-quarters confinement on
Capitol Hill; permissive rules of debate and dogged adherence to the
practice of internal democracy; the absence of formal leadership
roles; a compulsion to garrulity and contention; policy-making conducted in a hubbub of irrelevant activities—all these would seem
more than enough to offset whatever advantages smallness of size
and negligibility of citizen pressures upon the legislative establishment gave to those who would mobilize Congress for policy action.
There was another aspect of the congressional community, however, which inhibited the processes of majority formation perhaps as
severely as all these combined. This was a social structure which
tended to institutionalize the sectional or regional differences among
the members, and which probably aggravated the problems of
achieving consensus far beyond any internal sources of cleavage to
be found in the modern Congress.

Outside the chambers themselves the members did not, for all the closeness of their confinement, intermingle freely or associate widely. Instead they segregated into mutually exclusive, closely knit voluntary associations, forming a segmented social structure of face-to-face peer groups. These were the boardinghouse fraternities which almost all legislators joined when they came to Washington —the members who took their meals together, who lived together at the same lodginghouse, and who spend most of their leisure time together. Originating before the move to Washington and continuing at least until the Civil War, the congressional messes, as the members called their fraternities, were the basic social units of the Capitol Hill community. It is likely, as will shortly be seen, that they were the basic units of its political structure as well.

Within the larger governmental community, members segregated on the basis of branch affiliation. Within the congressional sub-community, members segregated principally on the basis of sectional affiliation. Legislators had a decided aversion to sharing their mess table, their living quarters, and their leisure hours with colleagues from regions other than their own and much preferred to live in groups restricted to men having approximately the same geo-cultural affiliation [42] (see Table 7). While most members saw to it that they had at least one companion from the same state in their mess, and while it was not unusual for a substantial portion of a state's delegation to gather under the same roof, few boardinghouse groups were comprised exclusively of members from the same state, and only rarely did an entire state delegation reside together.[43] Living in regionally mixed groups was preferred to living alone, but the truly cosmopolitan groups were few. Even when members from distant parts of the country formed a mess group, most often the group was dominated by a majority from the same state or region.

Ranging in size to as many as thirty members in one mess, the typical boardinghouse group was, then, a party of southerners or of westerners or of New Englanders, a conclave of New Yorkers, Jerseymen, and Pennsylvanians, or perhaps "a sett" of Virginians and Marylanders.[44] Within the congressional messes, Senators and Representatives mixed freely, bridging in their extraofficial life

TABLE 7

COMPOSITION OF BOARDINGHOUSE GROUPS[a]

	1807 (N = 154)	*1809* (N = 163)	*1816* (N = 194)	*1822* (N = 219)	*1828* (N = 249)
Percent living in groups representing: [b]					
a. one state	11.3	13.4	7.7	11.4	4.0
b. one region	72.4	69.4	74.2	66.8	68.9
c. different regions	13.2	14.7	15.0	15.5	18.5
Percent living alone	3.1	2.5	3.1	6.3	9.6
	100.0	100.0	100.0	100.0	100.0

Source: *Congressional Directories* for 1807, 1809, 1816, 1822, 1828.

[a] Percentages are of the total number of legislators with known residence.
The purpose here being to demonstrate patterns, category *a* includes larger boardinghouse groups in which there was no more than one "outsider" from another state; category *b* includes larger boardinghouse groups in which there was no more than one "outsider" from another region, as "region" is defined in note *b* below.

[b] Subject to the modifications noted below, the regional categories used here are as follows:

New England: Massachusetts, Connecticut, Rhode Island, Vermont, New Hampshire, Maine
Middle Atlantic: New York, New Jersey, Pennsylvania, Delaware, Maryland
South: Virginia, North Carolina, South Carolina, Georgia, Florida, Alabama, Mississippi, Louisiana
West: Tennessee, Kentucky, Ohio, Illinois, Indiana, Missouri, Arkansas, Michigan

Strict adherence to these categories would assign many states having a common border and sociocultural complex to different regions. The better to reflect common geocultural ties between members of the same boardinghouse group, messes are considered to represent a single region where all but one of the states represented in the group are of the same region, and that one exception is a state having a common boundary with one or more of the other states represented in the group. For example, a mess composed of four men each from New Jersey, New York, and Connecticut (the last a New England state but having a common boundary with New York) is considered to represent a single region.

their constitutional separation in official life. The young mixed with the old, the newcomers with the old-timers, the lawyers with the farmers, and the farmers with the merchants. But politics did not, for all this, make strange bedfellows on Capitol Hill. For these were not the important differences among sojourners in power, outward bound to the varied cultures of a new nation. In a heterogeneous society most members sought provincial companionship, setting themselves apart from men different in their places of origin and differently acculturated. They transformed a national institution into a series of sectional conclaves.

As their predominantly sectional composition suggests, few messes were chance groups of men who happened to find themselves at the same lodginghouse. Some legislators from the same state or region would travel together to the capital each fall and form themselves into a boardinghouse group upon arrival, perhaps recruiting others into their group to fill up the house.[45] Others "made up" their groups after arrival, sometimes with the boardinghouse proprietor or proprietress acting as intermediary.[46] Persons not members of Congress were rarely accommodated in the same house with legislators even in the early years when accommodations were scarce, and by 1828 a handbook for newcomers noted that "it has become an invariable custom for the members of Congress to mess by themselves." [47]

Mess group affiliation was recognized as a mark of identification among legislators. Conversationally members might be referred to as one of innkeeper "Dowson's crowd" or as a member of keeper "Coyle's family." Some boardinghouse groups were given distinctive names, such as the "Washington Mess" (so identified in the *Congressional Directory* for 1809) and the "War Mess," a fraternity of War Hawks in 1810–12. In further recognition of the importance of the boardinghouse groups the early *Congressional Directories*, rather than listing members in alphabetical order or by state, listed them by boardinghouse, each group roster headed by the name of the boardinghouse keeper and the groups listed in order of the proximity of their lodgings to the Capitol.[48] One surmises, therefore, that mess membership was regarded as a permanent affiliation for the duration of a session, with little shifting of individuals from one fraternity to another. The tendency was, moreover, for certain lodginghouses to be regarded as the "property" of certain regions from one Congress to the next, and take-over by an alien group was cause for ill feeling.[49]

Life within the boardinghouses combined the qualities of the fraternity house with those of the political club, bringing "together around the common mess-table kindred spirits engaged in the same pursuit" [50] and "insuring comradeship at all hours, and spirited but seldom acrimonious talk at meal-times." [51] It was a thoroughly communal existence. Since very few legislators brought their wives or families to Washington, boardinghouse society was for the most part one of "unvarying masculinity." [52] Manners were informal: members "threw off their coats and removed their shoes at pleasure. . . . The formalities and observances of society were not only disregarded, but condemned as interferences with the liberty of person and freedom of speech and action." [53] Summoned to the dining hall by the breakfast or dinner bell "like scholars in a college, or monks in a monastery," [54] messmates took their meals seated at one long table called the "ordinary," served by the proprietor or major-domo on plates handed down from the head of the table. All members of the group were placed on an equal footing, considerations of rank and precedence being entirely absent. At Conrad and McMunn's boardinghouse on Capitol Hill, Vice President Jefferson, recalled one of his friends,

lived on a perfect equality with his fellow boarders, and ate at a common table. Even here, so far from taking precedence of the other members of Congress, he always placed himself at the lowest end of the table. Mrs. Brown, wife of the senator from Kentucky, suggested that a seat should be offered him at the upper end, near the fire, if not on account of his rank as vice-President, at least as the oldest man in the company. But the idea was rejected . . . and he occupied during the whole winter the lowest and coldest seat at a long table at which a company of more than thirty sat down. [55]

Characterized by the distinctive manners and customs of its region, "each mess was an organized community in itself," with social distance maintained between the messes. [56] Within the group, "our association on the floor, and . . . in our . . . lodgings, led to the reciprocation of friendships which remained intimate and cordial during the continuance of our mutual Congress life"; outside the group, "intercourse for the most part was polite, but cold and general." [57] Encounter between members of different fraternities appears to have been limited largely to the five or six hours daily when everyone was assembled for work in the Capitol, and even then some accounts suggest that mess groups selected a bloc of neighbor-

ing desks on the floor itself.[58] Visiting between the messes after
hours was said to be infrequent. "The company is good enough,"
wrote a Representative of mess life, "but it is always the same, and
. . . I had rather now and then see some other persons."[59] If not
avoided by choice, visiting was discouraged by lack of privacy and
space within the boardinghouses. "Our not being able to have a
room each is a great . . . inconvenience," wrote one of the party
activists in the early Congress.[60] Guests would have to be received
in the common room or parlor, a "hot oven full of senators and representatives"[61] and "abounding with noise and intrusion,"[62] where
the members assembled after dinner to play cards, tell tales, talk
over the events of the day, "& then for politics."[63]

It is precisely on this point of greatest interest, "politics," that the
descriptive accounts of boardinghouse life tantalize, abounding with
allusions but devoid of specific information on the "consultations"
or "conferences" or "parlor assemblages" that seem to have been a
regular feature of mess life.[64] Perhaps because these gatherings
were so much a part of the routine or perhaps because they were
meant to be clandestine, the community record reveals no more
about the inner political life of the congressional messes than it reveals about the conferences of the Supreme Court justices at their
lodginghouse. The official record of roll call votes, however, offers
evidence which persuasively argues that the after-dinner "parlor assemblages" in the congressional boardinghouses were "caucuses" in
fact if they were not so in name, and which explains why legislators
occasionally applied the term "party" to their boardinghouse fraternity.[65]

For the members who lived together, took their meals together,
and spent most of their leisure hours together also voted together
with a very high degree of regularity. One hundred sixteen roll call
votes in the House of Representatives were selected for study, and
the voting behavior of each boardinghouse group on each roll call
was analyzed.[66] In almost 75 percent of the resulting 2,657 cases
analyzed, messmates voted unanimously or with only one dissenting
vote within the group (see Table 8). In only 11 percent of the cases
did as many as one third of the members of a group dissent from
their group's vote.[67]

TABLE 8

BOARDINGHOUSE GROUPS AS VOTING BLOCS, HOUSE OF REPRESENTATIVES, 1807–1829 [a]

	1807 10th Cong., 1st sess.	1809 11th Cong., 1st sess.	1816 14th Cong., 2d sess.	1828 20th Cong., 2d sess.	1829 21st Cong., 1st sess.	ALL CONGRESSES Number	Percent
Number of roll calls	32	17	28	19	20	116	
Number of groups	17	21	23	28	29		
Number of cases	544	357	644	532	580	2,657	
Cases of unanimity	44.7%	70.9%	38.5%	47.4%	42.4%	1,243	46.8
Cases of no more than one dissent in the group	26.3%	20.2%	28.9%	25.8%	33.1%	729	27.4
Totals: Cases of group "agreement"	71.0%	91.1%	67.4%	73.2%	75.5%	1,972 [b]	74.2 [b]
Cases in which two-thirds or more of group members agreed	87.0%	98.0%	90.5%	89.2%	83.3%	2,365	89.0

[a] Only groups of three or more Representatives were analyzed. "Absences" were disregarded with the following exception: where more than half a group's members failed to vote, this was considered to be the group's "vote" and any members casting an actual vote were considered dissenters. In the case of groups having only three Representatives, "agreement" in the above table means that at least two members voted similarly (or failed to vote).

[b] Table 9 analyzes the distribution of these agreements on roll calls of high and low House cohesion.

Moreover, boardinghouse fraternities voted as blocs quite independently of the size of the majority vote in the whole House—
independently, it would therefore appear, of the voting cohesion of
the majority and minority parties in the House.* Since a unanimous
vote in the whole House would necessarily mean perfect unanimity
in all boardinghouse groups, it might be expected that, as the size of
the House majority increased, so would the incidence of agreement
significantly increase within the subgroups that were the congressional messes. If such had been the case, the high incidence of group
agreement shown in Table 8 would be less significant as a measure
of the importance of these groups in the voting structure of the
early Congresses. Table 9 demonstrates that this was not the case,
however, on the 116 roll calls analyzed here. Boardinghouse groups
voted as blocs on the closely contested issues in the House just as
they did on the less controversial issues, decided by a large majority
margin. Moreover, the incidence of bloc voting by messmates not
only failed to rise but tended to decline slightly as the size of the
majority vote in the whole House increased. The more evenly divided the House sentiment and the more closely contested the issue,
the greater, apparently, was intrabloc "discipline" and the reliance
upon messmates for political cues.[68]

The voting performance of the congressional messes clearly suggests, then, that legislators looked for policy guidance, as they did
for companionship, to colleagues from the same locale or region,
and that these intralegislative fraternal associations were influences
of major significance upon the members' voting behavior.† This is

* The assumption here is that fluctuations in the size of the House majority
from issue to issue meant fluctuations in the cohesiveness of both the parties. It
is not reasonable to infer, particularly in view of data presented in the next
chapter, that one of the parties was consistently cohesive, while the other was
erratic.

† As with Representatives, Senators who were messmates tended to vote
together. Thus, for example, of the six groups of Senators living together in
1809, two groups voted with perfect unanimity on all ten roll calls taken in the
short 1st session of the 11th Congress; one group voted unanimously on nine
of the ten roll calls; two groups voted unanimously on eight; and the remaining
group voted unanimously on five. Perfect unanimity was thus achieved in 83.3
percent of the sixty cases.

Any extended analysis of boardinghouse group cohesion for the Senate, however, would include too few of the total membership, and the groups analyzed

not to assert that boardinghouse fraternities were the only source of guidance nor the only politically significant associations on Capitol Hill.* But no other grouping of legislators was institutionalized in the social structure of the congressional community. No other grouping was reinforced by such constancy and intensiveness of social inter-action between the members as the boardinghouse fraternities. And, as the following quotation illustrates, for no other type of grouping was political conformity asserted to be the moral obligation of the individual member, nor individual deviation from the group at-tended with such drastic sanctions. When the presidential election of 1824 was thrown to the House, Representative Stephen Van Rensselaer of New York violated an agreement among his mess-mates to cast their votes for Crawford, and voted for Adams instead. What ensued is best told in the words of one of General Van Rens-selaer's messmates:

When the election was over, as I was leaving the House, I saw [Van Rensselaer] coming to me, I hurried forward to avoid him . . . when I got home, I ran up in my own room, but had not been long there when he followed, he came in, he looked wretchedly, tears were running down his cheeks, "forgive me, McClean," said he, stretching out his hand. "Ask your own conscience General and not me," said I turning away. Since then he has been in coventry. A similar scene took place with V.B. [Van Buren] and the other gentlemen of the mess, we let him continue with us, sit at the same table with us, but we do not speak to him. He is beneath anything but contempt. . . . He has betrayed those with whom he broke bread.[69]

would be too small, to yield significant comparisons with the House of Repre-sentatives. The reason is that most Senators preferred to share living quarters only with Representatives; and when they did share with colleagues in the up-per chamber, usually only two, and rarely more than four, were affiliated with the same mess.

The fact that few Senators had boardinghouse fraternity ties with other Senators, and the small size of the senatorial contingents in any one fraternity, probably conduced to greater flexibility and fluidity of voting patterns in the Senate. It seems reasonable, however, to infer a similar importance for sectional influences in Senate voting patterns as in the House, given the predominantly sectional composition of the messes with which most Senators were affiliated.

* The voting cohesion of boardinghouse groups and state delegations is com-pared in Table 10. That of boardinghouse groups was, on the whole, higher on the 24 roll calls there analyzed.

TABLE 9

BOARDINGHOUSE GROUP AGREEMENTS ON ROLL CALLS OF HIGH AND LOW COHESION, HOUSE OF REPRESENTATIVES, 1807–1829 [a]

	Number of roll calls	Number of agreements	Percent of agreements
Low cohesion set	29	531	27.0
Range of indexes: 0.6–10.0			
Mean of indexes: 5.0			
Low-intermediate cohesion set	29	535	27.1
Range of indexes: 10.4–23.0			
Mean of indexes: 15.4			
High-intermediate cohesion set	29	441	22.3
Range of indexes: 23.2–37.4			
Mean of indexes: 30.0			
High cohesion set	29	465	23.6
Range of indexes: 37.8–76.8			
Mean of indexes: 50.3			
	116	1,972	100.0

[a] The 116 roll calls here analyzed are the same as those analyzed in Table 8. Table 8 also indicates how the 1,972 boardinghouse group agreements here analyzed were distributed as between different Congresses. (See Table 8, note b.) As indicated in Table 8, note a, "agreement" means cases where, half or more of the members of a boardinghouse group voting, they voted in unanimity or with only one dissenting vote; and cases where all members or all except one member of the group failed to cast a vote.

The Rice Index of Cohesion is used here, as throughout this work. (See Stuart A. Rice, *Quantitative Methods in Politics*.) Arithmetically this index is the difference between the percent favoring and the percent opposing a motion. Thus, an index of 0.0 indicates a tie vote; an index of 50.0 indicates a 75 percent majority on the issue decided; and an index of 100.0 indicates a roll call on which no dissenting vote was cast. As the range of indexes indicated above suggests, roughly three quarters of the roll calls selected for analysis involved issues on which less than a two-thirds majority was mustered in the House.

To construct the "sets" used in this table, the cohesion index of each roll call was figured, and the roll calls were then arranged in ascending order of cohesion. The 29 roll calls having the 29 lowest indexes of cohesion were segregated as the "Low Cohesion Set" in the table above; as the range of indexes identified for this set indicates, these were roll calls on which the issues were decided by very close votes in the House. The next 29 roll calls in ascending order of cohesion were then segregated as the "Low-intermediate Cohesion Set," and so on for the other two sets. The number of boardinghouse group agreements in each set of roll calls is entered in the second column in the table; the percentage of agreements each set contributed to the total number of agreements is entered in the third column in the table.

By seeking primary-group affiliations at Washington with colleagues most like their own constituents at home, legislators not only built parochial influences into the structure of the congressional establishment but made their responsiveness to these influences a matter of moral obligation.

While legislators might disdain a posture of servility to constituents, there can be little doubt, then, that they preferred those community arrangements which would enhance their ability to play the constituency agent in Washington. Such, indeed, was the value they placed on the role of the legislator as constituency agent that they appear to have organized their entire community around it. Permissive procedures afforded maximum freedom for advocating different constituency interests. Internal democracy conferred equality of status, prerogatives, and power opportunities upon the surrogates of those interests. Denial of recognition for leadership roles and avoidance of interbranch and interregional associations protected them from personal influences which might have conflicted with those interests. Chosen cycles of rendezvous at Washington and dispersal to the hinterlands ensured more exposure to constituents than to colleagues. And personal associations were chosen at Washington which reinforced constituency allegiances outside Washington: sectional fraternities put legislators in a primary field of influence within the governmental establishment which tended to duplicate the sectarian influence of their constituencies at home.

A system more superbly adapted to the articulation of constituency needs, more exquisitely sensitive to the mandates of provincial electorates, could scarcely be imagined. The remarkable thing is that such a system took root on Capitol Hill at a time when the level of constituency attention to the doings of the Washington community, and the level of constituency demands upon it, were perhaps at their lowest point in history. Political utility for the members partially explains it, to be sure. Boardinghouse fraternities tended to ensure that decisions made at Washington would not be so out of line with constituency sentiment as to endanger chances of reelection—for those who wished to stay in Washington. Permissive rules of proceeding provided needed opportunities to particularize, clarify, or obscure one's position for the official record, as constituency mood or local election prospects dictated. Yet rules so utterly permissive of obstructionism seem quite to exceed the electoral survival needs of legislators so remote from their constituents. And a social system which went to such extremes in insulating legislators from personal influences not in harmony with constituency allegiances seems quite to exceed any objective need they had for keeping themselves attuned to the moods of a distant and undemanding electorate.

Their isolation at Washington and the relative freedom of behavior this afforded invite attention, therefore, to the sources of such a social system in the values and attitudes of the legislators themselves, and especially in their psychology about power. For surely it can be no coincidence that power-holders who shared the cultural stereotype of power as evil should choose community roles and arrangements at Washington which tended to identify them with persons and interests outside the institutions of power. The antipower values of the governors would seem to explain, better than citizen demands upon them, the emergence of a constituency-oriented culture and social organization on Capitol Hill. Ambivalence about power among men in power would seem to explain, better than their needs for political survival, why they preferred the behavior of constituency agents to the behavior of rulers.

Causes aside, what emerges from the community record of the legislative branch is a social system which tended to ensure the integrity of the constitutional principle of representative government, just as the social system of the larger community tended to ensure the integrity of the constitutional principle of "separation of powers." But the dogged commitment to internal democracy and the fragmentation into sociopolitical blocs that have been discovered on Capitol Hill also raise—even more cogently for the congressional community—the same question that was raised by the antipower values and the fragmented structure of the larger governmental community. How could a system pregnant with such sources of conflict within itself perform the task of resolving conflict outside itself, in the nation at large? For it does not suffice for legislators at

Washington merely to reflect, in their own values and organization, the varied and conflicting interests of the society they represent. What it takes to govern a people is something quite distinct from what it takes to represent a people; and the needs of rulership are not the needs of constituency spokesmanship. If a representative body is to perform adequately as an institution of governance, there must be some means for reconciling conflict among the representatives themselves. There must be some means for subordinating conflict to accomplishment of common goals.

What machinery was there, then, in the congressional community of Jeffersonian times for resolving the conflicts made inevitable by its structure, its values, its work, its composition? What was there to prevent an anarchy of groups in a community of segregated sectional conclaves? What was there to bind these conclaves, and the fragments of the nation they represented, together in a functioning whole? What resources were available to mobilize Congress for action when action was needed? We turn now to seek the answers to these crucial political questions.

CHAPTER 6

RESOLVING CONFLICT

The majority political party was the one institution on Capitol Hill which promised to bring comity, stability, and direction to a community of contending minority blocs. Partisans with a philosophy approved by the electorate, sufficiently numerous to dominate policy, and deployed across a structure of blocs, the majority party had the promise of making a representative establishment into an establishment capable of governing. If the leading historical interpretation is to be accepted, the party fully realized that promise. The prevailing view is that party dominance of govermental processes was the outstanding characteristic of the Washington community during the Jeffersonian era. Ostrogorski forcefully stated this view in 1899 by asserting the existence of a Republican party which "enforced discipline, which compelled obedience to the word of command from whatever quarter it proceeded," with party decisions being "binding in honor . . . on every adherent of the party . . . who did not care to incur the reproach of political heresy, or apostasy." [1] Writing eighteen years later, Ralph V. Harlow, whose *History of Legislative Methods in the Period before 1825* has been taken as the leading authority on the subject, used similarly unequivocal language in summarizing the "Jeffersonian régime." In an "eminently successful attempt to overcome friction," he wrote, the Republicans "really built up a highly centralized system" in Congress:

The party following was drilled to act together in caucus, where the individual member was induced to relinquish his cherished privilege of blocking the wheels of action. But the caucus was only the rehearsal, so to speak, and there was always the possibility that in the regular performance in Congress some unruly Republican might cast off party trammels and vote as he pleased. To guard against such a contingency . . . [there was] a recognized leader in the House, whose duty it was to see that members "voted as was right." . . . Good Republicans . . . who insisted upon the right of independent judgment, were promptly read out of the party. It seemed a far cry to democracy.[2]

Rediscovered after decades of obscurity, Harlow's interpretation has received increasing attention and wide acceptance among recent writers.[3] That the Jeffersonian era saw the establishment of party government on Capitol Hill has become the leading viewpoint among historians and political scientists alike.

Concerning it, three points of evidence must be raised at the outset. First, legislators did not, during the Jeffersonian era, acknowledge party affiliation as a matter of record—a fact which itself suggests something less than the strong sense of party identification that is implied by the leading interpretation.[4] The membership of the congressional parties cannot therefore be identified, and even their numerical strength from one Congress to the next cannot be known with certainty.[5] In consequence, no assertions about party discipline in the Jeffersonian era can be based on direct evidence about party voting performance on legislative policy issues. Informed guesses can be made, and significant clues revealed, by examining the voting behavior of known blocs and other groupings smaller than the congressional parties. But for the most part the quality and character of congressional party performance must be established on evidence other than roll call votes.[6]

Second, the leading hypothesis of disciplined parties does not derive from even limited inquiry into congressional voting and it takes little if any account of the community behavior of legislators. The principal evidence on which it rests is a host of statements in the historical record indicating preconcerted voting, group discipline, caucuses, "cabals," settlement of issues "out of doors," and the like. Typical of these statements are the following:

Virginia moves in a solid column, and the discipline of the party is as severe as the Prussian. Deserters are not spared.[7]

The opposition . . . is drilled to act in phalanx on every question.[8]

No Saint in the Calendar ever had a set of followers less at liberty, or less disposed to indulge in troublesome inquiry, than some, at least, of [the Republicans in Congress whose policies were] attended with a severe and efficacious discipline, by which those who went astray were to be brought to repentance.[9]

Judging from my own perceptions, I cannot refrain from concluding that all great political questions are settled somewhere else than on this floor.[10]

It is said a *Jeffersonian caucus* met last Friday evening.[11]

The Jacobins, finding themselves unable to manage their business on the questions in the House, have adopted the plan of meeting in divan and agreeing on measures to be pursued and passed. . . . The wickedness of such a course has never been equalled but by the Jacobin club of Paris.[12]

Comments such as these suggest clearly enough the presence of group discipline and preconcerted voting. But to infer from them the presence of *party* activity and *party* discipline may be very much in error. These statements may be accounted for by the activities of boardinghouse groups or other voting formations besides political parties, understood in the modern sense as aggregations which overlap state or sectional lines.[13] Discovery of boardinghouse groups and their political behavior, in particular, means that commentaries suggesting group discipline and preconcerted voting can no longer suffice to establish even an inference of cohesive congressional parties.

Third, the wide currency that is being given to Harlow's interpretation by recent writers makes it necessary also to point out the political bias of his sources. His assertion of a party-dominated Congress is at variance with the views of all visitors and foreign observers, as well as with the observations made by members about their own party. Outsiders' accounts and insiders' observations about their own party coincide in picturing minimal collaboration and a legislature only sporadically preserved from its "proneness to anarchy" [14] by the "rope of sand" that Jefferson called his congressional party.[15]

There is only one set of sources which presents the image favored in modern commentary on political parties in the early Congress.

This is the portrait drawn by partisans of their political opposition. Such coincidence is not surprising. For when the evidence cited in support of the leading interpretation is scrutinized, it is discovered to originate largely from Federalist sources and to be a portrayal of the Republican majority in Congress. Federalist allegations of secret party caucuses on policy issues, of subservience to leaders, of whip-cracking discipline, and of punishments for deviation furnish the main evidence for Harlow's similar assessment of Republican party behavior during the Jeffersonian era. It is not very wide of the mark to say that the original authors of the "strong party" view were the Federalists, and that their partisan image of the Republican party has become the now-accepted image of the majority party in the Congresses of 1800–1828.

Conspiracy theories have ever been politically useful, and never more useful than to the losers in power in a culture which mistrusts power. In the early republic, party explanations of political events were precisely that—a mild version of conspiracy theory. To the needs and inclinations of the losers, they were especially well suited. Insinuations of slavish subservience to powerful leaders and of conspiratorial settlement of issues outside the formal proceedings provided them with a politically useful explanation for their own defeats, a propaganda weapon to disorganize the winners by playing upon their own antipower values, a chance to claim sanctimoniousness for themselves and to identify for all interested constituents the villains of the political drama.[16] This is not to say that their allegations are worthless as evidence: where there is smoke, there may be fire. But what were, in effect, accusations of deviance from American values and community norms—accusations by the losers that the rules of the game had been violated—are not a strong enough foundation to support a theory of highly disciplined congressional parties.

With these perspectives in mind, what concrete indications of party activity does the community record of the early Congress yield, and what was the quality of that activity?

The best positive evidence of party activity is the congressional nominating caucus. Indeed, had it not been for this institution the very existence of a congressional party, or of any institution serving to bind together the different political fraternities of Capitol Hill, would be difficult to prove.

In effect a nominating convention, the caucus was a group of legislators, more or less united behind one presidential and one vice-presidential aspirant, organized for the principal purpose of capturing the Presidency by legitimating and promoting their candidacies. After agreeing upon a slate, the participants customarily made their recommendations public in a formal circular drawn up and signed in "their individual characters as citizens." [17] A committee of correspondence, composed ordinarily of one legislator from each state represented in the caucus, was designated to communicate the caucus recommendations to the various states, their duties presumably including the job of rounding up support for the slate in their respective constituencies and state legislatures.[18]

It is uncertain when the first caucus was held; probably the first organized attempt by legislators to capture the Presidency occurred after Washington had disclosed his intention not to run for a third term. At the new capital, nominating caucuses met in the Capitol itself in late winter or early spring preceding a presidential election. The first of these appears to have been held in 1804, the last twenty years later: a total of six quadrennial convocations all held under Republican auspices, that is, by legislators claiming loyalty to Jeffersonian principles.[19] In every case but that of John Quincy Adams the caucus nominee won the Presidency.

Clearly, then, there was some degree of organized party effort in the early Congress, an attempt to make a binding majority out of the organized minorities that composed the congressional community. The existence of a party of legislators able four times out of five * to control, in effect, accession to the Presidency seems so far beyond the capabilities of the modern congressional party that it appears both logical and persuasive to postulate an impressively powerful legislative party in Jeffersonian times. Yet surface appearances may be deceptive. Ability to make Presidents does not neces-

---

* One of the six caucuses—that held in 1820—proved abortive and no nomination was made.

sarily mean ability to run Congress, nor, paradoxical though it may seem, does it mean ability to achieve party solidarity.

The fact is that even in the performance of its nominating function the majority party presents anything but the monolithic appearance which the leading interpretation has attributed to it. At least five of the six nominating caucuses convened by the Republicans in Washington were attended with symptoms of acute cleavage among the members. * In 1808 schism occurred over the desirability of having a caucus at all. The authority of anyone to call a caucus was challenged, with the result that the Senator who sent out the invitations—he had chaired the previous caucus—resigned his "chairmanship." [20] Moreover, according to the report of a participant in the caucus, only two short of a majority of legislators failed to attend: 27 Federalists who had not been invited, and 60 Republicans who "refused to attend," including at least one disaffected party faction.[21] James Madison was, to be sure, nominated almost unanimously by the "party" caucus. But it was a caucus that was boycotted by roughly 43 percent of the Republican party membership in Congress: hardly the picture of a monolithic or cohesive party.

A majority of the whole Congress, and an estimated 39 percent of the Republicans in Congress, failed to participate in the next caucus held in 1812.[22] Thus Madison's second nomination, like his first, was apparently accomplished by a caucus largely restricted to a pro-Madison group and by no means inclusive of the Republican membership. To achieve agreement even among the eighty-two Republicans who attended the 1812 caucus may have required considerable effort, this caucus being delayed several months beyond its usual time for convening.

Controversy over whether to hold a caucus at all erupted again when the time came to nominate Madison's successor. No one seemed willing to take the initial responsibility for calling a caucus, and with time running out as Congress neared the end of the session, an anonymous caucus call was posted conspicuously in the tempo-

* The 1804 caucus is not known in sufficient detail to assess the degree of party solidarity then achieved.

rary Capitol in the spring of 1816. A large majority of Republicans failed to attend and no action was taken at the meeting. Turnout noticeably improved in response to a second caucus call, signed by an Ohio legislator. Boycotted by roughly 20 percent of the party membership, the second caucus was thrown into an uproar by Henry Clay's introduction of a resolution putting the group on record as denying the legitimacy of caucus nominations. This sabotage effort failing, stalemate was narrowly averted on the choice of a nominee. Monroe won the nomination by the slim margin of eleven votes over Secretary of War Crawford. Despite their evident need to muster maximum voting strength in caucus, some of the Monroe partisans refused to attend the meeting on grounds of principle. Given the 20 percent Republican absenteeism, moreover, it is entirely possible that Monroe's majority vote in the caucus did not represent majority choice in the Republican party.[23]

The next caucus, in 1820, was boycotted by a large majority of the Republican membership and attended by "not more than forty members. . . . The delegations from Pennsylvania and North Carolina agreed unanimously among themselves not to attend."[24] In a year when a President from Virginia—Monroe—was standing for renomination, all but two members of that state's delegation in Congress refused to participate in the nominating caucus. The forty members who attended the caucus failed to nominate anybody.

In 1824 there were five serious contenders for the presidential nomination, all members of the Washington community: three cabinet officers (Adams, Calhoun, and Crawford) and two members of Congress (Senator Andrew Jackson and Speaker Henry Clay). Only 24 percent of the Congress attended the caucus then held, in which Crawford received 64 of 68 votes cast.[25] Clearly the "party" caucus comprised only the Crawford faction of the party.

A nominating caucus which could not even produce, by 1824, majority agreement within the party, let alone mobilize its majority in Congress, was clearly ready for discard. In fact it did collapse, 1824 marking the demise of this institution for all time.[26] Folklore has it that the people rose up in wrath to overthrow "King Caucus" in the presidential election of 1828, and retrieved a birthright usurped by the ruling clique in Washington. But Andrew Jackson was flaying a

dead horse in the campaign of 1828. For a Senator whose presidential ambitions had been frustrated by his fellow legislators in 1824,
"King Caucus" and a ruling clique in Washington were convenient
fictions to propagate in his next bid for the Presidency.[27]

The lesson conveyed by the congressional nominating caucus—
that the reigning party of the Jeffersonian era was singularly unsuccessful in achieving solidarity and discipline—thus appears to be
quite the reverse of what has been made of this institution by modern writers.

A second test of the party's capacity for action is afforded by
speakership elections in the House of Representatives. Whatever
else legislative parties may do, organizing the House by staffing its
elective and appointive offices is one of their elementary functions.
Electing a presiding officer would seem to be one endeavor in which
the incentives for party solidarity would be very high, especially in
the Jeffersonian era, since it was then the Speaker who staffed the
committees and designated their chairmen. An added stimulus to
party solidarity in speakership elections was that a majority, not
merely a plurality, was required under House rules to win the office.

Yet here again, as in the nominating of presidential candidates, inability or unwillingness of the members to close ranks around a
party candidate was the outstanding characteristic of party performance. The number of candidates running in a speakership election is a fairly reliable indication of the parties' ability to agree upon
candidates; and a persisting pattern of contests limited to two candidates, one major and one minor, would clearly indicate majority and
opposition party cohesion around their respective standard-bearers.
But only four of the thirteen speakership elections on which the
official record provides adequate information from 1798 through
1827 resembled what is the normal situation in the modern Congress. In the remaining nine elections, the number of candidates varied from only one to as many as ten running on the first ballot in a
single contest.[28]

Looking at candidacies in speakership elections over the entire period up to the Civil War reveals, moreover, some interesting
changes of pattern. Figure 4-A shows the number of first-ballot
candidates in each election, 1798 through 1859, who had a following

FIGURE 4. SPEAKERSHIP ELECTIONS, 1798 TO CIVIL WAR[a]

A. *Number of speakership candidates polling at least twelve votes*

B. *Percentage of votes polled by candidates other than the two leading candidates: the "nonparty" vote*[b]

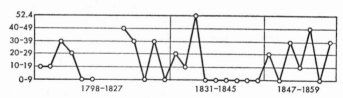

C. *Percentage of the "nonparty" vote polled by third- and fourth-place candidates combined*[c]

of at least twelve members.* The erratic pattern of votes and candidacies in the Jeffersonian era contrasts sharply with the period 1831–45, when two contestants, and no others with a following of twelve or more colleagues, were the rule.[29] Such a pattern was the exception in the Jeffersonian era, with two of the thirteen elections being "no-contest" elections, and seven of the remaining eleven elections bringing out factional candidacies in varying number.

The political implication of this contrast is that—in so far as ability to agree upon a speakership candidate significantly indicates the quality of party performance in general—nothing approaching a stable party system emerged in Congress until the Jacksonian era. This implication is further supported by Figure 4-B, which plots what may be called (rather more aptly for the post-Jeffersonian period, to be sure) the "nonparty" vote: that proportion of the total vote in each speakership election which went to candidates other than the two leading candidates. In a House with a stable two-party

---

* Twelve members comprised slightly more than 10 percent of the total House membership at the beginning of the Jeffersonian era.

NOTES TO FIG. 4

ᵃ Speakership elections occurring in the following Congresses cannot be included because the official record for these Congresses divulges only the name of the winning candidate: 1st through 4th (beginning dates 1789–95); 7th through 9th (1801–5); 12th (1811); 14th (1815); and 21st (1829). The regular Speaker in the 5th Congress becoming ill, a Speaker pro tem was elected in 1798; the official record gives sufficient information for this election, but not for the election of the regular Speaker, to be included in this table. Speakers resigned in the 13th (1813), 16th (1819), and 23d (1833) Congresses, necessitating two speakership elections in each of these Congresses, all of which are included in this table.

Where more than one ballot was needed to achieve the necessary majority, figures for the first ballot are used. The large majority of elections required only one ballot.

ᵇ Two elections in which there was virtually no opposition to the winning candidate are indicated by an interruption in the graph line. Both of these (1817 and 1819) were elections of Henry Clay.

ᶜ The "nonparty" vote means the total number of votes polled by all candidates other than the first- and second-place candidates. This graph includes only those elections (having four or more candidates) in which the nonparty vote was at least 10. The actual numerical size of the nonparty vote, in the elections included in this graph, ranged from 10 to 115, the average being 42 votes. One election (1814) in which there was a nonparty vote of 12 had to be excluded from consideration because the record did not identify how these 12 votes were distributed among the lesser candidates. These considerations eliminated eight elections in all—six in the period 1798–1827 and two in the period 1831–45.

system, the number of votes polled by candidates other than the
first two candidates would presumably approach zero in election
after election, the indication of such a pattern being, of course, that
each of the two parties had agreed upon its choice for Speaker. This
pattern, as shown in Figure 4-B, did not emerge until after the Jeffersonian era, and it then emerged with extraordinary clarity. For an
unprecedented period of six consecutive Congresses, beginning with
Jackson's last two years in the White House, party defections in
speakership elections were held to a level below 10 percent of the
voting membership of the House. Erratic performance and party instability are again indicated for the Jeffersonian period.

Internal analysis of this nonparty vote (Figure 4-C) permits the
further observation that Representatives who failed to support either of the two leading candidates voted in a far more coherent, organized fashion in the Jeffersonian period than subsequently. In the
period 1798–1827 there was a marked tendency of the nonparty
vote to concentrate around no more than two candidates, the third-
and fourth-place candidates polling, between them, an average of 87
percent of the whole nonparty vote per election. Such a concentration of votes implies a degree of organization among party dissenters
(or "independents") which was not approached in any other period
before the Civil War. As parties presumably came to play a more
prominent role in speakership elections following 1827, the irregu-
larly descending line of Figure 4-C shows the nonparty vote tending
progressively to dissipate and splinter among numerous "insignificant" candidates, until, by the period 1847–59, the third and fourth
candidates together polled not much more than half (54 percent
average) of the nonparty vote.[30]

Taken together with the erratic performance signified in the
first two graphs of Figure 4, the heavy concentration of nonparty
votes around the third and fourth candidates in the period 1798–
1827 may thus be reasonably interpreted as a symptom of a pronounced tendency toward factionalism during the Jeffersonian period. The votes indicate, in other words, repetitive, serious group
bids for power *outside* a party system. To this extent, the graphs in
Figure 4 tend to confirm precisely the sort of systemic qualities that

the bloc structure of the congressional community leads one to expect; and they indicate further the failure of the congressional parties of Jeffersonian times to overcome the cleavages inherent in this community structure.

Beyond the comparative insights they afford, the second two graphs of Figure 4 raise an inference of general interest concerning party development which may not be out of place to mention here. They suggest that changes in the "anatomy" of party dissent (Figure 4-C) were a more significant feature of the emergence of legislative parties than changes in the over-all incidence of party dissent (Figure 4-B). Averaging, by historical period, the percentage of party votes in each of the elections shown in Figure 4-B reveals that the level of party voting—to the extent that this is crudely indicated by the percentage of total votes going to the two leading speakership candidates—did not increase over the entire period up to the Civil War. Rather, it underwent a slight net decrease, starting with an average of 79.8 percent of the total vote during 1798–1827, rising seven points to 87.1 percent during 1831–45, then dropping eleven percentage points to 75.9 percent in 1847–59. This long-term stability in level of party voting, coupled with a progressive splintering of the nonparty vote among numerous insignificant candidates (Figure 4-C), suggests that the emergence of a lasting party system in Congress did not involve the lessening of party dissent so much as it involved the disorganization or individuation of the party dissenters (or "independents"). Figure 5 illustrates the proposition.

The conjecture—and it can be nothing more—that party dissent became less organized, more situational as legislative parties grew in prominence seems logical enough: growing disuse of small-group organization to bid for power and intensified efforts to mobilize large-scale voting strength would seem to go together, and to describe, in a crude way, the transition from factional politics to party politics.[31]

There is one other aspect of speakership elections that presents intriguing possibilities. This is the striking similarity of party performance during the Jeffersonian era and that in the last twelve years before the rupture of the Union. The decade ending in the

　　　　　　　　　　Capitol Hill

FIGURE 5. SPEAKERSHIP ELECTIONS, 1798–1859
*Changes in level of party voting versus
changes in structure of nonparty voting as correlatives
of legislative party development*

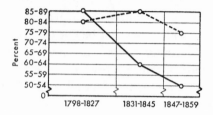

The broken line indicates the level of party voting (percent of total vote polled by first- and second-place candidates combined, averaged by historical period).

The solid line indicates the percent of the nonparty vote polled by third- and fourth-place candidates combined (Figure 4-C, averaged by historical period).

outbreak of the Civil War is generally thought to have been a period of mounting party disintegration, suggestive of spiraling conflict within the governing group itself. This disintegration is presumably what the first two graphs in Figure 4 picture for the period of 1847–59, with the parties unable to close ranks around speakership candidates. The similarity of performance in the immediate pre-Civil War period and in the Jeffersonian era provides, therefore, much to muse upon. What is suggested here is this historical sequence: instability within the congressional establishment during the Jeffersonian era, with factional tendencies pronounced; instability giving way to stability and party prominence in the Jacksonian period; then another period of instability beginning in Polk's administration and ending in the disintegration of the congressional community, the withdrawal of the southern delegations, and the dissolution of the nation. What was it, one wonders, that made the seeming instability inside the governmental community from 1800 to 1828 end so differently from that of 1847–59? Tentative answers may emerge as this study progresses.

Speakership elections in the Jeffersonian era, then, lend no support to the leading interpretation of a party that successfully "overcame friction" and "drilled" its members to "act together." Especially when compared with the period 1831–45, the erratic performance on speakership elections suggests quite the opposite. It suggests either a minimal degree of party involvement in the selection of an officer whose role would clearly have been of great usefulness to a legislative party, or a conspicuous failure to achieve consensus and cohesion in performing this elementary function of a legislative party.[32]

There remains the question of whether the congressional parties were involved in policy-making, as distinguished from President-making and Speaker-electing, and whether the majority party was able to impart stability and direction to the everyday performance of legislative government. If modern political experience is relevant, party concert upon the choice of a presidential and a speakership nominee is normally achieved with far less difficulty than party agreement on policy. Could a congressional party unable to close ranks for even the purpose of capturing the Presidency or the speakership do so in the daily, dissension-producing task of deciding policy? Because the usual test of party cohesion on policy issues—performance on roll call votes—cannot be reliably applied in the Jeffersonian era, this question can be answered only in terms of probabilities, not certainties. In lieu of direct evidence of party coherence on policy, the next best approach seems to be to ask whether party members organized themselves for policy action, what sorts of opportunities they created for harmonizing their views, and what degree of leadership effort was exerted to produce party solidarity. For of all voluntary associations, legislative parties cohere least spontaneously. And of all historical periods, in the Jeffersonian era party coherence on Capitol Hill is least to be expected in the absence of visible organization and visible efforts to rally the party members in common cause.

Boardinghouse blocs created peculiar obstacles to party solidarity which need to be specified here because they were of a magnitude to be surmounted only by a very considerable effort indeed. At the very least, rallying the party would involve contending, and contending successfully, against that host of influences which led the members to segregate into blocs in the first instance. Mobilizing the party for policy action would require coordination and cooperation among men from different regions in a community where men from different regions tended to avoid each other's company.[33] If boardinghouse fraternities were one-party in composition, there would be the additional managerial problem of cementing an enduring alliance of sectionally biased blocs each of which had a political life quite independent of the party, and each of which tended to maintain its internal solidarity irrespective of party cohesion.[34] In other words, the task of achieving party solidarity on the Hill would be the task of the Constitutional Convention of 1787 all over again: binding sections of the nation into an association capable of governing. The Constitution could bring together, at the seat of government, the states and the sections of the nation; but it could not make them work together.

If, on the other hand, men from opposing parties were mingled in the boardinghouse fraternities, an even greater obstacle to party solidarity would have been raised. In this case, rallying the party would tend to require that members vote in disagreement with messmates—this in a community where political conformity among messmates appears to have been strongly sanctioned.[35]

Seen in community context, then, party solidarity in the Jeffersonian Congress meant the achievement of agreement (individually or en bloc) among men who had chosen to have as little to do with each other as possible, and also, perhaps, the willingness of members to "betray those with whom they broke bread." It further meant successful counteraction of the profusion of other obstacles to party solidarity deeply rooted in the nature of the representative institution and in the values of its members: from rapid turnover of personnel to permissive rules of debate; from sectarian constituency interests to antipathies of cultural background; from ambivalence about power-seeking to a high valuation upon individualism and personal independence. It is not very likely, then, that parties could have been an important presence in the congressional community unless they were organized. And it is not very likely that party coherence on policy could have been achieved without an uncommonly active and persistent leadership effort to achieve it.

As to organization, one searches the community record in vain for evidence that common party affiliation was the basis of any associational activity whatever in the everyday life of Capitol Hill. Not only did legislators fail to identify themselves with parties in the official record, but they failed to assemble into party groupings for the conduct of legislative business, as in today's Congress.

The practice is for those who arrive first to choose their seats, and the choice is invariably respected.

There is no such thing known as a political division of seats. Members of the same politics certainly often choose to be placed near to each other, and sometimes the entire representation of a particular State is to be seen as near together as possible. But there is no rule in the matter.[36]

Neither did the party membership meet together outside of working hours. The widely prevalent notion that the Republicans "from the seventh Congress on . . . made regular use" of party caucuses for thrashing out differences on policy and "drilling" the rank and file to "act together" far overreaches any facts that have come to notice in this study.[37] And the assertion, equally widespread in scholarly literature, that the President and the cabinet attended these purported caucuses [38] has no foundation in discernible fact. These assertions have the double flaw of resting almost exclusively on Federalist propaganda as evidence and of employing an ambiguous definition of caucusing which mistakenly equates presidential nominating caucuses and caucuses by small groups such as boardinghouse fraternities with party caucuses on policy issues.[39] Albert Gallatin, himself a Republican party activist in the House before being appointed Jefferson's Secretary of the Treasury, recalled that during his six years in Congress from 1795 to 1801 "there were but two of those party meetings called for the purpose of deliberating upon the measures proper to be adopted." [40] Nothing in the published record of the congressional community from 1801 to 1828 plausibly suggests that the frequency of such party caucuses was greater then, unless one is to treat evidence of what a few Federalists thought the Republicans were doing as if it were evidence of what the Republicans actually did. The record indicates only two party caucuses on legislative issues for the entire period, both concerning crisis issues—the passage and the repeal of the Embargo Act prior to the War of 1812.[41]

Proving a negative is of course always difficult, and lack of reliable evidence of party policy caucuses does not conclusively disprove their existence. But the six nominating caucuses that were held at Washington during the Jeffersonian era appear recognizably enough in the written record of the community. It seems improbable that party meetings on controversial policy issues, held regularly over a period of almost thirty years, could have gone unrecorded in the many informal chronicles of the governmental community that have been published. Especially unlikely is it in a small, isolated settlement which provided no facilities for assemblages of such large size save the Senate and House chambers, the White House, and the ballrooms of a very few taverns—all of them offering not much more privacy than a fishbowl. To be sure, visitors to the Capitol who insisted upon satisfying their curiosity about the caucus were shown a cavernous crypt, originally intended as George Washington's tomb, and told that this was "The Caucus." [42] Suggestible outsiders went away with their suspicions of iniquity confirmed. A few scholars, alas, have taken the congressmen's joke seriously, too.

If "assembly" never sounded for the party platoons dispersed in their barracks on Capitol Hill, how could they have been "drilled" to march together?

If the party did not meet, neither did it attain, but momentarily, the status of an organized group in the congressional community. What degree of formal organization the party did achieve was only for the brief duration of its convocation as a nominating caucus, when the members elected a presiding chairman and tellers to count the votes. These offices expired with the adjournment of the caucus itself. In the periods intervening between caucuses the party had no officers, even of figurehead importance, for the guidance or management of legislative processes. Party members elected no leaders, designated no functionaries to speak on their behalf or to carry out any legislative task assignments. The party had no whips, no seniority leaders. There were no Committees on Committees, no Steering Committees, no Policy Committees: none of the organizational apparatus that marks the twentieth-century congressional parties as going enterprises, save for a prototype "campaign committee" whose job it was to stir up support for the presidential nominee outside of Congress.[43] Rather than the favored analogy to troops arrayed for battle and responding to the orders of their commander, a more likely analogy for the congressional party is what David B. Truman has called, in another context, the "unorganized" or "potential group":[44] a group without sufficient intensity or regularity of interaction among its members to sustain even the bare bones of a formal organization.

By a generally accepted notion among political scientists, voluntary associations for political purposes have their origin in shared attitudes which, under appropriate stimuli, give rise to heightened social interaction. Heightened social interaction gives rise, in turn, to formal organization, with an attendant "division of labor" inside the group into leadership and followership roles. When we observe minimal interaction among the members of the congressional party, none but a vestigial formal organization temporarily achieved once every four years (even that conspicuously failing to elicit consensus), and no designated leadership positions, this is prima-facie evidence that there was a minimum of shared attitudes among the party members. If the analogy between the congressional party and the "potential group" is justified, therefore, it would seem that no more influence upon policy should be attributed to the congressional party than is attributed to the unorganized in politics generally. Still more seriously to be doubted is the asserted capacity of the majority party to subordinate conflict to cooperation for common goals and to offset the disintegrative tendencies in its host community, when the party had, by the standards applied here, none but an episodic organizational reality in the life of the Capitol Hill community.

Was there, then, "informal" party leadership—party leadership without party organization? Here the written record presents the same problems of evaluation as on the question of party discipline. That there were leaders on Capitol Hill, in the sense of activists striving to win support for their views, cannot be doubted. That party partisanship had some degree of relevance for these efforts is to be presumed. The record contains references enough to "Republican leaders" and "leading men," just as it does references to preconcerted voting, settlement of issues out of doors, caucuses, and the like. But such commentaries suggesting leadership activity can no more suffice to establish the presence of *party* leadership than commentaries suggesting voting discipline can suffice to establish *party* discipline. The question is whether there were leadership roles looking specifically to the achievement of party solidarity and providing that persistence of effort which, in the absence of party caucuses or other formal organization, was presumably required to maintain any semblance of party cohesion.

Prevailing interpretation answers this question in the affirmative, and identifies two distinctly party leadership roles in the Congress of the Jeffersonian era. One is said to have been the position of "floor leader" in the House during Jefferson's eight years as President. Following Jefferson's retirement, the role of party leader is said to have shifted to the speakership under Henry Clay.

Considering first the Jeffersonian practice, it is evident that conspicuous efforts at leadership were made in Congress at the President's initiative during the years 1801-8. As Harlow has rightly pointed out, Jefferson innovated the presidential practice of singling out certain members of Congress for confidential consultation and to assist in the passage of presidentially preferred bills.[45] Congress having failed to designate or recognize authoritative spokesmen to deal with the President, Jefferson selected his own points of entree to Capitol Hill, relying upon legislators who were apparently willing to lend their influence to the accomplishment of his legislative objectives.

To call these voluntary presidential agents leaders of the congressional party, however, is to blur, without warrant in the evidence, the distinction between these two types of roles. Being an agent of the White House alone could scarcely have enabled a legislator to lead a Congress united in little else but its hostile attitudes toward leadership and power-seeking; and no evidence has been found suggesting any special sources of influence which could possibly have enabled Jefferson's agents to see to it that "the dictates of the Commander-in-Chief were obeyed" by the party rank and file.[46] Logic and evidence both are at variance, moreover, with the view that there was only one position of purported leadership held by "the personal representative of the President." [47] A Chief Executive reputedly skilled in politics would not have been very astute to place the entire burden of White House spokesmanship on one man in a community whose members were quick to pin the label of lackey upon colleagues too conspicuously identified as presidential collaborators.[48] And reliance upon a single legislator would not seem a very apt strategy for suffusing Jefferson's influence through a community of segregated sectional blocs. On the contrary, restriction of the presidential entree to a single legislator would suggest considerably less influence for President Jefferson than the leading interpretation attributes to him, unless his spokesman possessed extraordinary disciplinary tools or bargaining resources which no writer to date has suggested and which are nowhere indicated in the historical record. In a congressional establishment lacking organized parties and recognizing no leadership of its own, restriction of presidential access to one legislator suggests restriction of presidential influence to the bloc or other intraparty group with which that spokesman was associated.

In this connection, it is perhaps significant that the men most often named in secondary sources as having been presidential spokesmen —William B. Giles, John Randolph, Wilson Cary Nicholas (all of Virginia), and Caesar Rodney—are typically referred to in the original sources as leaders not of the "Republican party" but of the "administration party," the "palace troops," the "ministerial phalanx," and such. These labels seem to connote what would today be called the "presidential wing" of the congressional party. The leaders identified by Harlow may have been leaders of a proadministration faction only: that quartile of the Republican party in Congress who were thought to "have no other enquiry but what is the President's wish" [49] and who were "implicitly led by the administration." [50]

Direct evidence, though fragmentary, tends to confirm Jefferson's reputation as a wise politician, however. It suggests that he avoided reliance on any one agent, varying his spokesmen with the issues and employing more than one spokesman at the same time.[51] Jefferson himself named two legislators whom he was using contemporaneously for "confidential" communication before 1806, and hinted there were more.[52] Elsewhere he named still a third legislator, and wrote that he was but "one of those calculated to bring cohesion to our rope of sand"—Jefferson's metaphor for his congressional party.[53] More than one spokesman and shifts in presidential reliance from one to another set of spokesmen are evident on three specific legislative issues reported in historical studies—a bill providing for the government of the Louisiana Territory, a presidential request for authorization of sanctions against Britain for maritime incursions, and a request for appropriations to purchase West Florida.[54] And, while the names of Randolph, Giles, Nicholas, and Rodney appear more frequently, at least twenty Republican legislators in the eight years of Jefferson's administration are either explicitly identified as leaders in the documentary record or are associated with activities strongly suggesting a role of presidential spokesmanship. In addition to the four named above, these are Campbell of Tennessee, Macon, Eppes, Logan, Stevens Mason, Varnum, Crowninshield, Breckinridge of Kentucky, Joseph Nicholson, Bidwell, Baldwin, Davis, Clinton, Bradley, Newton, and Anderson.[55] It cannot be verified beyond challenge that all or even one of these men were in fact leaders. But the plethora of names associated with leadership does demonstrate that different observers or participants in Congress *perceived* different leaders at different times and from different vantage points in the community.[56] To that extent they tend to confirm what the structure and values of the congressional community and the absence of permanent party organization have already suggested: the absence of specialized leadership roles. Probably the President did not establish in his own interest what congressmen themselves were unable or unwilling to establish in their interest: a recognized position of leadership over the majority party within the legislative establishment itself. Community analysis and political sense both support Jefferson's view that "a rallying point . . . is wanting" for the congressional party; "there is no one whose talents & standing . . . give him the lead." [57] If there was to be leadership of the congressional party, the President himself would have to provide it. Whether he succeeded in doing so will be explored in Part Four following.

As to the reputed party leadership of Henry Clay, Speaker of the House for about eleven years between 1811 and 1825, skepticism is likewise indicated. Of Clay's popularity on the Hill there can be no doubt. Every time the Kentuckian sought the speakership he seems to have won it by overwhelming majorities. Twice he had virtually no opposition, presumably winning the support of even the Federalists in the House. These impressive victories, coupled with the Speaker's prerogative of appointing the membership of the House committees, have suggested to several authors both the extent and the means of Clay's leadership. A "party leader determined to force through a sometimes unwilling assembly the measures which he advocated"; [58] "both Speaker and leader of the majority party, something that none of his predecessors had ever been"; [59] "the most powerful man in the nation from 1811 to 1825": [60] so Clay has been described by writers on the early Congress.

But a Speaker who won the chair by extraordinary majorities seems to have met failure more often than success in winning majority support on policy. Of the seven policy controversies in which he is said to have been a major protagonist, and which came before the House in the form of specific bills or resolutions, Speaker Clay won clear victories in only two—the Missouri Compromise of 1820 and the protective tariff bill of 1824, passed by a five-vote margin.[61] On internal improvements,[62] the compensation law,[63] the Spanish Florida negotiations,[64] support for South American revolutionists,[65] diplomatic recognition of Greece and the new South American republics,[66] and censure of Andrew Jackson for his conduct in the Seminole War,[67] Clay was defeated either by direct vote, by dilatory action, or by refusal of the House to pass necessary implementing legislation. And when the presidential election of 1824 was thrown to the House of Representatives Clay was revealed to have a following of no more than factional proportions.[68] While it was an important faction, with sufficient votes to give the election to Adams, one wonders from this event and from his conspicuous policy opposition to Presidents Madison and Monroe whether Speaker Clay was not the leader of an antiadministration faction within the Republican party, rather than the leader of the party itself.[69]

The Speaker's appointive power over the House committees had significant potential as a resource for party leadership—especially so, it would seem, because the committee system absorbed no inconsiderable share of the legislative power under Clay's regime. For it was during the Jeffersonian era, particularly in its latter half, that the committees evolved from temporary advisory groups into permanent "little legislatures," each having jurisdiction over different policy areas, with much the same policy-making prerogatives and administrative oversight functions in their respective areas as they have today.[70] Power to staff these sublegislatures and designate their chairmen thus gave Speaker Clay important patronage to dispense to his colleagues, and with it the possibility of creating a party directorate of key committee chairmen not unlike that thought to have prevailed under Speakers Reed and Cannon later in congressional history.*

But how did Clay use this patronage? The manner in which he distributed committee appointments helps explain the seeming paradox between Clay's impressive popularity and his unimpressive power over policy. A look at the boardinghouse group affiliations of his committee appointees in the 14th Congress reveals that he chose them from almost every boardinghouse fraternity, that he tended to give each fraternity one or two seats on a wide range of committees, and that he clearly avoided favoring any one fraternity with a voting majority on any one committee. As to the chairmen, Clay gave five of twenty-eight chairmanships to Representatives not living in boardinghouse groups, a ratio conforming to the ratio of Representatives living alone or in pairs to the number who were affiliated with boardinghouse fraternities. The remaining twenty-three chairmanships were distributed among fourteen fraternities, with the

---

* One important element in these Speakers' power was, however, lacking in Clay's time—a Rules Committee chaired by the Speaker.

larger fraternities receiving slightly favored treatment.* It seems clear, then, that Clay parceled out committee patronage so as to satisfy the largest number of individuals and blocs in the congressional community, the tendency being to give each fraternity house one or two votes in each of a number of committees. Such a method of patronage distribution was likely to bring Clay great returns in personal popularity. It helps explain why Clay, despite his pronounced partisanship on policy issues, was repeatedly returned to the chair by overwhelming majorities.

At the same time it helps to explain why Clay was apparently so unsuccessful in converting his impressive support in speakership elections into a policy majority. Under any mode of staffing, the growth of the committee system would have posed new difficulties for party leadership and new threats to party solidarity. By multiplying the number of groups involved in policy-making, the committee system multiplied also the opportunities for obstructionism; and by giving these new groups hegemony over different policy fields it introduced a whole new set of disparate organized interests into the congressional establishment, over and above the sectional cleavages of the fraternity system. Clay's staffing policy heightened, in three respects, these obstacles to party leadership and party cohesion inhering in the committee system. By mixing men from different fraternities on each committee, his staffing practices tended to import the sectional/fraternal cleavages of the larger legislative establishment into each of its sublegislatures, creating as many new arenas for interbloc conflict as there were committees voting on policy. Second, by giving different boardinghouse fraternities dominion, in the form of chairmanships, over different committees, Clay's staffing practices tended to widen the divergences of interest among the fraternity blocs themselves: to the differences of sectional interest among the fraternities were now added the new sources of con-

* Essentially the same pattern of distribution as among different boardinghouse groups is evident in the committee membership of the Senate (14th Congress), where committee staffing was done by open ballot without the agency of an appointing officer. This similarity indicates the degree of general membership support for Clay's method, and it further casts doubt on the contention that Clay played favorites with his own partisans in his committee appointments.

flict stemming from their seizure of different outposts of power in the committee system. And, third, if the likelihood of agreement among fraternity blocs was lessened, so also was the likelihood of agreement among the committee chairmen themselves, by virtue of their membership in different fraternity blocs. A committee chairman of naval affairs and a chairman of military affairs are not likely to share the same view of defense needs under any circumstances; give the one post to a bloc of seaboard easterners and the other to a group of westerners and the likelihood of agreement between them vanishes altogether. In brief, the way in which Speaker Clay distributed his committee patronage appears to have multiplied the arenas for sectional conflict, to have given new cause for conflict among sectional blocs, and to have aggravated the inherent sources of conflict among the committee chairmen.

It comes as no surprise, therefore, to find that disagreement was the rule, and agreement the exception, among Clay's leading committee chairmen in the 14th Congress. Their voting performance was so erratic and their voting cohesion so low, indeed, that they cannot realistically be considered a group at all, much less a collegial body unified in policy and responsive to the lead of Speaker Clay.[71] Nor is it surprising that Clay was not very successful in providing that "rallying point" for the party which Jefferson before him had so sorely missed on Capitol Hill. In words almost identical to Jefferson's in 1807, Justice Story described the condition of the congressional parties in 1818, during Clay's fourth term as Speaker: "There is no rallying point for any party. Indeed, every thing is scattered. Republicans and Federalists are as much divided among themselves, as the parties formerly were from each other." [72] Power to control committee assignments, theoretically the strongest weapon in the arsenal of a party leader, appears to have been, in practice, a boomerang. By his manner of using this appointive power, Clay virtually foreclosed any real chance of leadership for himself. And instead of unifying the majority party, his use of committee patronage appears to have aggravated the cleavages within it.

What if Clay had been more selective in his committee appointments, giving preferential treatment to one or a relatively few boardinghouse groups? The fraternal ties among his appointees would doubtless have contributed to their political solidarity, sufficiently so, perhaps, to neutralize their different committee interests and to constitute the key chairmen a party oligarchy under the leadership of the Speaker. But if Clay had shown such partiality in distributing key committee positions, how long would he have remained Speaker? One or two or three boardinghouses did not command many votes, certainly not enough to have ensured Clay's re-election to the chair; and what incentives would there have been for the deprived groups to reelect a Speaker who systematically excluded them from these strategic outposts of power? For the triumph of dominating policy through dominance of the committees, Clay would likely have paid by losing the speakership. It seems Clay had no choice but to forsake strong party leadership if he wanted to retain the speakership.[73] If there is paradox here, it is superficial only. For to pose it is merely to say that the structure of the congressional community tended to ensure what its values were seen to imply at the outset of this analysis: to be a person of great popularity in the democratic community on the Hill, one could not be a person of great power, a strong party leader.

The two foregoing instances, President Jefferson's enlistment of congressional spokesmen and Henry Clay's speakership, virtually exhaust the examples available in the historical record on the subject of majority party leadership in Congress from 1800 to 1828. For the opposition party, the nearest to a formal leadership is found in the formation, in 1813, of a committee of legislators from different boardinghouse groups:

> We have [reported Daniel Webster] several projects, and a good many good hands to give a lift. We are trying to organize our opposition, and bring all our forces to act in concert.
> There is recently appointed a kind of committee, to superintend our concerns, viz: Pickering, Webster, Wm. Reed, Baylies, Porter, Pitkin, Grosvenor, Oakely, Stockton, Ridgeley, Hanson, Sheffey, and Gaston.
> It will take us this session to find one another out.[74]

Three things are noteworthy about the above statement: first, that thirteen members were found necessary to represent a party comprising a distinct minority (purportedly only 36 members on the House side) [75] in a Congress less than half its present size; second, that it would take these men an entire session of Congress "to find one another out"; and, perhaps most significant, that this degree of effort was required not to resolve their differences but merely to coordinate the actions of men who were already partisans in the same cause. Webster's statement speaks volumes about the difficulties of keeping either a majority or an opposition party going in a community of transients with provincial loyalties, scattered into separate fraternities, suspicious of leaders, and ambivalent in their attitudes toward power.

From a community perspective on the legislative establishment, therefore, such commentaries by participants as the following seem to reflect reality far more authentically than Federalist allegations of powerful party leaders:

The Democratic party want an acknowledged, bold and determined leader in the House. . . . John Randolph . . . has more popular and effective talents than any other member of the party; but Smith, Nicholson, Davis and others are unwilling to acknowledge him as their file-leader.[76] (1803)

The fact is that the House of Representatives is so completely disorganized, having no man to lead them, and being split into twenty different opinions, that there is little prospect of their adopting or pursuing any regular plan. . . . There is great disunion.[77] (1806)

No one pretends to see the course, or to be able to preside over the destinies of the House or the nation. . . . Violent passions toward each other fill the adherents of Madison and Clinton. Virginia is torn into factions.[78] (1808)

Such has been the confusion and division among the [Republican] party, that no one has hitherto discovered sufficient influence to control any great or general question.[79] (1812)

There is no rallying point for any party. Indeed, every thing is scattered. Republicans and Federalists are as much divided among themselves, as the parties formerly were from each other.[80] (1818)

For the Jeffersonian period as a whole, a study of the congressional community must endorse the view of a foreign observer who came to study American government in 1828:

I found there were absolutely no persons holding the station of what are called, in England, Leaders, on either side of the House. . . . It is true, that certain members do take charge of the administration questions, and certain others of opposition questions; but all this so obviously without concert among themselves, actual or tacit, that nothing can be conceived less systematic, or more completely desultory, disjointed.[81]

On the subject of party leadership, then, as on every other facet of congressional parties explored here, the evidence seems not to confirm the important role claimed for these groupings by modern scholars. If the Jeffersonian experience be cited for its contrast to modern times, it cannot be cited, on the community record, to show the strength of party leadership in the early Congress. It should be cited to show, on the contrary, how very far the institutions of party leadership in the modern Congress have surpassed their primitive antecedents of the Jeffersonian era in vigor and in opportunities for the exercise of influence.

Vision cannot wholly be trusted in viewing political horizons so distant as 1800–1828. As nearly as a community study of the governing group can define those horizons, however, strong parties appear to be more the mirage than the reality of Capitol Hill in the Jeffersonian era. All signs indicate the general weakness of the congressional party, not its significance and surely not its dominance of government, as the hallmark of the Jeffersonian experience. Measured by behavior on speakership elections and presidential nominations, party performance was weak where it should have been strongest. Judged by the degree of recognition accorded them, parties appear to have been an insignificant social presence in a community whose members would not commit themselves in the public record to membership in any party, would not deploy into party groupings in their policy-making sessions on the floor of House and Senate, and would not assemble for party meetings outside the formal sessions except to nominate presidential candidates every four years. It is difficult to believe that in the conduct of legislative government the parties played more than a peripheral role, having no enduring formal organization, almost no caucuses on public policy questions, no legitimated leadership roles. All evidence indicates a majority party utterly incapable of managing conflict in a community whose structure, whose work, whose composition, whose values made conflict inevitable.

What was there, then, to bring stability to this multibloc community and to prevent disruptive conflict? One has to conclude that there were no institutionalized means for performing this indispensable function in a governing group, and that the behaviors and values productive of conflict far outweighed those contributing to the resolution or stabilization of conflict.

The community on the Hill simply did not invest very heavily of its time, its effort, or its values in the processes of majority formation—in the "accommodation and mutual sacrifice of opinion" which necessarily attends these processes and which is (as Jefferson so accurately put it) "necessary to conduct a numerous assembly." [82] Activity looking toward the building of majority consensus appears to have quickened only at caucus time, when it seemed that Congress had virtually to suspend its policy-making tasks in a feverish effort to organize itself for capturing the Presidency.[83] In the intervening periods, coordination of action and negotiation of differences among members of different boardinghouse fraternities seem to have been limited largely to the hours of the day when all were gathered together in formal session, and to have taken place at random at the firesides on the periphery of the auditoriums themselves.[84] Consensus-building and conflict-resolving were relegated to the sidelines, while contention and strife held the center of the stage: this is the image, both literal and figurative, presented by the early congressional establishment.

Outside the formal sessions, occasional liaison between different fraternities seems to have been accomplished by dispatching a delegation from one boardinghouse on a political errand to another:

Yesterday, on the bill for an extra session of Congress, I made an attack on [the] Administration. . . . The ground I took was so grateful to my friends that I had a deputation from Frost's boarding-house, consisting of Tallmadge, Upham, and Davenport, and another from the Washington Mess, consisting of Vandyke, Lewis, and Van Rensselaer, to thank me, and wish my speech should, as soon as possible, be put in a pamphlet.[85]

For purposes of political negotiation, such a method of communication between boardinghouse fraternities was, one would think, of limited utility because of the formalities involved. Rapprochement among contending factions apparently required elaborate etiquette, as indicated in this account by Henry Clay of an early effort at coalition between his own faction and that attached to Senator Andrew Jackson.

The greater part of the Tennessee delegation . . . called on me together, early in the session, for the express purpose, as I understood, of producing a reconciliation. . . . [This preliminary meeting having been satisfactory,] the Tennessee representatives, all of whom . . . boarded at Mrs. Claxton's, on Capitol Hill, gave a dinner, to which we [Jackson and Clay] were both invited. . . . We there met, exchanged salutations, and dined together. I retired from the table early, and was followed to the door by General Jackson and Mr. Eaton, who insisted on my taking a seat in their carriage. I rode with them, and was set down at my lodgings. I was afterward invited by General Jackson to dine with him. . . . He also dined, in company with fifteen or eighteen members of Congress, at my lodgings, and we frequently met, in the course of the winter.[86]

Not only does the record indicate a low intensity of consensus-building activity, but it is not at all certain that common party affiliations were habitually appealed to or were most significant in the efforts that were made to bind together different boardinghouse groups. For those in search of allies outside their own fraternity house, common provincial affiliations may have been exploited with as much success as common party affiliations. Table 10 suggests a high enough incidence of political agreement among Representatives from the same states * to indicate that common provincial affiliations among members of different boardinghouse fraternities were politically significant, as they certainly were among messmates.[87] While there is no necessary incongruence between sectional or state solidarity and party cohesion, it is quite obviously ominous for the party and the nation alike when stimuli toward sectional or state sol-

* Table 10 must be read with caution because state delegation cohesion shown therein partially reflects what was, in reality, cohesion among messmates. This is because more than one member from the same state was likely to reside in the same boardinghouse.

idarity within the legislative establishment are not accompanied by institutions or leadership efforts to bring states and sections together in common cause. Absence of strong party leadership and party machinery on Capitol Hill invited sectional appeals as perhaps the easiest mode of accumulating voting strength beyond the narrow circle of one's fraternity bloc. It invited precisely those sectional solidarities which were to shatter the parties and the nation alike in the second thirty years of the governmental community at Washington.

Why should there have been this utter lack of system in the congressional community for reconciling group differences in sufficient degree to produce sociologically and politically meaningful—as contrasted with merely numerical—majorities? Why should there have been so little exertion, apparently, to do what has to be done in order to acquire controlling power in a governing body proceeding by majority rule? To pose these questions is to come back again to the attitudes respecting politics and power that were widely shared in the governmental community and to the legislators' perceptions of their own roles as the people's representatives at Washington. For it can scarcely be accident that a community whose members were disposed to see immorality in power was also a community deficient in the behaviors and the informal institutions by which (majority) power is acquired. What, indeed, was the failure to develop any system for getting majority agreement if not another expression of the governmental community's aversion to the sorts of behavior that mark a man for a politician and a seeker after power? What, after all, but the legislators' antipower values created in them that compulsion to play the constituency advocate—the outsider in power —and to avoid the behavior of rulers? The psychology of the governors themselves would seem to explain better than any other single factor their deficiencies in the statecraft that is necessary to make a truly representative institution into an effective governing institution.

If the community structure and values of the governing group be crucial to an understanding of the early government, the image of a party-dominated Congress which now pervades the literature on Jeffersonian government ought therefore to be discarded. In its

TABLE 10

VOTING COHESION ON TWENTY-FOUR
ROLL CALLS, BY STATE DELEGATIONS AND
BOARDINGHOUSE GROUPS [a]

	MEAN OF COHESION INDEXES ON EACH ROLL CALL [b]		
	State delegations	*Boardinghouse groups*	*Deviation* [c]
10th Congress, 1st session	78.9	83.7	+4.8
	52.0	47.5	—4.5
	42.1	48.2	+6.1
	81.7	91.9	+10.2
	58.6	70.0	+11.4
	74.8	66.5	—8.3
14th Congress, 2d session	64.3	66.7	+2.4
	43.4	57.6	+12.2
	56.8	60.0	+3.2
	61.9	78.2	+16.3
	59.2	40.6	—18.6
	47.5	53.9	+6.4
	46.1	40.7	—5.4
	37.5	65.2	+27.7
	28.3	54.3	+26.0
	64.9	63.1	—1.8
	42.3	62.4	+20.1
	30.5	52.7	+27.2
20th Congress, 2d session	75.2	64.7	—10.5
	65.8	69.5	+3.7
	58.8	67.5	+8.7
	46.1	62.5	+16.4
	70.6	64.1	—6.5
	60.1	65.0	+5.1

[a] Only those boardinghouse groups and state delegations having three or more Representatives are included in the table; and only those voting situations were analyzed in which at least half, and a minimum of three, of the members of a boardinghouse group or state delegation cast a vote. Otherwise, "absences" were disregarded. All the roll calls analyzed here were included in Table 8. Of the 116 roll calls analyzed in Table 8, the first 6 occurring in the 10th Congress, 1st session, the first 12 occurring in the 14th Congress, 2d session, and the first 6 occurring in the 20th Congress, 2d session, were analyzed for inclusion in the above table.

[b] The Rice Index of Cohesion is used here. See Table 9, note *a*. Each figure in the first column represents the mean of cohesion indexes for all state delegations on a single roll call; the corresponding cell in the second column represents the mean of cohesion indexes for all boardinghouse groups on the same roll call.

[c] Negative deviation (—) indicates roll calls on which the mean was higher for state delegations.

place ought to be the image of a legislature whose members had yet to solve the basic problem of representative government—had yet to develop ways to rule through institutions designed to represent. In its place ought to be the image of an institution utterly unequipped to handle major social conflict: a legislature ever on the verge of group anarchy, awaiting only the catalyst of those passionately felt, deeply divisive issues which must sooner or later irrupt into the Washington community.

One portion of the States is banded against another; there is no feeling of community of interests; jealousies deepen into hostilities; the mine is laid, a spark at length falls, and the grand federal Constitution is blown into a thousand fragments.[88]

These words were not written on the eve of the Civil War, nor from any knowledge but knowledge of the governmental community at Washington. They were written by a foreign observer thirty years before the Civil War, at the close of the Jeffersonian era. And what inspired them was what he saw in the community on Capitol Hill.

CHAPTER 7

THE CONGRESSIONAL
ESTABLISHMENT: A
COMMUNITY PERSPECTIVE

Chapter 3 of this study ventured the prediction that a governing group who shared the prevailing cultural perception of power as evil would tend to favor community associations and behaviors which were sanctioned by the Constitution, in preference to the power-seeking relationships connoted by the political party. While more was involved than the group's attitudes toward power, this prediction proved correct as concerns the social organization of the larger Washington community. Instead of organizing their community around parties, the members organized separate societies around separate branches of government, carrying into their community relationships a constitutional structure intentionally inimical to party rule.

The prediction seems also to be borne out by the community behavior of legislators in their own establishment on Capitol Hill. Here again, what impresses is the essential conformity of community structure to constitutional norms.

Thus, the segregation of the members into politically cohesive boardinghouse fraternities created, inside the legislative establishment, a system of separated institutions sharing the power to govern. The separated institutions of the community structure were not, to be sure, the bicameral separations of the constitutional structure. But the subdivision of the congressional community into minority blocs was eminently conformable to the key organizing principle of the Constitution: given a legislature proceeding by majority rule, the fraternity system on the Hill divided the power to decide policy among groups no one of which, alone, possessed the means (in this case, the voting strength) to impose its own will on public policy. And what other sort of structure was better calculated to produce in the majority party the result approved by James Madison in his famous treatise on the virtues of political pluralism? "Either the existence of the same passion or interest in a majority at the same time must be prevented," he wrote in *The Federalist*, No. 10, "or the majority, having such coexistent passion or interest, must be rendered . . . unable to concert and carry into effect [its] schemes." What with the subdivision of the larger community into separate subcommunities, and the further subdivision of the subcommunity on the Hill into separate political fraternities, one hardly knows whom to credit with the greater genius for establishing structures designed to undermine party rule—the men who made the Constitution, or the pioneer politicians who made the governmental community.

As in the case of the larger community, too, conformity of social structure to constitutional norms implies a widely shared sense of identification with roles prescribed by the Constitution, as against partisan roles as party members. For the larger community, social segregation by branch affiliation suggests the paramount importance to the members of their constitutional roles as executives, legislators, or judges. On Capitol Hill, social segregation by sectional affiliation suggests the primacy of constitutional roles as delegates and spokesmen for outside, constituency interests. Such at least was the operational impact of a social system which put legislators in a primary field of influence restricted principally to colleagues most like their own constituents at home, which infused these fraternal relationships (in some instances, at least) with a moral obligation of group allegiance, and in which there was patterned avoidance of intersectional relationships not likely to harmonize with the members' constitutional obligations as constituency representatives.

And by building into their community structure at Washington the same sort of influences to which the Constitution made them subject outside of Washington, legislators carried the representative principle far beyond the formal requirements of the Constitution, just as they carried the principle of separated institutions well beyond the Constitution's directives.

What emerges from a community study of Capitol Hill is, therefore, a social system which gave probably greater sanction and encouragement to constituency-oriented behavior than any institutional norms or organizational features of the modern Congress. Such a structure is worth the more notice because of the Constitution's permissiveness vis-à-vis internal legislative organization and because of the further freedom of behavior that constituency inattention afforded to the governors on the Potomac. These circumstances call special attention to the sources of this community structure in the attitudes and values of the power-holders themselves, and particularly in their psychology about power. This is not to deny the presence of other contributing factors, one of them presumably being the political utility of the fraternity system. Their bloc voting suggests that sectional fraternities served the members as a trustworthy source of policy guidance in a community where relationships of trust were hard come by, and one which minimized the risk of political miscalculation—with possibly adverse electoral consequences—that was inherent in their isolation from their constituencies. But one must see more than mere coincidence in the power-holders' preoccupation with the morality of power, on the one hand, and their preference, on the other hand, for behaviors and associations inside government which identified them with persons and interests outside the institutions of power. Constituency-oriented behavior, in other words, justified the possession of power in a context of personal and national values which seems to have demanded justification for the possession of power.

Whatever degree of influence may be assigned to legislators' attitudes about power, one conclusion drawn from a community study of Capitol Hill is this: an institutionalized predisposition toward constituency-oriented behavior was present inside the congressional community of the Jeffersonian era quite independently of formal constitutional requirements for representative government, and well before the degree of constituency attention focused upon the Washington community had reached such a point as to require or even to suggest behavior of this sort.

Coupled with community values and organization that were evocative of conflict among different constituency agents was a notable lack of efforts and institutions to bind them together in common cause. The majority party provided a potential basis for cohesion in a community of contending minority blocs, but its success in realizing that potential appears to have been greatly exaggerated by modern writers. Weakness, not strength, of legislative parties in the Jeffersonian era is a second conclusion of a study of the congressional community.

The leading interpretation presumes a favorable environment for disciplined legislative parties which did not, in the first instance, exist on Capitol Hill. The sharp divergence of cultural backgrounds and constituency obligations and the high rate of turnover among the community's membership raised obstacles to party solidarity which could not have been easily surmounted even if there had been some means available for assimilating the large biennial influx of freshman legislators into the party fold. To these "givens" of the environment, stemming from the electoral provisions of the Constitution, was added a host of obstacles having no other origin than the attitudes and desires of the legislators themselves. The stress laid upon proving one's independence of party, coupled with positive sanctions upon primary-group allegiance; rules of proceeding which encouraged intraparty dissent, together with a marked indisposition toward that "accommodation and mutual sacrifice of opinion" so vital to party success; patterned social avoidance between men from different regions whose collaboration was essential to majority party solidarity: these exemplify a political culture on Capitol Hill that was positively uncongenial to strong legislative parties. What all assertions of strong parties have overlooked is that party discipline of the sort postulated would have involved behaviors in conflict with the manifest behaviors that were positively valued in the community life of the legislative branch.

It seems improbable, therefore, that anything approaching party discipline could have been achieved without some visible machinery to bring it about, some persistence of exertion to bring it about, and some more reliable evidence that it was brought about than the participants' allusions to voting discipline and party machinations which have been offered in support of the strong party hypothesis. Six simple criteria were accordingly used in Chapter 6 to test the leading hypothesis of a legislative institution dominated by a strong ruling party: the degree of solidarity achieved in the congressional nominating caucus; the degree of solidarity achieved in speakership elections; whether or not party membership was openly acknowledged on the Hill; whether or not party ties were reinforced by regularity of social interaction, as in legislative caucuses; the degree of formal organization achieved; the presence or absence of party leadership roles having more than transitory significance and having means or opportunities for the exercise of influence that were not available to legislators generally. On these criteria, it is the weakness of parties, not their strength, that emerges as the paramount historical fact. Parties on the Hill were largely unorganized groups. They were without an openly recorded membership, much less with differentiated leadership roles. Common party affiliations were unsustained by regularity of social interaction among the members as a collectivity. Party performance was weak where solidarity should have been easiest to achieve—in speakership elections and presidential nominations. And the only manifest institution for party action, the nominating caucus, disintegrated into warring factions before the close of the Jeffersonian era.

To what extent, under these circumstances, the majority and the opposition parties agreed within themselves on policy issues cannot be answered by a community study. Probably it cannot be answered at all, except conjecturally, for a Congress whose members left no apparent record of their party affiliations. A more important question, however, would seem to be whether the objective of party solidarity was widely approved or persistently sought by legislators. With a modicum of confidence, a community study answers this question in the negative.

The weakness of the party impulse and the absence of party organization in the early Congress tend to challenge two familiar propositions about legislative parties and to suggest new propositions in their stead.

First, the proposition that occupancy of the institutions of government enhances a political party's viability would seem to have questionable validity for the congressional parties of the Jeffersonian era. If this study is correct in finding major threats to party viability *inside* the governmental community—in a structure and a set of values among the governing group that were hostile to parties —then the reverse of the usual proposition seems nearer to reality. It would seem rather that, in the absence of intervening influences, occupancy of institutions of government would have as its natural consequence the progressive weakening of the congressional parties and the growing incapacity of the majority party to control questions of public policy. Separated institutions inside the governmental community and the attitudes reinforcing these separated institutions subjected the parties, in other words, to balkanizing influences which, if unchecked by unifying influences of comparable persistence and strength, would eventuate in their destruction altogether as meaningful entities. Culminating the factional tendencies that were evident throughout the Jeffersonian era, the final collapse of the congressional nominating caucus in 1824 and the disappearance of both Republican and Federalist parties from the national scene before the Jeffersonian era had run its course are consistent with this interpretation. The absence of party machinery or leadership in Congress to offset the divisive effects of community structure and values argues strongly for the paradox that being "in power" brought about loss of power, the withering away of what Tocqueville called the "great parties," and the disappearance of them both in the very act of trying to run the government. One is reminded of the physiological process by which an organism rids itself of an alien presence. It was as if the governmental organism had rid itself of parties alien to its constitution.

Some rethinking seems in order, too, concerning the proposition that the weakness of the congressional parties is related to the intensity of organized group pressures playing upon Congress from the outside. When the state of party organization in the Jeffersonian and in the modern Congress is compared, it is a reasonable conclusion that congressional parties fared far worse in the absence of "pressure politics" than they do under heavy pressure of organized citizen demands. And a community study of Capitol Hill suggests why it should have been so—why public indifference (or its operational equivalent: negligibility of organized citizen pressures upon government) contributed to the weakness of congressional parties. The structure of the community and the attitudes toward power reflected in this structure were such as to require strong, widely felt incentives as well as a "democratic" justification for the collaborative effort and for the power-seeking behaviors involved in the mobilization of party majorities. The nature of the community was such as to require justification for leadership, incentives for followership, and a rationale for men with different outlooks to conspire to agree. A high level of citizen interest, especially the sort that manifests itself in organized "pressures," would provide just such incentives for the legislators, just such justification for the deviance from customary community behaviors which vigorous parties required. Not so with an indifferent citizenry. Public indifference to the doings of the Washington community downgraded the political rewards of party collaboration on the Hill, denied to party "politicking" the important democratic justification of response to citizen demands, and tended—in the context of the governing group's values —to stigmatize, as power-seeking for its own sake, the behaviors essential to the maintenance of party rule.

The new proposition thus emerges that the attitudes and structure of the early congressional community tended to make outside pressures, or at least the believable appearance of outside pressures, an essential precondition for legislators' acceptance of, and indulgence in, the kinds of social behavior which go into the making of a successful legislative party system. However problematic they might eventually become for the parties, it would seem that citizen pressures, in some degree, were historically necessary for the development of vigorous legislative parties.

If the reasoning here is correct, then we have, for the congressional community, a provisional answer to the question posed at the close of Part Two: Would it be possible to sustain effective political command—ruling majorities, in the case of Congress—inside government in the absence of sustaining responses of interest and support among citizens outside government? The answer seems to be negative. Solution to the problem of building institutions of rule inside Congress would have to await solution of the problem of citizen indifference, of "government at a distance and out of sight." To put the proposition more sharply: there was a functional need for the development of an interested, attentive public outside Congress in order to attain that controlling influence over public policy which comes with the successful organization of a majority party inside Congress.[1]

The proposition may help explain two major political developments, both originating in the Jeffersonian era. It implies, on the one hand, pressures inside Congress, more urgent and more specific than those noted earlier in this work, toward a major readjustment in the relationships between the Washington community and the citizenry. In so far as the proposition functionally relates the search for controlling (party) influence inside Congress to the need for higher levels of citizen interest outside Congress, it forecasts a resort to the attention-getting behaviors and to the formulation of attention-getting issues which were to mark the political debut of the Jacksonians. It helps explain why electorate-oriented party organizations should rise, in the Jacksonian era, on the ruins of the Jeffersonian parties. And it suggests cogent reasons why these parties of the future should have been organized from the top down as much as from the grass roots up; why they should have been the inventions of the power-holders for eliciting the attention of the people as much as the inventions of the people for gaining access to the Washington community.

Alternatively to, and pending development of, a "democratic" readjustment in government-citizenry relationships, one can also see what might be called—for want of a more fortunate phrase— "antidemocratic" pressures at work inside the Jeffersonian Congress. One can see forces working toward internal institutional changes which would minimize the need for organizing majorities in order to control policy, as well as the (hypothesized) need for arousing citizen interest: forces working toward minority rule and away from majority rule. The rather sudden development of the committee system at the midpoint of the Jeffersonian era comes immediately to mind, involving as it did a considerable expansion in the scope of minority-group decision-making and a corresponding constriction of collective decision-making by the whole membership of each house of Congress. Clearly the fragmentation of the larger legislature into numerous "little legislatures" was consistent with a community organized into minority blocs and lacking any but the most primitive means of binding those blocs into working majorities for dominating collective decision-making. It would be erroneous not to see other, perhaps more immediate, stimuli to the development of the committee system, and these will be mentioned later in this work. But the standard interpretation which sees the committee system as a response to the problem of handling a large volume of technically complex legislation seems not very applicable to the Jeffersonian era.[2] Decision-making by the minority formations that were the congressional committees may well have been, in part, a functional adaptation to the early Congress' incapacity to organize itself for effective policy-making by majorities.

The third and final conclusion concerns the low priority accorded in a community of segmented social blocs to the mediation of conflict, as contrasted with very marked emphasis upon behaviors and attitudes productive of conflict. Quite irrespective of whatever party cohesion occurred on policy issues, the gross imbalance between conflict-producing and conflict-resolving behaviors and attitudes compels the conclusion that the congressional community was a fundamentally unstable social system. No impression emerges from the community record of Capitol Hill in the Jeffersonian era more clearly than the impression of a community lacking adequate means to resolve or stabilize the conflicts generated by its own structure and values, let alone those conflicts imported into it from the outside, to which, as a governing community, it was peculiarly susceptible.

What degree of instability a social system may have and still perform effectively as a governing system is a question little researched and not easily answered. Clearly one does not look for perfect stability in a society of power-holders. Conflict is inevitable among a society of representatives in a republican polity; and the American system of government has developed an unusually high tolerance for internal conflict. That it is not enough, however, for a governing society merely to represent clashing interests, merely to mirror the conflicts overt or latent in the larger society, seems equally certain. Still less does it suffice to institutionalize, after the fashion of the early Capitol Hill community, the sectional cleavages and conflicts of a new federal republic. To perform the inherently governmental function of resolving conflict in the polity at large, there must be some means for resolving conflict among the governors themselves, and some disposition to do so. There must be some means for displacing disintegrative conflict with harmless or constructive conflict; some means for preventing the indefinite escalation of conflict and for keeping it within manageable bounds. It would seem, too, that these means must be sophisticated and institutionally sanctioned in proportion as the sources of conflict are prolific and themselves institutionalized.

Such means, commensurate with the sources of conflict, are not discernible in the congressional community of Jeffersonian times. As a system for the effective representation of citizen interests the social system of Capitol Hill has probably never been surpassed in the history of republican government. But a fragmented social system of small blocs, more anarchic than cohesive, seems hardly to meet the minimal requirements for a viable system of managing social conflict, for performing "the regulation of . . . various and interfering interests" which the author of *The Federalist*, No. 10 acknowledged to be "the principal task of modern legislation." Far from serving as an institution for the management of conflict, the little democracy on the Hill seems more likely to have acted as a source of conflict in the polity. An ironic and provocative judgment is thus suggested by the community record of Capitol Hill: at a time when citizen interest in national government was at its lowest point in history the power-holders on the Potomac fashioned a system of surpassing excellence for representing the people and grossly deficient in the means for governing the people.

It would seem to follow, then, that while the congressional community could scarcely withstand any major divisive influences coming upon it from the outside, it was essentially dependent upon forces outside itself for internal stability in sufficient degree to perform its governmental function adequately. In view of this need for outside direction, the relations between the congressional community and the executive establishment on the other side of the River Tiber assume crucial importance. Could the Presidency, as an external force, supply that unifying influence which the congressional community lacked within itself? Or, alternatively, could the executive establishment take upon itself the tasks of a governing entity that Congress seems unable to have performed? These two political questions take us, in Part Four, to an exploration of presidential-congressional relations and, in Part Five, to a community analysis of the executive branch.

PART FOUR

THE PRESIDENCY
AND THE HILL

CHAPTER 8

STATECRAFT

To assert that the constitutional framers intended to prevent the President from exercising influence over men and policies on Capitol Hill would be an overstatement. But it seems beyond argument that the Constitution provided a wholly inadequate vehicle for presidential leadership of Congress. That the framers made the Chief Executive independent of the representative body was no inconsiderable accomplishment in a nation whose colonial experience gave every reason for mistrusting executive power. Nothing would have been more out of keeping with the post-Revolutionary political mood nor out of character with the organizing principles of the Constitution than for the framers to have admitted into it the concept of presidential leadership of the legislative branch.

As ratified, the Constitution indeed opened fewer and less promising avenues for legislative influence to the head of government than it did to ordinary citizens outside government. If the constitution gave the President the authority to propose action and recommend measures to Congress, it gave not only this but more to the citizenry: upon citizens but not upon the President it conferred the right to petition Congress—in modern usage, to mount "pressure" campaigns—and an all but unlimited freedom to organize as need dictates for the pursuit of legislative objectives. If the President was given a potentially important source of influence in the conditional veto over measures passed, the ultimate sanction against unwanted legislation was given to the voters, not to the President. None of the framers' objectives was more explicit than to deny the head of government any influence over the selection, tenure, or career advance-

ment of legislators. If the Constitution gave the President authority
to summon Congress in extraordinary session, nothing in the Constitution ensured a hearing for the President's views. Upon citizens
and states, but not upon the President, the Constitution conferred
the opportunity and the right to have spokesmen on Capitol Hill.
Far from providing legislative representation for the President's interest, the framers took special pains to avoid it. The ingenuity of
their devices for ensuring disharmony or at least divergence of
viewpoint between Congress and President—devices ranging from
staggered elections to different constituencies for the two—was
matched only by the elaborateness of their schemes to ensure frustration of action when different viewpoints proved irreconcilable.
There remained, as a potential instrument of leadership, the President's appointive power; but this was shared with the Senate for all
those executive positions which were, at Congress' option, made
subject to confirmation.

Of legal authority for presidential leadership of Congress, then,
the Constitution was nearly as bare as Mother Hubbard's cupboard.

No more promising avenues to presidential leadership were
opened by the social structure of the governmental community. If
the Constitution preferred constituents over the President for access
to the legislative branch, the retreat of legislators into a separate and
exclusive community of their own, and their deployment inside
their community into boardinghouse fraternities, ensured priority
to the influence of their associates over the influence of the White
House across the swamp. The Constitution and the structure of the
Washington community together thus tended to relegate the President to third place in the hierarchy of influence over the legislative
branch, after constituents and colleagues. And, just as the Constitution legally defined the President's position as an outsider to Capitol
Hill, the structure and values of the governmental community defined the President socially as an outsider. Tacit rules reinforcing
social segregation were especially stringent in the case of the President, and community custom, more explicitly than anything in the
Constitution, kept the presidential tiger from the gates of Capitol
Hill. Etiquette forbade the Chief Executive to set foot inside the

legislative compound for any purposes but inauguration, attendance at a few other ceremonial functions, and to sign bills on the last day of the session, the last being an accommodation to Congress and one which must have gone far toward neutralizing the political feasibility of the pocket veto.[1] Early-rising legislators might glimpse President Adams trotting around the Capitol on his dawn constitutionals, and President Jefferson might be seen on rare occasions at the Sunday sermon in the Hall of Representatives; but confinement in the White House was a rule never broken by any Jeffersonian President for missions of persuasion, political negotiation, or leadership to Capitol Hill.

The morass of the Tiber swamp intervening between the Capitol and the executive mansion, and the rutted causeway pretending to bridge it, were fitting symbols for what the community arrangements of the governing group offered the President by way of access to power on the Hill.

What, then, was left to the President for providing that "rallying point" which his party, and that stabilizing force which the Congress, so sorely needed? There remained precisely what presidential power in Congress has always largely, though not exclusively, depended upon: the exercise of political skill, of statecraft, by the occupant of the White House. The means and tools of leadership which the Constitution and the community culture all but denied to him the President had to improvise out of wit and ingenuity, as his political talents, circumstance, statutes, and good fortune permitted. Possibly the framers of the Constitution intended it this way— intended that leadership be politically achieved rather than legally ascribed. Probably they did not intend leadership at all. Probably they believed they had invented a system of government that would make leader-follower relationships unnecessary within the ruling establishment. More likely they never comprehended the risks of government by "separate and rival interests," never foresaw a Congress unable to control conflict within itself, and never foresaw that the Presidency would have to supply the unifying influence needed to secure the Congress and the fragments of the nation it represented against disintegration. For it would tax the imagination to believe that the framers intended so much to depend so largely on the chance of having a skilled politician for a President.

It is, therefore, statecraft more than institutions one must study in dealing with presidential-congressional relations during the Jeffersonian era. The task of analysis is infinitely the more difficult because of it: difficult because American political literature has yielded, to guide analysis, but one published work on the principal subject of statecraft; * difficult because the historical distance of the Jeffersonian era makes it impossible to recapture the subtleties involved in this most subtle of political relationships; difficult because of the inherent elusiveness of a relationship in which matters of personality and individual style are so pervasively involved and so vitally important; difficult, finally, because the relationship had to be in large measure arcane, and one can never be sure that all its most important aspects have found their way into the written record of early Washington.

Yet the historical record is not barren. It provides, indeed, somewhat more evidence of presidential efforts at leadership on Capitol Hill than of efforts made by legislators themselves. Part Four will attempt to answer, on the basis of this record, four principal questions. First, were there in the Jeffersonian era any circumstantial aids to the winning of presidential influence on the Hill? Second, what were the means devised and used by Presidents for this purpose? Third, were the means sufficient? Did they allow Presidents to perform from a distance and as outsiders the task of political management that legislators themselves would not regularly perform? Fourth, what explanations does a community study of the governing group suggest for the success or failure of presidential leadership in the period 1801–28?

As to circumstantial aids, four aspects of the political environment in Jeffersonian times would appear, on the surface at least, to have facilitated presidential influence on Capitol Hill.

There was, first, the predominance of foreign affairs over the domestic work of the governmental community. Except for the admis-

* No nation has been so dependent upon statecraft for the effective management of its conflicts and produced so little literature on the subject. Richard Neustadt's *Presidential Power* stands alone.

sion of new states and the administration of territories, the attention of the Washington community during the period 1801–28 was principally absorbed in that area of activity which has traditionally given large scope to presidential initiative, namely, foreign affairs: the war against the Barbary pirates; the acquisition of Louisiana from France; the tortuous negotiations with Spain for the acquisition of West Florida; the Seminole War; the working out of a policy toward the emerging nations of Latin America and the formulation of the Monroe Doctrine; the readjustment of relationships with France in the aftermath of her revolution, during a period which saw Napoleon's rise and fall; and the prosecution of the second war against the colonial parent of the young nation, the War of 1812. Predominance of foreign policy issues by no means assures a President of influence in Congress. But the tendency of such predominance, recognized generally by students of American politics, is to increase the political risks of opposition to the President, to elicit whatever forces there be for unity, and to heighten that dependence of legislators upon the President (in this case, for policy initiative and information) which is the keystone of presidential influence on the Hill.

Second, Presidents of the Jeffersonian era faced only negligible competition from organized citizen groups for access to, and influence among, legislators. The negligibility of organized citizen demands upon Congress was, to be sure, a mixed blessing. For if it tended to reduce the President's competition and saved Congress from what might well have been, in the Jeffersonian era, divisive influences the community could not have begun to cope with, it also denied the President the important supplementary source of support for his legislative objectives that lobbyists may provide. Nonetheless, the virtual absence of organized "pressure-group" representatives at the seat of government heightened the chances for the President to dominate the communication channels to Congress. It saved the voice of the White House from being lost in a general noise of lobbying.

Third, the method of presidential nomination by congressional caucus (and of presidential election by the House of Representatives when, as in 1801 and 1824, no candidate received an electoral majority) assured Jeffersonian Presidents of some degree of personal support on Capitol Hill at the time of their accession to office. This was not necessarily majority support, as discussion of the nominating caucus in Chapter 6 has indicated. Nor was the caucus without its liabilities to the President. For if it assured incoming Presidents a circle of partisans on the Hill, it also must have brought them into office with a passel of political debts to legislators, not so easily discharged without compromising the independence of their office as indebtedness to the politicians outside government who now manage presidential nominations. Nevertheless, the fact that congressional approval was virtually a precondition to attaining the headship of government gave Jeffersonian Presidents stature, at the time of their accession, as the men with the largest demonstrated support inside the governmental community, as well as a potential sphere of influence on Capitol Hill.

Last, all Presidents of the Jeffersonian era had service experience in Congress prior to entering the White House. Jefferson served four years as presiding officer of the Senate, moving directly from one of the largest boardinghouse groups on Capitol Hill to the executive mansion. Madison was a Republican leader in the House for a considerable period before moving to the Secretaryship of State and thence to the Presidency. Monroe had served four years, and John Quincy Adams five, in the Senate. All Jeffersonian Presidents were members of the governmental community at Washington when they were elected to the Presidency, and none came into the office without having had the opportunity to learn at firsthand the facts of political life on Capitol Hill.[2]

With these more or less favorable auguries, among the several unfavorable ones mentioned earlier, how did Presidents go about the work of preserving and enlarging that sphere of influence with which they came into office? The record indicates four presidentially improvised practices directly or indirectly related to the acquisition of influence in Congress: the selection of confidential agents among legislators themselves; the deputizing of cabinet members for political liaison with Congress; "social lobbying" of legislators at the executive mansion; and the use of a presidential newspaper. A dubious fifth may have been the political use of the President's appointive power. Of the Presidents holding office from 1801 to 1828, the first was the only one to employ all the techniques mentioned above and the only one, it seems, to pursue with vigor the task of leading Congress. Any exploration of presidential leadership of Congress must therefore have to do principally with Thomas Jefferson's eight years in the White House.

Jefferson's enlistment of legislators to act as his agents on the Hill has been noted in Chapter 6. The practice was to single out individual legislators for "confidential" communication who, privy to the President's wishes and presumably acting under his guidance, would steer desired bills through the legislative process. What Jefferson had to gain by this innovation in presidential-congressional relations is obvious enough to require no elaboration. So long as enough legislators—and the right legislators—could be persuaded to undertake the job, the President acquired not merely that legislative representation of his interest which the Constitution denied but also an indirect participation in internal legislative processes where direct participation was constitutionally proscribed. Equally important must have been the advantages to the President of having confidential sources of political intelligence from the Hill. Jefferson's apparently impressive record of legislative successes, which is widely believed to have resulted from "drilling" the membership in party caucuses, may well have been due instead to his foreknowledge of congressional sentiment afforded in part by these confidential agents, and the resulting opportunity to adjust the timing, language, and content of his legislative proposals accordingly.

What limits there were to the effectiveness of this technique, and the reasons why it ceased to have prominence when its innovator went out of office, will be assayed after the other presidential techniques have been described. At this point, however, it is necessary to take issue in part with the leading interpretation that congressional "leadership was neither the prerogative of seniority nor a privilege conferred by the House; it was distinctly the gift of the president." [3]

As previously noted, it is questionable whether the term "leaders" accurately denotes the relationship of these men to their fellow party members on the Hill. "Spokesmen" for the President would appear better to describe the legislative role of men whose position was not legitimated by seniority or by election of their colleagues, as leadership in the modern Congress is; of men who, on the evidence of the written record, enjoyed no opportunities for influence over legislative procedure that were not available to any other legislator; and whose only distinguishing characteristic indicated by the historical record was their special relationship to Jefferson.

Also questionable is the view implicit in the interpretation that the absence of party organization and of legitimated party leaders on the Hill worked wholly to the President's advantage. Recent understanding of the historical and functional relationship between the Presidency and the congressional party runs counter to this view, and would indicate rather that Presidents are more the beneficiaries than the victims of organized congressional parties with self-selected leaders.[4] That it was an advantage for the President to be able to choose the individuals with whom he would deal in Congress seems likely. But the circumstance which gave him this choice—namely, the failure of the congressional party to organize and select its own leaders—seems just as likely to have canceled out this advantage. The fact that his congressional agents were not legitimated as leaders meant, for one thing, that they could not speak authoritatively to President Jefferson for the party membership. Nor could they, on the President's behalf, approach the party's membership with the authority and the bargaining leverage that accrue to the elected leadership positions of organized congressional parties. Far more significant, the fact that these agents were not legitimated as leaders by their own colleagues must have heightened, to the President's great disadvantage, the conflicts inherent in a role which required loyalty to the White House in a community where independence of the White House tended to be a measure of a man's personal integrity. Lack of an elective base or other recognition of their legitimacy must, in other words, have made Jefferson's spokesmen far more sensitive to intralegislative pressures and sentiments adverse to the President than to party leadership in the modern Congress, which combines spokesmanship for the President with a demonstrated base of support within the congressional community. Circumstances can of course be imagined when spokesmanship for the President conferred some degree of status on Capitol Hill. But there can be little doubt that, given a congressional atmosphere resistive to the President, to be marked as a man under the influence of the Chief Executive was more a liability than an asset on the Hill; and that to be involved in a collusive relationship with the White House in any circumstances was to run a continuous risk of social stigmatization for sycophancy as one of the "toads that live upon the vapor of the palace." [5]

The record affords a vivid glimpse of these values being asserted against one legislator who had consented to act as administration spokesman. He was, in the words of a cabinet officer,

subjected to such sneering hints and innuendoes . . . as if he were a dependent tool of the Executive [that] he has suffered himself to be goaded . . . not only into disavowals of any subserviency to the views of the Executive, and to declarations in the face of the House that he did not care a fig for the Administration or any member of it, but into the humor of proposing measures which the President utterly disapproves. From mere horror of being thought the tool of the Executive he has made himself the tool of . . . [the] opposition.[6]

Almost certainly, the stressful nature of the role had much to do with the defection of Jefferson's most prominent congressional spokesman, John Randolph, in 1805–6. The overriding influence of legislative over presidential loyalties is suggested by Randolph's subsequent explanation of his conduct:

I came here prepared to cooperate with the Government in all its measures. . . . [But I soon] found that I might cooperate or be an honest man. I have therefore opposed and will oppose them. Is there an honest man disposed to be the go-between and to carry down secret messages to this House? No. It is because men of character cannot be found to do this business that agents must be got to carry things into effect which men of uncompromitted character will not soil their fingers or sully their characters with.[7]

The troublesome problem of divided loyalty was not so apparent, at least, in the case of cabinet members, and this may have been one of the reasons why all Jeffersonian Presidents used them for political liaison with Capitol Hill. Not only because they were members of the President's own executive community and formally subordinate to him, but also because the President had no staff of his own to dispatch on political missions to the Hill,[8] department heads figured prominently as intermediaries between President and Congress in every administration. Secretary of the Treasury Albert Gallatin was President Jefferson's principal executive agent for congressional relations, and he is the only high-level executive officer known to have resided permanently on Capitol Hill.[9] Henry Adams has written of this arrangement:

[The] close neighborhood [of his residence] to the Houses of Congress brought Mr. Gallatin into intimate social relations with the members. The principal adherents of the Administration in Congress were always on terms of intimacy in Mr. Gallatin's house, and much of the confidential communication between Mr. Jefferson and his party in the Legislature passed through this channel. . . . But the communication was almost entirely oral, and hardly a trace of it has been preserved either in the writings of Mr. Gallatin or in those of his contemporaries.[10]

President Madison regularly instructed his department heads to take advice concerning legislation to Congress and to discuss policy matters with congressmen, commenting as follows:

I remarked that where the intention was honest and the object useful, the convenience of facilitating business in that way was so obvious that it had been practiced under every past administration, and would so under every future one.[11]

Although President Monroe privately objected to official communications from Congress directly to department heads and bypassing the President,[12] he and his successor in office encouraged direct communication from department heads to legislators, extending their instructions to include political liaison with congressional committees:

It has always been considered as a practical rule [wrote Secretary of State Adams] that the Committee of Foreign Relations should be the confidential medium of communication between the Administration and Congress.

. . . The Chairman . . . has always been considered as a member in the confidence of the Executive . . . [and] the President has . . . directed me to communicate freely to him.[13]

To the extent that Presidents utilized cabinet members from choice rather than because they had no personal staff, the practice conceivably had some advantages over direct presidential liaison with legislators. The use of "front men" allowed Presidents to maintain, for what it was worth, the outward appearance of conformity to community norms which decreed social distance between the President and Congress. It also gave them a medium of influence perhaps more palatable to lawmakers than direct confrontation with the President himself, since cabinet members had inferior social status to elected persons; and it gave Presidents particularly good access to the congressional committees with which department heads had, then as now, much business. The use of executive agents also permitted what neither public messages to Congress nor personal transactions between the President and legislators did: a means for presenting and pressing upon Congress legislation in which the President did not want or could not afford to be directly implicated. Just such an instance occurred in 1805–6. Clearly intended for diplomatic ears, public messages threatening invasion of Spanish Florida were being sent to Congress by President Jefferson while his agents, ostensibly without White House authorization, were presenting a draft bill appropriating funds to purchase West Florida from Spain.[14]

And in theory department heads, as members of the President's official family, were more nearly subject to presidential direction and closer to the President's interests than intermediaries who belonged to the legislative branch. Theory and reality may have jibed for Jefferson, blessed with a Secretary of the Treasury who apparently kept his departmental interests subordinate to his obligations as presidential agent. For Jefferson's successors, the gap between theory and reality would become abundantly clear. Pending later discussion, the question might also be kept in mind of how likely the use of department heads for congressional liaison was to exert a unifying influence upon the President's party on the Hill.

A third power technique was the wining and dining of legislators at the executive mansion. If etiquette restrained the President from crossing the Tiber to make the acquaintance of congressmen, he could lure them across to the White House. Like the enlistment of congressional spokesmen for the President, legislative dinners were Jefferson's innovation and a device conspicuously employed by him alone among Presidents. Before and after his two terms in office, the President's after-hours social life was restricted almost exclusively to obligatory dinners and state functions, a once or twice weekly White House levee, and holiday receptions. Jefferson abolished the levee immediately upon assuming office and substituted small dinners held almost nightly when Congress was in session, with legislators predominating among the guests. The dinners were the talk of Washington. In the judgment of observant diplomats from abroad, for whom food and wine were standard accessories of political persuasion, they were the secret of Jefferson's influence.

Political purpose pervaded the conception and execution of Jefferson's legislative dinners, and if no one but foreign emissaries seemed to perceive the fact, that was but testimony to their political success.[15] Rarely more than a manageable dozen guests were invited at the same time, and each evening's dinner group was selected "not . . . promiscuously, or as has been done [by Jefferson's successors], alphabetically, but . . . in reference to their tastes, habits and suitability in all respects, which attention had a wonderful effect in making his parties more agreeable, than dinner parties usually are." [16] Guests received invitations penned in the President's own hand, often with a personal note; hundreds of mementos sent over the Tiber in those eight years later found cherished places in family albums. All legislators were invited, most more than once during the course of a session. Jefferson apparently made more of a distinction between Federalists and Republicans than did the legislators themselves in their own community. While Federalists received their share of invitations, the President seems never to have invited them at the same time with legislators of his own party, save for a maverick like Senator Adams, whom he regularly surrounded with Republicans at the dinner table, and who subsequently defected to the Republican fold. "He ought to invite them without regard to their political sentiments," a Federalist Senator grumbled; "the more men of good hearts associate, the better they think of each other." [17] But nothing would have been more out of keeping with Jefferson's desire to cultivate a sense of comity among his partisans on the Hill. Not only did he avoid mixing Federalists with Republicans, but fragmentary evidence suggests that Jefferson made it a practice to bring Republicans from different boardinghouses together around his dinner table, while Federalists were invited by boardinghouse bloc. Nor did Jefferson ordinarily mix cabinet members with his congressional guests. The field was reserved for the Chief Executive and legislators.

The dinners could not have been better staged. A round table was used, thus avoiding a place of precedence for the President and putting him among peers, at the same time that it prevented separate, private conversations. The risk of distraction and eavesdropping by waiting servants was averted by Jefferson's installation of a dumbwaiter situated near his elbow, bringing up victuals and potables from belowstairs to be served by the President himself: "You see we are alone," he announced, "and *our walls have no ears*." [18] A French chef was "his best ally in conciliating political opponents" and the finest of imported wines put "all their tongues . . . in motion." [19] "You drink as you please and converse at your ease," a bedazzled Senator wrote home.[20] The President's uniform for the occasion was nondescript, marking his for a humble station: slippers down at the heel, faded velveteen breeches, hairy (not quite threadbare) waistcoat. Politics seemed somehow the one subject never discussed, talked around but not about, with the conversation adroitly steered away from shoptalk: enough of that in the boardinghouses from which the guests had now escaped. An Adams might, however, come away with an idea of what the President's views were on a question of national boundaries; [21] another congressman on a prospective presidential appointee.[22] Dominating the situation but never the conversation, Jefferson "took the lead and gave the tone, with a *tact* so true and discriminating that he seldom missed his aim; which was to draw forth the talents and information of each and all of his guests and to place every one in an advantageous light and by being pleased with themselves, be enabled to please others. Did he perceive any individual silent and unattended to, he would make him the object of his peculiar attention and in a manner apparently the most undesigning would draw him into notice and make him a participator." [23] To farmers he talked of agriculture; to classicists, of philosophy; to geographers, of Humboldt; to lawyers, of Blackstone; for naturalists he brought out his elegantly illustrated bird books from Europe. Raconteur extraordinary, he played the buffoon with zest, and improved upon the Baron Münchhausen himself. "You can never be an hour in this man's company without something of the marvellous. . . . His genius is of the old French school." [24]

It was a virtuoso performance, and the foreign diplomats rightly saw method in it all. But they quite misjudged the first Virginian President in thinking that his manner was "put on." Jefferson in politics was Br'er Rabbit thrown in the briar patch.

Why Jefferson's three successors in office failed to continue the tradition can only be speculated upon. Perhaps the usefulness of the dinners lay in their novelty, and maybe there was little political mileage left in them by the time of Jefferson's retirement.[25] Perhaps their usefulness derived from the lack of competition elsewhere in the executive community; for in the administrations of Jefferson's successors, as will later be shown, congressmen did not want for a multitude of eager hosts and hostesses along executives' row. Perhaps the ever-swelling ranks of Congress, with reapportionment and the admission of new states, made small dinners impractical and dictated large receptions for congressmen (as in Jackson's time), invited in alphabetical segments according to the first letter of their last names. Perhaps none of Jefferson's successors had the inclination or the stamina to spend long hours nightly listening to congressmen after a hard day's work. Perhaps none saw the political opportunities in it.

In any case, none of the three Presidents following Jefferson had any opportunities remotely comparable to the legislative dinners for meeting informally with legislators. Madison reinstituted the levee, much to the delight of the diplomatic corps, who could once more parade in state attire, as well as of the townspeople, from bank president to musky stableboy, for the levee, announced weekly in the local newspaper, was open to all without invitation.[26] In Madison's time, the inimitable Dolley kept dignity uppermost at these affairs, and managed with the aid of a tall turban topped with "towering feathers" to preside over the throng.[27] She had the finesse but, alas, none of the objectives of the politician, and her very brilliance reduced her husband to an insignificant presence, sometimes unrecognized by his own guests.[28] "Being so low of stature, he was in imminent danger of being confounded with the plebian crowds; and was pushed and jostled about like a common citizen." [29]

How utterly useless this institution was for purposes of confidential communication with legislators is indicated by the fact that the Chief of Staff's pocket was picked at one of the levees; [30] and at another manpower had to be summoned to subdue a raucous domestic from one of the legations who had come to hobnob with society.[31] Hack drivers, after depositing their fares, did not scruple to hitch their nags to the White House post and drop in for a toddy themselves. "It is a mere matter of form," wrote a congressman; "you make your bow . . . eat and drink what you can catch . . . and if you can luckily find your hat and stick, then take French leave; and that's going to the 'levee.' " [32]

Madison's successor spent a small fortune in France and Belgium to refurbish the White House after the British had finished with it. But if Monroe gave congressional guests an acquaintance with elegance, what he got in return was a congressional investigation into his vouchers.[33] He had the misfortune, too, of an English wife given to stiff stately dinners, migraines, and prolonged periods of withdrawal from what had then become a viciously competitive social life.[34]

In daring and in sheer lavishness of output the second family of Adamses to occupy the White House outdid all their predecessors. They threw open the great east hall and had a ball where Adams' mother had hung out the laundry, even though the chamber was still partially unplastered during the son's regime. Dinner parties and dances became the order of the day, and while Adams enjoyed not a minute of it he surprised everyone by coming out "in a brilliant masquerade dress of social, gay, frank, cordial manners." [35] But Adams buried his puritan conscience only to have it rise upon him, like a phoenix, from Capitol Hill. Coming on top of the Monroes' elegance, the importation of continental entertainment styles brought forth chastisements from across the swamp, by legislators always predisposed to view White House social life as "the resort of the idle, and the encourager of spies and traitors." [36] Adams' particular reward for his efforts was a shower of rebuke for installing a billiard parlor in the White House at public expense.

Note in contrast, then, the virtues of Jefferson's social technique. The dinners allowed him to make the personal acquaintance of each legislator in a community whose membership was in constant flux, to appraise the strengths, prejudices, and foibles of the men he wished to lead, and to spot the potential troublemakers and the potential spokesmen for himself. They allowed the President to accomplish, under his personal supervision, what no institution on Capitol Hill existed to accomplish: to bring legislators belonging to different boardinghouse fraternities together in circumstances conducive to amicability and free from contention, and in such a way as to stimulate a sense of common party membership among them. They gave him an opportunity to build general good will in Congress which would give his agents a more favorable atmosphere in which to do their work and which would at the same time react favorably upon his efforts to preserve their loyalty by minimizing the risk to them of acting as presidential agents on the Hill. The personal acquaintances made through the dinners also afforded Jefferson knowledge about his party members independently of his agents, an independent source of political intelligence about congressional mood and opinion against which to evaluate the reports of his agents, and a means of assessing the performance and standing of his agents vis-à-vis other legislators. The dinners gave the President a chance to encourage a sense of personal obligation and indebtedness to him among the lawmakers: a chance to please, to flatter, and to make them feel important. Last, but by no means least important —community attitudes toward power and politicians being what they were—he was able to display himself as a plain human before the men he wished to lead. He gained the opportunity to disarm men mistrustful of power and authority, and to convince them that the fellow in the White House was an exception to the stereotype they and the country harbored of politicians and power-seekers.

None but Jefferson with his shabby dress, irresistible humor, and ingratiating manner could have carried it off. Well might he have said, with Shakespeare's King Henry,

> I stole all courtesy from heaven
> And drest myself in such humility
> That I did pluck allegiance from men's hearts.

Presidential newspapers deserve brief mention as a means of influence, though they were at best of secondary importance, and not so specifically directed as the other techniques to the persuasion of legislators. Here again the innovation seems to have been Jefferson's. Before the transfer of the government to its Potomac locale, he persuaded a Philadelphia editor and friend to transport his printing press to Washington, and Samuel Harrison Smith began publication of the *National Intelligencer* there on October 1, 1800.[37] Precisely what the relationship was between Jefferson and Smith cannot be told from the community record, other than their common partisanship in the Republican cause, and apart from the fact that Smith was also selected as official reporter for the congressional debates, receiving sundry public printing contracts as well. The *Intelligencer* was, however, universally acknowledged inside the governmental community to be, and was spoken of as, the "official" or "administration organ." It remained so until 1824, the last of the Jeffersonian Presidents using instead the *National Journal*, also published in Washington, as his principal publicity medium.[38]

Nor can the specific political uses to which Presidents put these newspapers be defined without a separate, comprehensive study of their content; and even then the difficulty of identifying the presidentially inspired items would be vexing, for the *Intelligencer* was not merely a partisan sheet but a legitimate newspaper in its own right, and one of high quality. It seems reasonable to suppose, nevertheless, that Presidents availed themselves of newspapers for much

the same reasons as the leadership in any organization employs organs of propaganda: to make and select "news" which will reinforce
attitudes favorable to the leadership and its objectives, and to counter other media communicating unfavorable attitudes toward the
leadership. Since the *Intelligencer* and the *Journal* had only local
circulation, they may be considered principally as organs of internal
propaganda, rather than a presidential device for reaching the larger
public outside Washington, although items appearing in the *Intelligencer* were occasionally reproduced in the partisan press of other
localities.[39]

A special virtue for Presidents lay, presumably, in the semi-
anonymity of communication that newspapers afforded them.
Without attribution of source, views might be expressed, awareness
of events might be revealed, rumors might be scotched or created,
of which Presidents could not take official cognizance. For purposes
of self-defense or counterattack, opportunity was offered them to
participate pseudonymously or covertly in the exceedingly vicious
political warfare of their day, where overt participation would have
lowered the dignity of their office.[40] In addition to providing cover,
use of newspapers by Presidents may well have been an effort to re-
coup some of the opportunities lost by their exclusion from the busy
network of extraofficial communication that was social life outside
the White House walls.[41]

Until 1816 the presidential newspaper appears to have dominated,
though it did not monopolize, the "mass" media inside the governmental community. It lost that preeminence in Monroe's administration, and by the 1820s the President shared the local propaganda
field with at least four factional newspapers. They were under the
patronage, respectively, of the Secretary of the Treasury, the Secretary of War, the Secretary of State, and Andrew Jackson.[42]

As to patronage, the definitive work on early public administration states unequivocally that "the institution of bartering patronage
for legislation . . . did not exist." Leonard White has found that
before Jackson "no President . . . undertook to buy leadership with
patronage. . . . The practice of using patronage to get votes in either House was rare and would have been thought corrupt." [43] As

White implies, then, community attitudes and values tended to fore-close the use of patronage as an instrument of pressure upon Congress. More than this, they did not offer any but the most equivocal sanction for the partisan use of the President's removal and appointive power. No President before Jackson either subscribed to or practiced on more than a small scale the principle that vacancies ought to be created to make way for partisan appointments. Such a practice would, as Jefferson saw it, "revolt our new converts, and give a body to leaders who now stand alone." [44] "There is a Scylla as well as a Charybdis," John Quincy Adams commented on the question of partisan appointments to maintain favor with the party or nonpartisan appointments to maintain general good will.[45] Jeffersonian Presidents steered the middle course, thus helping to neutralize what has long since been recognized as one of the most potent weapons of presidential leadership.

It is "probable," as White also points out, that no President "failed on occasion to smooth the path of legislative accommodation by a suitable appointment." [46] But even where community values did not restrict partisan use of the President's appointive power, it is certain that availability of positions did—and not alone because "the number of vacancies was relatively small." [47] Another reason was that the principal responsibility for staffing the appointive offices did not rest with the President. Precisely how many of the appointive positions were the President's to dispose is not known.[48] Jefferson stated that six hundred of the roughly twenty-seven hundred civil appointive positions were "named by the President" when he came into office; [49] it is not clear from his choice of phrase whether he was referring to the number of positions *de facto* falling under the President's disposition, or the number he was authorized by law to appoint. In the postal service alone more than this number were put by law under the appointive jurisdiction of the Postmaster General. The entire service throughout the Jeffersonian era—a very large proportion of the government's personnel complement—was appointed by the service chief, and "it was unusual for the Postmaster General to consult the President, or to be called in by him to receive executive advice" on appointments.[50] It seems that most of the revenue collectors were appointed by the Secretary of the Treasury; in Jefferson's administration Gallatin cleared his choices for these important jobs with the President. Treasury officers subordinate to the collectors were, in turn, appointed by the collectors themselves, subject to approval by the Secretary of the Treasury. As to the civil staff at Washington, "department heads . . . [made] their own selections of clerks and subordinates without reference to the President." [51]

What principally remained to the President seems to have been therefore the relatively small number of district attorneys and marshals (only 24 each in 1801), territorial governorships, diplomatic and cabinet posts, and judgeships.[52] It was presumably in this limited area that the main opportunities were offered to "smooth the path of legislative accommodation by a suitable appointment."

But here the President's choice was by no means free, for all these positions required Senate confirmation. This fact, considered together with the President's implicit or explicit political obligations to legislators deriving from the mode of presidential nomination by congressional caucus, makes it not at all surprising that legislators figured very prominently among the presidential appointees to high-level executive positions. Diplomatic posts went ordinarily to legislators:

[The President] said he did not approve the principle of appointing members of Congress to foreign missions, but as it had been established in practice from the first organization of the present Government, and as the members of Congress would not be satisfied with the opposite principle, he did not think proper to make . . . a [different] rule for himself.[53]

As to cabinet posts, two of every three appointees from the administration of John Adams through Jackson's second administration had seen previous service on Capitol Hill, and well over half of the 49 cabinet appointees during this period (28, or 57 percent) were initially brought into the executive branch from a last preceding government service in Congress.[54] Not all of these went immediately to cabinet posts; ten of the 49 appointees were elevated to cabinet rank after first serving in other executive posts, most of them diplomatic. Of the remaining 39 who were appointed directly to the cabinet from outside the executive branch, 23 (59 percent) were appointed from a last preceding government service in Congress, 20 being members of the congressional community at the time of their appointment; 14 (36 percent) were appointed from a last preceding service in state government; and only two (5 percent) were appointed directly from private life without recorded previous government service.[55]

The practice of appointing legislators to high executive places, considered together with a presidential nominating procedure which put incoming Presidents under obligation to legislators for having won the Chief Magistracy, would seem to indicate that the prestige patronage available to Jeffersonian Presidents was employed more to repay their own pre-inaugural political debts on Capitol Hill than to create congressional indebtednesses for purposes of winning influence on the Hill.

Indeed, the choice of legislators personally as beneficiaries of this patronage may have hindered more than it facilitated presidential leadership of the legislative branch. Consider the dilemmas posed for the President in thus bringing about the transfer of important men in Congress from one to the other side of the Tiber. If executive appointments were given to repay political services pre-inaugurally rendered, who would be left behind on Capitol Hill to render party services to the President after inauguration? How helpful was it to Presidents in mobilizing party majorities and winning friends on the Hill to have removed from the congressional community, by executive appointment, the very men who had helped organize the congressional backing that had given them the Presidency? No wonder Jefferson was constantly on the search for men to replace his congressional spokesmen, and resorted to letter-writing campaigns imploring trusted friends to run for Congress where they might act on his behalf.[56]

If, on the other hand, executive appointments were used to co-opt rivals, pacify factional leaders, and woo potential opposition, which of the two courses of action would have made less trouble for the President: to leave potential adversaries on the Hill, disaffected,

there to become marplots; or to bring them into his own executive
family and confer upon them the organizational apparatus of an executive department or the prestige and responsibility of a diplomatic
post? "Why, good God!" Jefferson replied when President Monroe
asked his advice about dispatching Andrew Jackson to the diplomatic post farthest from American shores, as minister to St. Petersburg; "he would breed you a quarrel before he had been there a
month!" [57] And whose was the hostage thus brought across the
Tiber to the executive reservation? The President's, the better to
bargain with the Hill? Or the Hill's, the better to bargain with the
President? Who would call the tune for the legislator-become-
department-head—his old friends in Congress, or the President?
President Jefferson's much-quoted comment is suggestive: every executive post filled, he wrote, "me donne un ingrat, et cent en-
nemis." [58] His words might be kept in mind pending inquiry, in
Part Five, into President-cabinet relationships.

Not only, therefore, was the constitutional authority to remove
and appoint public officers largely unexploited by Jeffersonian Presidents for the purpose of winning influence on Capitol Hill. It
would seem that the manner and the restrictive circumstances of its
exercise in Jeffersonian times entailed large liabilities to the power
interests of the President.

These, then, comprised the known inventory of presidentially
improvised tools for achieving influence on Capitol Hill from 1801
to 1828: enlistment of individual members to work confidentially
for the President from positions inside the congressional community; enlistment of cabinet officers to work as presidential agents
from positions outside the congressional community; personal contact with legislators through entertaining them at the executive
mansion; employment of intracommunity public propaganda media;
and appointment of legislators to executive offices.

Did they suffice for the purpose employed, and enable the President to supply that unifying influence which a representative legislature needed if it was to govern effectively? For Thomas Jefferson
they apparently did, but not for his successors in the Presidency.

CHAPTER 9

POWER WON AND POWER LOST

All studies of the period are agreed on Thomas Jefferson's successful leadership of Congress—on "the extraordinary compliance that
Jefferson drew from his party followers in the two Houses." [1]
There is nothing in the record of the Washington community to
challenge the essential point, though the record does suggest a few
reservations about the accepted view of Jefferson's leadership. Pre-
ponderance of legislative successes over failures is difficult to prove,
since there was no announced legislative program of the President
to serve as yardstick; and while executive bill drafting was known
throughout the Republican era, there is no way of identifying precisely which bills reflected the special desires of the President.[2]
Based more upon the efforts Jefferson made to lead than upon legislative results, and relying largely upon the often colored testimony
of contemporary legislators, most studies tend, too, to overstate
Jefferson's influence. Unaware of the bloc structure of the congressional community, all studies tend to discount the factionalism that
was latent throughout Jefferson's regime and manifest in the party
split of 1806, when Representative Randolph and his "Tertium
Quids" broke with the administration. And the congressional party's
desertion of President Jefferson in 1809 on the question of the embargo is too often denied its necessarily important place in any assessment of Jefferson's leadership.[3]

It is important, moreover, to recognize that—with the exception
of the embargo—Jefferson's policies, being essentially conservative,
did not need the intensity of leadership effort that legislative victories on bold new policy departures tend to require. The two broad

programmatic features of Jefferson's administration were enlarge-
ment of the national frontiers and retrenchment in the national
government. Making the nation bigger was scarcely a goal to kindle
significant opposition, and objections in Congress (most notably on
the Louisiana Purchase) found little echo in the constituencies. Fru-
gality and fiscal conservatism (severe retrenchment in the defense
establishment, decrease in the national debt, abolition of direct taxes,
disbanding the internal revenue service) were hardly difficult matters on which to obtain cooperation from a Congress dominated by
a states' rights party and facing an undemanding electorate. Had
Jefferson adopted Secretary Gallatin's proposal for a 20 million dollar internal improvements program, a more meaningful evaluation of
his leadership would be possible. But Jefferson effectively quashed
this pioneering proposal, while endorsing its objectives, by suggesting to Congress the need for a constitutional amendment to make it
legal.[4] In assessing Jefferson's leadership, therefore, the observation
that a "compliant" Congress gave the President nothing to veto during his eight years in office must be balanced by the observation that
Jefferson asked for little, besides the embargo, that gave a Republican Congress hard political reasons for opposition. And even the
embargo, intended to coerce Britain and France into cessation of
harassments against American overseas trade, experienced little difficulty in getting through Congress. Congressional approval was facilitated in 1807 by outraged public opinion over a British naval attack,
within sight of Hampton Roads, upon an American warship which
had refused permission for a boarding party to search its crew for
deserters. Not until after the eastern seaboard began to feel the drastic economic effects of lost overseas trade did the citizen protest
arise which occasioned Congress' resistance to, and ultimate defeat
of, the President on this issue.[5]

   With these reservations, the accepted view of Jefferson's leadership is nevertheless persuasive. The Randolph splinter movement
was contained, owing more perhaps to the "universal misanthropy"
of Randolph himself than to any institutional brakes.[6] No other major offensive against the President was launched from Capitol Hill
until after the embargo had been laid, and Congress made no major

forays against the President's executive subordinates, through investigations or otherwise. Assertions of congressional supremacy thus remained harmlessly verbal, receiving no institutional implementation. Jefferson furthermore succeeded, against a ground swell of citizen discontent, in carrying the congressional party with him on a series of progressively harsher measures to implement the embargo during his last year in office. It does the record no violence, then, to say that during the better part of Jefferson's two administrations a relatively successful *ad hoc* experiment in party government under presidential leadership was being undertaken at Washington.

But this experiment lasted at the longest for only seven of the twenty-eight years of the Jeffersonian era, and came to an abrupt end ere its leader had departed Washington. All historical studies are equally agreed that there occurred in 1808–9 a sudden and drastic decline in the influence of the Presidency which was never recouped for the remainder of the Jeffersonian era. "The sudden collapse of the embargo policy through Republican defection ended Jefferson's leadership," Leonard White observes, "and marked the beginning of a long decline in the influence of the Presidency." [7] "The whole structure of Mr. Jefferson's administration toppled over and broke to pieces in its last days," wrote Henry Adams.[8] Jefferson lost the support, retaining merely the acquiescence, of his own cabinet on foreign policy.[9] He was deserted by his own spokesmen and agents on Capitol Hill.[10] The party, and even the Virginia delegation, ceased to follow his lead. "I am [now] . . . chiefly an unmeddling listener to what others say," Jefferson wrote in December, 1808; "never did a prisoner, released from his chains, feel such relief as I shall on shaking off the shackles of power." [11]

Madison inherited the wreckage. "New subdivisions and personal factions [in Congress] equally hostile to yourself and the general welfare daily acquire additional strength," Secretary Gallatin advised the President from his post on Capitol Hill;

measures of vital importance have been and are defeated; every operation, even of the most simple and ordinary nature, is prevented or impeded; the embarrassments of government, great as from foreign causes they already are, are unnecessarily increased; public confidence in the public councils and in the Executive is impaired, and every day seems to increase every one of those evils. . . . [It is impossible] to produce the requisite union of views and action between the several branches of government.[12]

Matters worsened as war clouds gathered. In a crisis posing the gravest threat to national independence, effective control over the nation's security was seized by a Congress unable to chart a consistent policy because it was rent with factions, now one, now another ascendant. Having deprived the President of economic sanctions against Britain and France, Congress would not commit itself to force of arms, the only practical alternative for preventing British naval interdiction of American shipping. Instead, it fell back on a temporizing "nonintercourse" policy which telegraphed to all the world the nation's unwillingness to fight, perpetuated the sources of domestic discontent with the embargo, and yet was even less enforceable than the embargo. The further depredations on American shipping which this policy invited put some groups in Congress in mind of war. But revenue losses attendant upon the embargo and nonintercourse policies—exports dropped 80 percent in value during the first year of the embargo—put other legislators in a mood for economizing. Both prevailed. War Hawks succeeded in pushing the nation into war; economizers denied the President sufficient funds to prepare for or to prosecute war. Committee chairmen bottled up tax bills in committee, while others destroyed the United States Bank by refusing to vote a renewal of its charter.[13] The year before war was declared the executive thus found its tax revenues drastically reduced while at the same time it was deprived of its chief source of loans, its chief fiscal agency, and its chief instrument against inflation. In the face of impending hostilities, appropriations for the Army and the Navy were slashed.[14] Congress refused the President's request for staff help for the Secretary of War on the ground that a salary of $3,000 apiece for two Assistant Secretaries was a needless expense and would create additional patronage for an already overpowerful President.[15] Requests for authority to reorganize the military establishment were refused on the same grounds.

While the House simultaneously demanded war and economy,

the Senate busied itself in seizing control over presidential appointments.[16] A Senate clique refused Madison's choice for Secretary of State and installed an incompetent to handle the nation's diplomacy at a time when diplomatic talent alone might have saved the nation from a war it was not prepared to fight. Madison was given a Secretary of State who breached cabinet security, intrigued against him on Capitol Hill, and who was so inept that he had to be instructed to conduct all diplomatic dialogue in writing so that the President could be certain of what was being communicated and could ghostwrite the Secretary's papers.[17] Opportunity to negotiate a settlement, presented by Russia's offer of mediation, was all but foreclosed to the President by the Senate when it rejected Secretary Gallatin, its erstwhile political guide, as the President's special envoy to St. Petersburg. Confirmation was refused after Gallatin was already on the high seas, and notice of his lack of authority to act for the United States was not received until after he had presented his credentials to the Tsar. Two other diplomatic appointees as well as Madison's appointee to the Supreme Court were likewise refused confirmation.[18]

Congress had become "unhinged," Madison wrote to Monticello.[19] "I know of no government which would be so embarrassing in war as ours," brooded the former President.[20] His prophecy was fulfilled, and what ensued seems, in the twentieth century, like a nightmare from the nation's childhood. With a politically disabled President and congressmen scuffling among themselves for the helm, the nation drifted leaderless into war, utterly at the mercy of events. The "honnor of the Country is gone," wrote a congressman, "& the Government is paralized." [21] A disorganized Congress—part hawk, part dove, part collusionist, "sub divided into Sections, half, quarter, and fractional Sections, and each . . . too wise to be led by the other" [22]—could not possibly unify a divided citizenry. The second war for independence saw insurrection incipient along the Atlantic coast, disunion threatened, sedition openly preached from the pulpits of New England, the Vermont militia ordered by its governor to desert from national service, and the Commonwealth of Massachusetts negotiating for an alliance with the enemy.[23] A Congress suspicious of the military pushed the nation into war with half a dozen regiments for a regular army and no general staff; a navy mostly of sail-and-oar gunboats with one cannon apiece to do battle with the world's greatest sea power; and a war office and admiralty staffed by two Secretaries, a handful of clerks, and no advisers either civilian or uniformed.[24] A miserly Congress plunged the Treasury into bankruptcy and sent the government hat in hand to private banking houses. With the entire salt-water fleet bottled in harbor by the Royal Navy and enemy raiding parties roaming free on American soil, the bankers caucused and decided to lend money only in return for the privilege of dictating instructions to the government's peace negotiators at Ghent. The government refused to yield sovereignty to financiers; the bond issue was not subscribed; and the bankers financed the enemy war effort by investing in British Treasury notes instead.[25] A last-resort administration bill to recharter the United States Bank was defeated because the Secretary of the Treasury and House supporters could not agree on details. For lack of one congressman's vote the government ran out of cash, unable to pay the troops.[26] A Congress unable to govern considered arming itself to fight. In the midst of a tumultuous debate on a motion to take to the field, a British squadron sailed in and sacked the Alexandria waterfront. Congress decided to go home instead, a week after the British left. "Gentlemen," the Speaker had warned, "if we do arm and take the field, I am sure we shall be beat, if there is not more order kept in the ranks than in this House." [27]

The disorganization of the government and the discord of the populace communicated itself to the military and made the nation's capital a monument to the greatest disgrace ever dealt to American arms. One year after Congress had fiddled while Alexandria burned, the enemy was all but made a gift of Washington, funds for the defense of which had been provided on the eve of attack—not by congressional appropriation but by local Washington banks.[28]

An inept commanding general was permitted to consume the six weeks preceding British occupation trying to make up his mind where to engage the enemy, without troubling to reconnoiter their approach.[29] Military intelligence was so lacking that the Secretary of State was horsed to find out how near and how many the British were; and only the accident of a warning shout from a volunteer scout prevented the President himself from proceeding across a bridge outside Washington directly into the advancing enemy column.[30] The American officer corps chose almost the moment of battle to air grievances against the Secretary of War, informing the President by messenger that "every officer would tear off his epauletts if Genl Armstrong was to have anything to do with them." [31] A preliminary skirmish and a glimpse of redcoats on the outskirts of Washington sufficed to put seven thousand fresh American troops to rout before a footsore British force of forty-five hundred; unfired muskets, thrown away, marked the path of retreat.[32] "The victors were too weary and the vanquished too swift" to allow the pursuit of the Americans beyond the undefended capital, British Admiral Cockburn explained in his official report.[33]

If the invaders had thought to lay siege to the government they were bound to have been thwarted in any event. For the government was not merely physically absent from the capital. It was politically nonexistent. Congress had responded to the emergency by disbanding for summer vacations. The cabinet had dispersed to all points of the compass. The President roamed alone in the countryside while Washington burned, a tragic figure among a receding tide of deserting troops. And a perverse citizenry who demanded a magician for a President, and expected victory without sacrifice or inconvenience to themselves, found voice enough for revilement. A country housewife refused sanctuary to Mrs. Madison and cursed her out of the house because the President had called her husband's militia unit into service.[34] Insulting remarks about Madison were inscribed on the blackened stone rubble of the Capitol.[35]

There is more to be remembered about the War of 1812 than "The Star-Spangled Banner," or Andrew Jackson's victory at the battle of New Orleans, fought after Europe had already decided to give the new nation peace.

Except for disunion itself, Madison's administration saw the fulfillment of every worst prophecy of the governmental community's structure, its attitudes toward politics and power, and its remoteness from the citizenry. Jefferson's leadership having already collapsed, the Presidency was restored politically to the place defined for it constitutionally and structurally in the community—a position as outsider to, and lacking leadership authority over, the establishment on Capitol Hill. This unifying influence removed, all the divisive forces inherent in the social organization and values of the congressional community were loosed. The party shattered to pieces and Congress could not govern, plunging into factional strife at the very moment of rejecting presidential leadership. Leadership of the nation thus fell to a legislative body whose organization and values rendered it wholly unequipped to lead, and obliged it to follow, a distant and divided citizenry. Policy initiative thus passed to a Congress unable to mobilize itself, much less the populace, for the pursuit of any consistent policy. A nation on the brink of military disaster was thus embarked upon erratic and mutually contradictory courses of action dictated by transitory factional combinations at the seat of government. It was total victory for the principle of government by "separate and rival interests." The Presidency slept; effective power resided nowhere; an anarchy of groups reigned over the nation. As a wise historian put it, "government, in the sense hitherto understood, became impossible." [36]

Prospects seemed favorable for the restoration of presidential leadership under Monroe. Madison's successor won eight years in the White House by two of the most impressive electoral landslides in history. The opposition party was swept under, and the "era of good feelings" witnessed not one memorable policy controversy at Washington that aroused significant citizen interest outside the capital. And, while it was neither planned nor exploited for the purpose, a presidential tour of defense installations gave Monroe an opportunity to demonstrate his personal popularity such as no other Jeffersonian President had.

Yet none of these advantages converted themselves into power for the President on Capitol Hill. Neither peace nor prosperity nor nearly total triumph at the polls put the congressional party together again: "Every thing is scattered. Republicans . . . are as much divided among themselves as the parties formerly were from each other," reported Justice Story in 1818.[37] As a satisfied citizenry reverted to political indifference, Monroe watched his congressional party consume itself in factional warfare and, in the final collapse of the caucus in 1824, give up the chance to nominate Presidents rather than agree upon a nominee. He confronted a hostile Speaker who let no opportunity slip to embarrass his administration. By his own testimony, he found himself bereft of helpers or defenders inside Congress "except members who occasionally appear as volunteers, and generally even without any previous concert with the Executive." [38] He watched his own executive branch become the punching bag against which Congress put muscle on its newly developed committee system. "I have never known such a state of things," Monroe wrote Madison, "nor have I personally ever experienced so much embarrassment and mortification." [39]

On domestic policy the record is barren of any evidence of presidential leadership. Initiatives and solutions on the two major domestic issues of Monroe's time—slavery in territories and protectionism for American industry—were almost wholly congressional. The Missouri Compromise of 1820 and the protective tariff of 1824–25 bear not the slightest trace of presidential influence. Monroe successfully contested Congress' lead on one occasion by vetoing an internal improvements bill; Congress successfully contested the President's lead on the domestic matter he seems to have pressed most urgently—authorization and financial aid for an exploratory expedition to the Yellowstone.[40] On foreign policy, especially the Latin American question, Congress continued to intrude itself with such lack of restraint that the Secretary of State had to give the resident British minister a lecture on the authoritativeness of the executive in this regard.[41] Not leading Congress but preserving his own independence of action and his own supremacy in diplomacy in the face of "violent systematic opposition" by Congress "seems to absorb all the faculties of [the President's] mind," commented Secretary Adams.[42] Monroe succeeded to the extent of timing diplomatic recognition of the South American republics and "announcing" the doctrine that bears his name.[43] Significantly the Monroe Doctrine was not submitted to Congress for approval.

"The Executive has no longer a commanding influence," Justice Story reported from his vantage point on the Hill in 1818; "the House of Representatives has absorbed . . . all the effective power of the country." [44] With this view no legislator appears to have disagreed at any time in Monroe's administration. Said Speaker Clay to Secretary Adams two years later, Monroe "had not the slightest influence on Congress. . . . henceforth there was and would not be a man in the United States possessing less *personal* influence over them than the President." [45] A Senator commented that "the very President who is just re-elected with but one dissenting voice throughout the Union . . . has actually . . . fewer real friends and admirers, and less influence than any of his predecessors had." [46] The Presidency slept for another eight years.

It can be said of Adams as of Madison that the last Jeffersonian President could not have played a less significant role if he had been absent from Washington altogether. Moving to recapture policy initiative immediately upon his inauguration, Adams proposed to Congress what his two predecessors had vetoed—a national program of internal improvements. But it was as though the very source of this initiative sufficed to set Congress against what it had previously proposed. Adams' bold new policy departure, calling not only for federally supported highway and waterway systems but also for a national university and government support for the sciences, was laughed out of court on Capitol Hill. "I fell," wrote Adams, "and with me fell, I fear never to rise again . . . the system of internal improvement by means of national energies. The great object of my life, therefore . . . has failed." [47] Within two years of taking office Adams "lost all opportunity to lead" when, for the first time, both houses of Congress fell into the hands of factions opposed to the President.[48] "My own career is closed," Adams confided to his diary.[49] With "uncontrollable dejection of spirits," he retreated into private hobbies and office routine to await second-term defeat.[50] Untended, his relations with Congress degenerated to the lowest point in the Jeffersonian era. One fourth of the membership of Congress refused even to pay courtesy calls at the White House, and the President's son was assaulted by a Jackson man in the Capitol when he came to deliver a presidential message.[51] Adams' situation may have been hopeless from the moment he stepped into the executive office, acceding to the Presidency with the support of neither the caucus nor a majority of the voters, winning the election in the House of Representatives only to have that victory discredited by charges of a corrupt bargain between himself and Henry Clay, and facing a Congress determined from the beginning to make him the second single-term President in history.

Jefferson's years in the presidential mansion were thus the exception to the rule: an atypical and unrepresentative episode in the early history of the Presidency. For the Jeffersonian era as a whole, the question of whether the improvised tools of influence sufficed to secure presidential leadership over Congress must be answered firmly in the negative. Indeed, they did not even suffice to prevent a nearly total eclipse of presidential power on the Hill lasting two decades.

Why should this have been the case? Why should Jefferson's experiment in party government under presidential leadership have withered on the vine? A fundamental explanation is that the experiment was conducted in a hostile institutional, psychological, and national cultural setting. Its objective was basically at cross-purposes with the constitutional order of the governmental establishment, at cross-purposes with a social and political order inside the governmental community that had been created by the governors themselves, and at cross-purposes with deep-seated values and attitudes which sustained both these structures. It would be too much, perhaps, to say that the experiment was doomed from the beginning. But it is a real wonder that, with such a powerful combination of factors against it, the experiment worked for even a brief while.

Yet something more than this general explanation seems necessary to account for the sharp contrast between Jefferson's experience in dealing with Capitol Hill and that of the three succeeding Presidents. Despite the odds against the perpetuation and institutionalization of presidential leadership, Jefferson's administration did demonstrate that Presidents could command significant influence on the Hill. What, then, is the explanation for the very marked *change* in the power position of the Presidency vis-à-vis Congress that began in Jefferson's last year in office?

Current literature favors the view that presidential leadership collapsed because the President lost, and congressional activists gained, control over the party machinery that Jefferson had established in Congress.[52] Evidence previously presented argues strongly that there was no congressional party apparatus to capture in the first place; but even if there had been, to state that congressional leaders gained control over the party begs the question of why the President lost it.

A partial explanation of the contrast between Jefferson's power position and that of his successors perhaps lies in the novel circumstances of the first Republican Presidency. Jefferson had the advantage of riding the crest of a public reaction against the Federalists. He came to power with a congressional party fresh from victory, still having momentum from the organizing effort which helped produce that victory, and still rallied around a distinctive political creed. These transitory aids to a President's efforts to keep his congressional party intact were not operative for Jefferson's successors. The party for them was beginning to experience the disintegrative effects of its accession to separate institutions of power and of high turnover rates among its congressional personnel; and a political creed hostile to government spending—especially defense spending—could serve no longer to unify, but only to divide, a governmental party with a war on its hands. Then, too, an opposition party was still active, still a threat, during Jefferson's incumbency. The disappearance of the Federalist party during the regimes of Madison and Monroe removed still another stimulus toward Republican party unity, lessening the need for closing party ranks in order to be secure in the positions of power.[53] At the same time the practical extinction of the Federalist party left no outlet for effective opposition except within the Republican party, the very totality of the Republicans' victory thus sowing the seeds of their own disintegration as a party.

Another partial explanation for the decline of presidential leadership after Jefferson is lack of leadership drive or ability in Jefferson's successors. Modern understanding of presidential power demands respect for the view that a President's desire and capacity for leadership have much to do with the degree of influence he is likely to achieve on Capitol Hill. Even today, when institutions exist to facilitate presidential leadership of Congress and when the need for such leadership is widely acknowledged, the power of the office cannot be divorced from the personal qualities of the man in the office. Presidents are not likely to command wide influence on the Hill without working for it, without knowing how to work for it, and without some taste and talent for the techniques of getting it.

That Jefferson had these qualities and that his three successors in office did not seems a reasonable interpretation of the record. He was the only President to employ all the tools or techniques of power enumerated in the preceding chapter. He was the only President who was persistent and innovative in statecraft. He was the only President to 1829 whose performance in office indicates anything remotely approaching aptitude or liking for the politics of leadership. A subjective evaluation, based on the persistence and ingenuity of his efforts to influence Congress, would be that Jefferson alone achieved that psychological liberation from his party's and his culture's attitudes toward executive power which seems an essential precondition for the development of personal expertise in the pursuit of power.[54]

In contrast, Monroe—so Leonard White argues—"believed that the President should allow Congress to make up its own mind on domestic matters without influence from the Chief Executive." [55] Constitutionally orthodox, such a view would seem to have precluded even any effort at presidential leadership. There is good reason for believing that Madison's own ideological commitments similarly inhibited his desire and capacity for leadership of Congress. A background as the nation's most effective advocate of "separation of powers" (in *The Federalist*, No. 51) and of the theory of government by contending factions (in *The Federalist*, No. 10) may have served Madison well as an opposition leader in Congress before 1800. But it would seem to be poor preparation for a role of presidential leadership. As for Adams, his diary reveals a public servant extraordinarily perspicacious about and experienced in the inner power struggles of the Washington community, who demonstrated, moreover, very considerable political skills in the field of diplomacy when serving as Secretary of State. His apparent aversion, however, to political connivance in the high office of the Presidency seems to have prevented him from effectively exploiting these assets in his own power interests as Chief Executive. This aversion could only have been abetted by the abuse heaped upon him for appointing the congressman responsible for his victory in the House election to the Secretaryship of State—perhaps Adams' only major essay at political bargaining with his own colleagues.

It would therefore appear to be no coincidence that the only President from 1801 to 1829 to have won significant influence on the Hill was also the only one who has acquired, justly, the reputation of a politician in office. Only in Jefferson, it seems, was the desire for accomplishment united with the attributes necessary for accomplishment: a desire for power and a gift for getting it.

Yet political virtuosity does not make all the difference between powerful and powerless Presidents, and Jefferson's performance was by no means unflawed. At least two glaring political errors were made by Jefferson which did not pass unnoticed even at the time. One was his selection of John Randolph as a presidential spokesman on the Hill. Wholly without feeling for the politics of compromise, mercurial, idiosyncratic, with a consuming passion for verbal exhibition and a compulsive psyche which vacillated between undue attraction to and deep abhorrence of figures of authority, Randolph was to say the least a very poor choice of channel for the President to his party on the Hill.[56] Jefferson's other mistake was to announce at the outset of his second term that he would not seek a third. His "disclosure of this fact, thus early," observed a Senator, "is an unnecessary and imprudent letting down of his importance. It lessens greatly his influence on the government. Most men seek the rising rather than the setting sun."[57] It is no surprise that Randolph's breach with Jefferson, and the first major split in Jefferson's congressional party, followed soon after this announcement. Also in the interest of better perspective on the state of the political art in

Jeffersonian times, it bears noting that neither Jefferson nor any of his successors to 1829 fully exploited even those power advantages conferred by the Constitution. To recall Andrew Jackson's well-known political use of the veto and patronage suffices as illustration of the fact. Jeffersonian Presidents felt constrained to apply the veto only against measures of doubtful constitutionality [58]—a stricture which Jackson rejected out of hand, along with the tradition of avoiding removals from executive office on partisan grounds.

Granted the importance of political skill and granted Jefferson's distinction in this respect, the "great man" theory still falls short as a total explanation of the drastic change in the power position of the Presidency beginning in 1808. It is most obviously inadequate because the change occurred not after but during Jefferson's incumbency. Not only the time but also the circumstances of Jefferson's loss of power on the Hill challenge an interpretation which would attribute changes in presidential power exclusively to variations in the leadership skill of Presidents. The circumstances were that Jefferson had insisted upon continuance of a policy, the embargo, which was arousing clamor in the constituencies. Being the only policy of Jefferson's administration which aroused widespread interest and significant opposition outside the capital, the embargo provided the only test of presidential leadership under conditions comparable to those prevailing in modern times. Jefferson's leadership failed that test. Congress abandoned the unpopular embargo policy just as it abandoned the unpopular compensation policy in 1816: the energetic efforts of a politically skilled President to preserve the one policy had no more impact upon Congress than utter presidential indifference on the other policy. For all Jefferson's virtuosity as a politician, it counted for nothing on the Hill when good political reason arose for legislators to resist the President's lead.

One is therefore obliged to seek a further explanation for the fact that the collapse of presidential leadership in 1808-9 established the pattern for the next twenty years. In the author's opinion, two factors claim equal consideration with lack of political skill in Jefferson's successors. One was the weakness of the President's resources for leading Congress: the weakness of the early Presidency as a bargaining position. The other was internal institutional changes on Capitol Hill which were beyond control from the White House and which in all probability rendered any degree of political skill useless to Presidents for recouping leadership of the legislative branch.

The President's leadership resources were weak in the sense, first, that they were not exclusive to the Presidency. Enlistment of congressional agents to promote and protect one's interests, entertainment of legislators at home after hours, use of public media of propaganda, and employment of departmental patronage to discharge and create congressional obligations were every one of them resources of influence available equally to cabinet-level executives. In Jefferson's time there is no evidence that these resources were being utilized by any executive but Jefferson himself. After Jefferson, as Part Five will show, their utilization became common practice among cabinet members. The point to note here is that the usefulness of these resources to the President was largely dependent upon the failure of his subordinate executives to exploit them in their own interests.

The President's leadership resources were weak in the further sense that, however adequate for eliciting affirmative responses from a permissive Congress, they were not of the sort that enables a President to "pressure" affirmative responses out of a reluctant or resistive Congress. Persuasion is the necessary tactic for leading an independent legislature whose support a President cannot command; and the principal source of a President's persuasiveness is the strength of his bargaining position. It follows that the Chief Executive must have "currency" with which to bargain if his leadership is to survive the sorts of challenges to be expected from an independent Congress. Rewards must be available for inducing legislators to cooperate with the President, and risks must be posed for noncooperation: the self-interest of the legislators must, in some degree, be made to connect with "going along" with the President.[59] Precisely this essential ingredient seems to have been lacking in the leadership resources of the Jeffersonian Presidents. Only one of the tools of influence used by them touched the self-interest of the legislators, namely, patronage; and use of patronage for bargaining purposes was eschewed by Jeffersonian Presidents. Threat of veto was another possible sanction, also unused, however, for bargaining purposes.

Nothing else seems to have remained, nothing, certainly, remotely comparable to the sources of pressure which a twentieth-century President can summon in behalf of his legislative objectives. Reference has earlier been made to the absence of organizational resources for exerting pressure upon Congress. Jeffersonian Presidents had no personal staff—no king's men—to carry on the work of lobbying; they were dependent upon department heads having obvious political and organizational interests of their own to promote on Capitol Hill. There were no organized interest groups whose bargaining resources a President might have enlisted in bringing pressure to bear upon legislators. There was no national party committee to supplement, with its own tools of influence, a President's efforts to secure congressional party support. There was no organized party within the Congress, with its tools of influence over the rank and file, to lend aid to a President.

Moreover, the opportunities to perform useful services for legislators—no inconsiderable source of leverage for a modern President—were negligible. The practice of presidential endorsement of legislators running for reelection did not exist. The opportunity to direct campaign aid to legislators at election time—money, publicity, personnel—was precluded by the absence of a national party committee or any other organ with such services to dispense. The minimal involvement of national government in the domestic affairs of the country precluded any significant opportunities to reward cooperative legislators with "pork" for their constituents; and what local patronage was available was most of it dispensed by department heads and service chiefs. Detailing of staff and experts to help congressional committees or legislators who supported presidentially endorsed legislation was unheard of: there were no executive experts or staff to detail for the purpose; there was no technically complex legislation requiring expert service. The Washington bureaucracy was too small and too accessible to make legislators dependent upon the Chief Executive's help in expediting their administrative requests.

The impressive bargaining advantages a modern President has as representative of a national citizen constituency were precluded altogether because the Jeffersonian Presidency had no popular electoral base. Protégés of kingmakers on the Hill, Jeffersonian Presidents could not claim popular backing for their candidacies. None could even lay claim to having won his own election, since whatever campaign work was involved was presumably carried out by a caucus committee of legislators. No President ever went on a campaign tour. Stumping was unknown; exposure to the people was negligible.

It follows that no Jeffersonian President could exploit the bargaining advantages of citizen spokesmanship, and none tried to claim such a role for themselves. This role was preempted by legislators, inevitably to the disadvantage of the President in a community where citizen spokesmanship provided the most acceptable cover for power claims. It follows, too, that the President could not benefit from any aura of popular prestige or charisma, as President Jackson did: "Were it not for the fear of the out-door popularity of General Jackson," Senator Webster observed in 1830, "the Senate would have negatived more than half his nominations." [60] No President could claim a popular mandate for policies requested of Congress. None could plead campaign commitments to a party platform in support of his legislative objectives; rather it was legislators who were in the better position to claim policy commitments from Presidents, all of whom got into office by the pleasure, as it were, of the men on the Hill. Even more important, the absence of public campaigning meant that no Jeffersonian President could claim the independent electoral strength and the popular following which today tie the vocational security of many congressional party members to the presidential coattails. This source of legislators' dependence upon the President was lacking in Jeffersonian times, and with it was lacking what is today one of the most important incentives for party members on the Hill to cooperate with the Chief Executive: the incentive of building a legislative record that will enhance his, and therefore the party's, chances for victory at the next election.

"Nor," as Leonard White has noted, "did any President 'go to the country.' The facilities for such a course were almost wholly lacking, and probably none of the four [Jeffersonian] Presidents . . . possessed the personal qualities that would have made such an appeal either feasible or successful." [61] No Jeffersonian President sought forums outside Washington for communicating his views; and in an isolated capital where reporters were rarely to be found press releases and press conferences could not be. The ability to reach the outside public and the opportunity to guide opinion; the ability to appeal over the heads of Congress to their constituents; the chance to command national attention for himself and his policy objectives: these important sources of leverage were denied to the President of a nation still in the predawn of the communications revolution.

Against this background, the Jeffersonian Presidency seems to have been no bargaining position at all. Leadership was, to be sure, possible without carrots or sticks: Jefferson demonstrated that. But leadership without services or sanctions, without coattails or a constituency, and without organizational resources or access to mass communications could hardly have survived serious challenge from Capitol Hill. Truer insight was never shown than by a legislator who observed, even as Jefferson's power was at its zenith, that the President's techniques of influence were "temporizing expedients the [ultimate] success of which is doubtful. If a really trying time should ever befall this administration, it would very soon be deserted by all its troops, and by most of its principal agents." [62] Small wonder that the President's leadership collapsed so swiftly in 1808 and so permanently for the remainder of the Jeffersonian era. It was dependent on little more than the charms and wits of the man in the office; on the political naïveté—or unhuman self-denial—of the President's cabinet members in not utilizing in their own interests the techniques of influence demonstrated by the President himself; and on the pursuit of policies which did not arouse widespread controversy in the constituencies. In a word, continuance of Jefferson's leadership largely depended on the continuance of circumstances that were abnormal in American politics.

Internal institutional changes on the Hill further contributed to the political incapacitation of the Presidency after Jefferson. These changes were of two sorts. First, there were changes in the number, size, and composition of the fraternity blocs, changes which enormously complicated the task of securing party cohesion. There was, second, the development of the committee system, which made the mobilization of party majorities increasingly insufficient for purposes of attaining leadership over Congress.

Consider first the burgeoning difficulties, as the Jeffersonian era advanced, of whipping up a majority. Admission of new states and reapportionment due to population growth swelled the ranks of Congress by almost half again its size from the beginning to the close of the Jeffersonian era. By 1828 the President had to get the support of 48.3 percent more legislators, in order to have a policy majority, than Jefferson did in 1801—itself a situation which demanded redoubled leadership effort simply to maintain the leadership position that Jefferson had won. But that was not the half of it. While Congress increased nearly 50 percent in membership, the number of fraternity blocs increased by roughly 350 percent during the same period (see Table 11). Upon entering the Presidency Jefferson had but eight such groups to deal with in all, and it is a fair inference that support of four of these voting blocs was sufficient to produce a policy majority in the House of Representatives.[63] Adams, by contrast, confronted a House subdivided into no less than twenty-eight boardinghouse blocs, not counting members living in pairs. To obtain the majority that Jefferson could achieve by rallying four fraternities, the last Jeffersonian President would have had to rally triple that number of groups, assuming the unlikely circumstance that he succeeded in getting the unanimous support of each of the thirteen largest boardinghouse blocs on the Hill. Realistically, a coalition of perhaps fifteen or sixteen fraternities in addition to scattered votes from nonaffiliated congressmen was necessary to secure majority support in Congress.

Nor was the progressive splintering of the congressional community into ever smaller and more numerous fraternity blocs the whole of the difficulty confronting Jefferson's successors. From a purely arithmetical standpoint, appeals and leadership efforts looking to the mobilization of state delegations offered a more efficient avenue to majority formation as the Jeffersonian era advanced. For while

TABLE 11

THE CHANGING CONTEXT OF MAJORITY FORMATION, HOUSE OF REPRESENTATIVES

	1801	1807	1816	1828
A. Number of groups having three or more members				
Boardinghouse groups	8 [a]	17	23	28
State delegations	15	15	18	20
B. Minimum number of groups comprising a simple majority of the House				
Boardinghouse groups	4 (est.)	7	10	13
State delegations	4	4	5	5
C. Size of groups				
Percent of members living:				
Alone or in pairs		8.2	22.9	25.3
In groups of 3 to 5		10.1	20.8	31.5
In groups of 6 to 9		31.2	45.4	17.9
In groups of 10 or more		50.5	10.9	25.3
Percent of members comprised in state delegations of:				
1 or 2 members		7.1	3.4	2.9
3 to 5 members		11.3	0.0	6.6
6 to 9 members		25.0	34.1	27.8
10 or more members		56.6	62.5	62.7

[a] Boardinghouse lists (*Congressional Directories*) are not available for any year before 1807. Authority for the identification of 8 boarding-house groups in 1801 is found in a letter of that year written by Albert Gallatin. Henry Adams, *Gallatin*, p. 253.

boardinghouse blocs were shrinking in size and growing rapidly in number, state delegations were expanding greatly in size and increasing only very slowly in number. Table 11 indicates that it was toward the end of Jefferson's second term that state delegations became an arithmetically more viable organizational base for majority formation than the fraternity system. By 1828 a minimum of five state delegations, as against a minimum of thirteen boardinghouse blocs, could yield the President a majority.

Yet precisely in the degree that mobilization of state delegations became more advantageous to the President it must have become more difficult to accomplish. For one thing, a gathering trend toward two-party states, with the approach of the Jacksonian era, introduced sources of cleavage into the state delegations that were rare earlier in the Jeffersonian era, when one-party states appear to have been almost the invariable rule.[64] For another, it seems not unlikely that the practice of electing Representatives by geographic districts instead of at large was on the increase in the Jeffersonian period.[65] Giving each Representative a separate and distinct constituency to represent, the single-member district system tends to project the interest cleavages in the state electorates upon the state delegations in Congress, presumably lessening the areas of common interest and hence the incentives to political collaboration among members of the same delegation. The most palpable impediment to the bloc mobilizaton of state delegations—and a phenomenon which may have reflected both the trends noted above—was that legislators belonging to the same state delegations tended to scatter ever more widely into different boardinghouse fraternities as the Jeffersonian era advanced. Analysis of boardinghouse lists reveals that the number of individuals sharing living quarters with one or more colleagues from the same state dropped from 81.5 percent of all Representatives in 1807 to 56.4 percent in 1828. The number of legislators living in boardinghouse groups comprised exclusively of members from the same state dropped from 11.3 percent of the combined Senate and House membership in 1807 to 4.0 percent in 1828, while the percentage living in interregional groups rose slowly but steadily from 13.2 percent to 18.5 percent over the same period of time. Members tended, in other words, increasingly to avoid primary-group ties with colleagues from the same state at just the time when closer association among state colleagues might have become much more rewarding to the President by facilitating the accumulation of blocs of delegation votes.

As a consequence, state delegations and boardinghouse fraternities became increasingly disparate structural elements in the congressional community. By virtue of their overlapping membership in these two types of groups, legislators tended to become ever more subject to two potentially conflicting fields of influence within their own community: the interstate influences of their fraternity group and the perhaps more narrowly focused interests reflected within their respective state delegations. Concerted action by, and loyalty to, colleagues from the same state became increasingly harder to reconcile with loyalty to one's primary group. It is this conflict which is epitomized in the incident involving Representative Van Rensselaer, reported in Chapter 5, when the presidential election of 1824 was thrown to the House of Representatives. Van Rensselaer was caught between pressures from the New York delegation to vote for Adams and pressures from his messmates to vote for Crawford. Resolving in favor of Adams, he was made to eat the bitter bread of banishment for having "betrayed" his fraternity brothers. Such conflicts as these must have been felt by many congressmen in the later Jeffersonian years. Indeed, escape from them may have been one of the reasons why growing numbers chose not to associate with any fraternity.[66]

Jefferson, then, had the double advantage of a relatively few groups to deal with on the Hill and a fraternity group composition in which state delegation ties and fraternity ties were generally in harmony. For Jefferson's successors, increase in the number and decrease in the size of boardinghouse groups diminished the possibility of concerting them sufficiently to maintain a working majority; while the possibility of mobilizing the bloc strength of state delegations, as an alternative, was diminished owing to burgeoning sources of cleavage within the delegations, one of them being an increasing diversity and disparity of fraternal obligations within the delegation memberships.

What happened, in brief, was that the congressional community became afflicted with a politically dysfunctional "metabolism" which created an ever more acute need for the stabilizing influence of presidential leadership but which at the same time made any possibility of presidential leadership ever more remote. Trends the Presidency was helpless to arrest and which it lacked the tools to counteract tended progressively to diminish the hope of successfully utilizing the two—probably strongest—types of group ties in the congressional community for purposes of rallying majority support. Without any compensatory growth in leadership resources, it seems doubtful that any President after Jefferson could have preserved his congressional party from these disintegrative trends in its host community. Political virtuosity, surely, could not alone have stabilized a social system undergoing fission. Considering the circumstances, Presidents after Jefferson may have been political realists, after all, in eschewing the effort to lead Congress.

The rise of the committee system, coming on top of these developments, sealed the doom of presidential leadership. Beginning in earnest during the War of 1812, the evolution of the committees from *ad hoc* advisory groups into permanent "little legislatures" paced the decline of presidential leadership. By 1825 the committee system had taken on most of its modern features—seniority rule and the House Rules Committee excepted—and had absorbed broad powers of initiative, amendment, and quasi-veto in legislation, as well as supervision of executive administration. By Jackson's first term, foreign visitors to Washington were making the same observations about the committee system that American scholars were to make half a century later:

These committees have separate apartments, in which the real business of the country is carried on . . . no bill connected with any branch of public affairs could be brought into Congress with the smallest prospect of success, which had not previously received the initiative approbation of these committees. . . . the members of the cabinet are, in truth, nothing better than superintending clerks in the departments over which they nominally preside. . . . [The] standing committees . . . in fact, manage the whole business of the executive departments.[67]

That committee preeminence challenges the preeminence of the White House as a claimant for influence on Capitol Hill is widely enough accepted to require no argument here. There is need only to specify briefly the ways in which the development of the committee system was bound to have contributed to the collapse of presidential leadership in the Jeffersonian era.

First, the advent of specialized sublegislatures introduced a new set of "separate and rival interests" into a congressional establishment already splintering into ever more numerous voting blocs. The committee system multiplied the number of organized groups to compete for attention and for power with the President. At the same time it provided new fodder for factional contention within the President's party. To the regional cleavages already built into the fraternity system were added the clashing interests and outlooks that are bound to result when different groups are given hegemony over different subject matters of policy. Moreover, since the committee system was organized around the same functional interests as the executive branch—foreign affairs, military affairs, finance, and so on—it encouraged the exportation of interdepartmental conflicts across the Tiber into the legislative establishment, and paved the way for the kinds of departmental partisanships that are familiar in the modern Congress. If an officer of wide popularity such as Speaker Henry Clay, armed with appointive powers over the committees, could not keep the congressional party knit together in the face of these new divisive influences, still less was the likelihood that an unarmed President could do so from a position outside Congress.

If the growth of the committee system made the mobilization of party majorities more problematic, it lessened, at the same time, what Presidents could accomplish by mobilizing a party majority. In Jefferson's time ability to command majority support within Congress went far toward conferring the ability to dominate legislation, for the President then had only one legislative arena to dominate—the floor proceedings in Senate and House, where majorities decided policy. Not so for Jefferson's successors. If they would lead Congress, two legislative arenas must need be dominated: the plenary sessions, where majorities prevailed; and the proceedings in committee, where minority groups prevailed. Thus, Jefferson's strategies for building majority consensus would not likely have sufficed to confer leadership over a Congress many of whose important decisions were no longer made by majorities at all. Obsolescence of Jefferson's tools for influencing Congress, not merely lack of leadership ability, may help explain why Presidents after Jefferson failed to make conspicuous use of them.

Jefferson, moreover, was able to refer his legislative requests to persons of his own choosing on the Hill, selecting those who could be counted upon to push them forward. With the development of the committee system, Congress referred the President's legislative requests to groups of its own choosing. A President with modern bargaining tools might have prevailed upon the Speaker to appoint sympathetic chairmen to some of the critical committess; without them, no President could expect any Speaker, however personally disposed toward accommodation, to show favoritism to the President's men in distributing his committee patronage. Least of all personages on Capitol Hill did Speakers have anything to gain by partiality to the White House in a community where independence of the White House tended to be a measure of personal integrity. There was nothing any President could have done to prevent what actually happened in 1827: every committee in the Senate and House was staffed with either a majority or a chairman opposed to the President.[68] Raising the possibility that White House requests would fall into unfriendly hands, committee reference also made it easier for Congress to evade or refuse action on these requests. For purposes of resisting the President's lead, the committee system conferred on a wide range of small groups the capacity to postpone action on the President's legislative proposals, to alter the substance of those proposals, and to develop facts and sentiments adverse to favorable action before the proposals ever reached the floor for collective decision. Committees made it easier than ever before for a clique or faction, or even a strategically placed individual in Congress, effectively to oppose the President without having to mobilize substantial voting strength in opposition to the President.

In creating sublegislatures Congress practically liberated itself, also, from even the weak bonds of dependence upon the Presidency which Jefferson had been able to exploit for leadership purposes. Committees provided Congress with its own organs for exercising policy initiative, investigating policy alternatives, obtaining background information, and supervising the administration of measures passed. Dependence upon the President for these functions was correspondingly reduced; and in so far as information or guidance was wanted from the executive branch at all, committees provided the means for getting it directly from the departments themselves.

Finally, the committee system pushed the Presidency into the background and brought cabinet members to the forefront of executive dealings with Congress. With the establishment of congressional agencies for overseeing the work of the executive departments and passing upon substantive legislation affecting these departments, it was unavoidable that interaction should be intensified between the department heads and their superintending committees on the Hill —intensified to the degree that, as one scholar has observed, cabinet-committee relationships became the principal "medium of inter-communication" between the two branches of government.[69] Thus it was that a subsystem of political relationships between department heads and their supervising congressional committees came to supplant, as the principal arena of confrontation between the executive and legislative establishments, the direct relationship between the President and his congressional party that Jefferson had enjoyed. The committee system caused the President to lose dominance over the communication channels to the community he needed to lead, and gave executive subordinates better access to the vital centers of legislative decision than the President himself had. Men whose positions made them "the natural enemies of the President," as department heads have been called, became the principal spokesmen for the executive branch before Congress.

The committee system, in short, ensured the end of a political relationship between President and Congress which was fundamentally at odds with the structure and values of the governmental community to begin with, which was impossible to maintain in the face of systemic trends within the congressional community, and which existed as long as it did only because a permissive Congress tolerated it. For the second half of the Jeffersonian era, the whole question of presidential leadership of Congress was "academic": nothing short of dramatic innovations in the style and in the political resources of the Presidency would make it possible again. The important question, after Jefferson, was whether the President could maintain the loyalty and cohesion of his own executive branch in the face of committee pressures from Capitol Hill—in the face of assault upon the executive establishment by a Congress so divided, so leaderless within itself.

It is a weak Presidency, then, that emerges from this exploration of presidential-congressional relations in the Jeffersonian era. A brief taste of power under Jefferson, and then the Presidency was reduced to political impotence, failing to provide that leadership of the legislative branch which the Constitution did not intend the executive branch to provide and which the congressional community did not provide within itself.

Such was the combination of factors conducing to this decline that powerlessness in congressional dealings seems a predictable fate for the early Presidency. Modern experience as well as logic teaches that no President is likely to distinguish himself in congressional leadership if he lacks the ambition and, in reasonable degree, the political skills to exercise such leadership; and these appear to have been conspicuously absent in all Presidents from 1801 to 1828 with the exception of Thomas Jefferson. But the best of political talent could not have conferred enduring leadership upon a weak presidential office. Given a Constitution which failed to authorize a leadership role for the Chief Executive—much less to confer the sanctions essential to the exercise of leadership in any organization— availability of extraconstitutional power resources was as much a prerequisite for presidential leadership as the possession of leadership ability. And not one of the really important resources for influence that are available to modern Presidents for leading Congress were at hand for Jeffersonian Presidents. A Presidency without carrots or sticks, services or sanctions, coattails or a constituency, organizational resources or access to mass communications—such a Presidency could not have sustained leadership of Congress under any but the abnormal circumstances of a Congress which had no serious ground to contest presidential leadership.

Lack of leadership aptitude in the incumbents and shortage of leadership resources available to the office are two factors familiar to political analysis which would seem sufficient, alone, to have ensured the failure of presidential leadership. A community analysis of the governmental establishment suggests that this failure should be explained not solely in terms of what the office and the men in the office lacked, however, but also in terms of a political culture at Washington which was positively unreceptive to presidential leadership.

Shortage of leadership skill and resources in the White House, as on Capitol Hill, was partially the manifestation of antipower attitudes among the power-holders themselves. A community ethos hostile to leadership and followership roles per se was especially hostile to any effort toward supplanting the constitutionally orthodox relationship between President and Congress with a superordinate-subordinate relationship. A community inclined to equate citizen spokesmanship with virtue itself provided little rationale for leadership of citizen spokesmen by an office which could not claim citizen spokesmanship for itself. A pervasive mistrust of power-seeking, among the governors themselves, must have inhibited the desire of Presidents to lead as well as the willingness of legislators to follow; and an underlying sense of the wrongness of presidential influence over the legislative branch made presidential leadership a covert affair which could neither be acknowledged in practice nor defended in principle on either side of the Tiber.

Antipower attitudes nourished a community structure hostile to presidential leadership. Community arrangements, reflecting the preferences of the governors themselves, went far beyond the Constitution in isolating the President from those he would lead in Congress, assigning the Chief Executive and legislators to separate camps as members of mutually exclusive social entities. A subcommunity structure on Capitol Hill split the President's potential followership into organized minority blocs, introducing durable sources of cleavage among them that were unknown to the Constitution, that were independent of disagreements on passing policy issues, and that were destructive in tendency of the one instrumentality on Capitol Hill—the political party—which might have facilitated presidential leadership. These built-in sources of cleavage proliferated, moreover, as the Jeffersonian era advanced. A 350 percent increase, from 1801 to 1828, in the number of primary-group voting blocs and an increase of nearly 50 percent in the size of Congress created purely mechanical and communication problems of rallying majority support which the early Presidency clearly lacked the resources to surmount. Changes in the composition of these voting blocs, furthermore, introduced new sources of cleavage and lessened any realistic hope of mustering majority voting strength on the alternative basis of state delegation solidarity. And the development of the committee system, besides adding still another source of cleavage to the congressional community, created a new arena of policy-making that was elusive of influence even by a President who might succeed in rallying majority support on Capitol Hill.

Studying the Jeffersonian experience in its community context thus opens new perspectives upon the nature and role of the Presidency as a leadership position.

The resistiveness of the American governmental system to presidential leadership, first of all, has been much greater than the conventional legal, historical, or institutional analyses of the Presidency would suggest. The problem of presidential leadership was not merely to find ways around the language and intent of a Constitution which did not equip the presidential office for leadership. The task was to find ways of counteracting or circumventing the manifest attitudes, the preferred organizational behavior, and the systemic trends of the governing society itself. The Jeffersonian Presidency was wholly unequal to that task. As a leadership office, the Presidency was therefore a failure. It could not have been, under the conditions prevailing in the Jeffersonian era, anything but a failure.

Second, it would seem, from the perspective of a community study, that converting the presidential office into a vehicle for leadership of Congress required basic changes in the style and structure of American national politics. Passing crises and other empowering events were not, as the Jeffersonian experience amply demonstrates, sufficient. The preeminence of foreign policy; war and the gravest threats to national security; lack of organized opposition outside government and political quiescence in the country; consistent dominance of Congress by the President's party; overwhelming landslides at the polls for the presidential candidate: none of these sufficed to convert the early Presidency into a leadership position. To confer enduring leadership capacity upon the White House, nothing less than the revolution in government-citizenry relationships that came with Jacksonian democracy would seem to have been adequate. Continuing attention and interest on the part of the citizenry would liberate the Presidency from psychological bondage to antipower attitudes and from institutional bondage to a kingmaking Congress. Democratically exploited, an attentive citizenry would give the Presidency coattails and a constituency, and a role of citizen spokesmanship equal to that of Congress. It would give the Presidency a forum for appealing over the heads of a resistive Congress. An articulate and demanding electorate would sustain a party organization outside of government which would provide the President with services and sanctions to use in his dealings with Congress. It would lay the groundwork for the organization of congressional parties and it would ultimately bring organized citizen interests into the political arena, each equipped with resources for persuasion which a President might enlist in behalf of his legislative objectives. Giving the Presidency a national citizen constituency would never suffice to guarantee presidential leadership of the legislative branch. But the Jacksonian revolution, which marked the beginning of a major constituency-building effort, would seem to have been a necessary prerequisite for leadership in the White House—as much so as it seems to have been for the emergence of leadership in Congress.

Third, the need for presidential leadership would seem, from the perspective of the Jeffersonian experience, far more acute than is generally recognized. The eclipse of the Presidency after Jefferson signified the loss of the only stabilizing influence then available upon a governing society on the Hill that was inherently unstable. Had the loss of presidential leadership been compensated by the development of self-leadership or other stabilizing devices within the congressional establishment, the long-range viability of that establishment as a governing institution would be less subject to question. But theories to this effect cannot be reconciled with the community record of the legislative branch. New leadership did not arise on Capitol Hill to supplant that of the President. The congressional party did not change masters, as some have argued: it ceased to have masters. The party did not evolve toward an organized action group, toward greater cohesion, once Jefferson's leadership had collapsed. On the contrary, loss of presidential leadership was attended by disintegration of the majority party into warring factions, by an accelerating fragmentation of the social and political system on Capitol Hill, and by the development of a committee system which not merely introduced new divisive forces but also offered legislators a means of exercising power which minimized the need for building stable majorities.

If, therefore, presidential leadership made the difference between a Congress capable of managing major social conflict and one incapable of doing so, the failure of presidential leadership after 1808 must be interpreted as an event of profound significance in the political history of the republic. Until such time as presidential leadership was regained, or until new stabilizing influences developed on Capitol Hill, one-third part of the government had failed in one of the fundamental tasks of government. Well beyond the halfway point from 1789 to the Civil War, a congressional community doggedly committed to its own internal democracy, progressively anarchic within itself, and jealous of its independence from the President had failed to provide security against the rupture of the Union itself.

One alternative remained in the Jeffersonian era: that the executive establishment might itself perform these necessary functions of a government. To this political question the final chapters are addressed.

PART FIVE

THE EXECUTIVE
ESTABLISHMENT

CHAPTER 10

SEPARATE BATTALIONS

Outwardly differing from the congressional community in virtually every respect but their common language and their attitudes toward their vocation, the community of executives west of the Tiber exhibited few of the instability- and conflict-producing features distinctive of the establishment on the Hill.

Instead of a society of transients and short-term servers in government, one finds a highly stable community membership on the west bank of the Tiber. The drastic reconstitutions of membership that occurred every two years on Capitol Hill were never experienced, during the Jeffersonian era, by the executive community. Personnel turnover was limited principally to the topmost positions in the executive branch—the President, the Secretaries of the four departments, and the Attorney General—and even in these positions changes tended to be infrequent. While no Jeffersonian President left office with his original cabinet intact, none but Jefferson commenced his administration with a wholly new cabinet. Below the cabinet positions was a permanent officialdom, recruited in substantial part from the local population of the District and its environs.[1] "A solid and unchanged official substructure," secure in fact if not in law against partisan removal from their jobs, the civil staff "tended to come from an identifiable section of the population; they were not infrequently succeeded by their sons, and they often found places for their relatives . . . and they grew old in office."[2]

No conflicting party allegiances divided the membership of the executive community. Presidents and Secretaries all had a common party affiliation; as for the civil staff, whatever conflicts of partisan commitment they had were kept well concealed—doubtless one of the secrets of their vocational security in a historical period when there were no civil service laws to protect their tenure. No conflicting constituency allegiances, obligations, or commitments divided a community none of whose members were elected but the President. The compulsion to represent the home folk, to vaunt one's regional loyalties and to play the constituency advocate that was so prominent a source of clash and conflict on the Hill was an attribute lacking in executive behavior. Nor did the intense primary-group allegiances of the congressional boardinghouse fraternities exist west of the Tiber. Boardinghouses were not only few but frowned on in executive society as *déclassé* at best, scandalous at worst. For the few high-level executives who chose to reside in a boardinghouse, the arrangements bore little resemblance to the mess life that was favored by legislators on the Hill; usually a separate suite of rooms was engaged and the executive dined separately, sharing only the downstairs parlor with the other paying guests.[3] Following the Chief Executive's example and rejecting that of legislators, executives made a practice of bringing their families to Washington, each family residing in a separate dwelling. Instead of close-knit sectional conclaves as on Capitol Hill, then, the basic unit in executive society was the family household, "each family standing as it were by itself and caring only for itself, unconnected by any of those ties of common interest, which unite the permanent inhabitants of other cities." [4]

The contentiousness generated by mass-participation policy-making in a public forum was wholly alien to the executive community. Decisions were not publicly arrived at; policies were not openly debated; and the chance to participate in their formulation was restricted almost exclusively to a small minority of the membership occupying the topmost positions in the executive branch. There was no institutional device provided in the executive establishment for collective action by all its members. Executive society at work was executive society segregated into orderly work groups —departments, divisions, bureaus—housed in different office quarters, having a minimum of interaction, each concerned with different subject fields of public policy.

Spared the frictions attendant upon mass-participation policy-making, the executive community was spared also the unstabilizing and anarchic tendencies inherent in the democratic social system found on the Hill. In no facet of its corporate existence, either at work or at leisure, was executive society an equalitarian society. Inequality was locked into the differential pay scales of executives, ranging from an annual salary of seven or eight hundred dollars for most clerks (in 1800) to a salary of twenty-five thousand dollars for the President.[5] Inequalities in perquisites, unknown on Capitol Hill, were evident in the size and accouterments of executives' office quarters, in the length of vacations they were able to take, in the hours of the day spent in work.[6] Inequalities in rank, status, and authority, undiscernible on the Hill, were endemic to bureaucracy: a hierarchy of superordinate-subordinate relationships gave every executive but the President a superior officer to whom he was accountable and whose authority to issue orders was not subject to challenge from below.*

Rank and status differences in the administrative structure appear, furthermore, to have carried over into extraofficial life, giving rise to a social structure which reflected and complemented the official hierarchy of the executive branch. A three-tiered hierarchy of status groups best describes executive society. In the lowest tier were the ancillary employees, clerks, and civil officers below cabinet rank —a permanent cadre who acted as caretakers of the government during the summer season while their superiors and Congress were vacationing. This contingent appears to have lived a separate class existence within the community. They mingled largely with each other and with townspeople in their leisure activities, intermarried within the group, developed their own social circles and rank orders, and stayed clear of the governmental politics of their superiors, obtaining their political outlets in town affairs instead.[7] A deprived class, unable to get decent salaries from a penurious Congress, they took after-hours employment to supplement their

---

* It is not meant to imply that no limits existed upon the authority to issue orders. Nor should the structure of authority referred to here be confused with a structure of power. To what extent the power structure coincided with the authority strucure will be explored later in this work.

incomes, formed a benevolent society to care for their sick and aged, and discharged their grievances in politically innocuous ways.[8] In a ludicrous parade which parodied both their own low status and the pomp and ceremony of their superiors, they marched through the President's portico attired in rags and cardboard, cornstalk muskets at right shoulder arms, thumping on tambourines and braying like asses, and proceeded up Pennsylvania Avenue to make a mock assault on the Capitol with pop guns.[9]

Cabinet-rank officials and their families formed the second status-tier or "high society" of the executive community, together with high-ranking military and naval officers, the diplomatic corps, and the relatively few "gentlemen" of the town. This group was socially distinctive for its high level of material culture, the semitransient status of its members in the community, its cosmopolitan group composition, and, as will shortly be seen, a relatively high intensity of social interaction within the group in the form of reciprocal entertaining. In the secretarial echelon high social status was thus combined with immediate command over the entire organizational apparatus of executive government, dominance (in the later phases of the Jeffersonian era) over the communication channels to the Hill, and preferential access to the Presidency itself—inasmuch as all Jeffersonian Presidents came into the office from the Secretaryship of State.*

At the summit of executive society, literally in a class by itself, was the "First Family." Peerless in his legal status, the President had a peerless social status as well, marked by his occupancy of the largest residence in the capital and the only one provided at public expense; by a salary more than quadruple that of his highest-ranking subordinate in the community; by his exemption from the usual rules of etiquette requiring other executives to return calls paid to their homes; and by a special rule of etiquette which precluded, on grounds of dignity, personal appearances at any social function outside the executive mansion. King without a court, or even so much as a receptionist or a personal guard to control access to his person, the President was also obliged to give audience to all comers, from

* For Thomas Jefferson, service as Vice President intervened.

supplicants off the street, passing vendors, wayfarers, curiosity-seekers, and bearers of grievances of every conceivable sort, to bearers of diplomatic credentials from sovereigns abroad. With the "crazing cares" of these visitors, who consumed a major part of every working day, Presidents would doubtless have been glad to dispense; but it was precisely their preeminent status that made them the most sought-after personages in Washington.

As a final point of contrast with the congressional community, executives invested very heavily of their time, money, and effort in the cultivation of personal acquaintanceships. For legislators the end of the workday marked a period of social withdrawal, an escape into their respective fraternity houses. For executives, however, the close of the workday signaled the commencement of a busy round of "at homes," teas, card parties, receptions, dinners, and balls. Suggesting the importance of such socializing in the life of the executive community, roughly as much time appears to have been allotted to it as was reserved each day for the conduct of public business, the daily routine for Secretaries being six hours at the office and the remainder of the day, often until midnight, consumed in entertaining. Sociability was officially decreed, indeed, by a presidential document promulgated for the specific purpose of "bring[ing] the members of society together," and prescribing the rules of social initiative and response.[10] Sociability was thought important enough to justify considerable financial sacrifice, too. Secretaries spent more than three times the amount on transportation—horses, horse feed, coachmen—for shuttling themselves between parties than legislators spent on themselves for room and board; the Secretary of State found that keeping fashionable and maintaining a hospitable household alone cost considerably more than the whole of his $6,000 annual salary.[11] Not to use one's leisure time in sociability was to give offense. Secretary Adams was reprimanded for neglect of his social obligations by an anonymous newspaper advertisement, and felt obliged to cut his workday short in order to "indulge . . . others by mingling in society, partly to repel a reproach . . . of a reserved, gloomy, unsocial temper." [12] Illness was considered no better excuse for social aloofness than overzealous attention to office work: Secretary Clay's wife "is obliged to go to other peoples parties, sick or well, for fear of giving offence.[13] Personability and social aptitudes—qualities wholly uncultivated in legislative society—were emphasized to the point of becoming a basis for rating a man's political prospects in the executive community. An individual whose "manners are extremely conciliatory and popular" was thought to be "silently but surely . . . adding to his influence," [14] while a Secretary's withdrawal to a remote residence was taken to indicate the "disappointment of his ambition." [15] Inattention to social appearance was thought to reveal political indifference, and a façade of good spirits had to be maintained at all costs: "Suffering must be suppressed . . . cheerfulness . . . must be assumed." [16] No sharper contrast can be imagined to the community of legislators, with their aggressively individualistic public behavior and their dogged denial of any social obligations beyond their own fraternity group, than an executive society where "people consider it necessary to be agreeable,—where pleasing . . . becomes a sort of business, and . . . enter[s] into the habitual calculations of every one." [17]

Executive society was distinctive, then, for the absence of those very characteristics which were politically problematic for the community of legislators on Capitol Hill. By one sort of logic, a community having a stable membership, a social and legal hierarchy, compulsory sociability, no divergent electoral constituencies, and no opposition party should not have experienced the severe internal cleavages that brought the congressional establishment to the verge of disintegration by the close of the Jeffersonian era. By one sort of logic, the executive establishment should have been far less needful of, or at least far less resistive to, presidential leadership than a representative legislature.

But it was another sort of logic that prevailed west of the Tiber. In fact, the executive establishment became less of an organic, cohesive entity than the legislative establishment on Capitol Hill. In fact, the executive community harbored within itself sources of cleavage and conflict as deeply divisive as those on Capitol Hill, and requiring no less astute leadership to manage.

An enduring source of contention was the colony of foreigners comprising the diplomatic corps. The representatives of other sovereigns brought to the executive establishment cultural antipathies and a disparity of power interests far sharper than any to be found on the Hill, and an undercurrent of antagonism which no outward conformity to the niceties of etiquette could conceal. Being thrown together in Washington's wilderness seemed merely to multiply the opportunities for acting out, in their social relations, the conflicts of national interest among them. A prolonged and bitter social warfare between the British and French legations at Washington accompanied the hostilities between the sovereigns they represented, culminating in a near-fight between the British and French ministers at a White House dinner which the President prevented by intervening with his saber at the ready.[18]

Frictions within the corps were family disputes, however, compared to the cold war that characterized relations between Americans and foreigners at Washington. The attitude of the Old World diplomats is best reflected in their habitual reference to the Americans as "the natives"—unlettered, vulgar, impressionable, and, in their political novicehood, easy marks for political manipulation. Foreign envoys insinuated themselves into the politics of their host community in ways that would today be intolerable, but which were then considered no impropriety against a new nation not even meriting the recognition of being dealt with by envoys of full ambassadorial rank. They lobbied freely for advantageous tariffs on Capitol Hill, curried favor with legislators by sumptuous dinners, offered political guidance and propaganda services to enemies of the administration when it suited their purpose, and on at least one occasion exploited the weakness of a bibulous Senator to incapacitate him on a key foreign policy vote.[19] They hired native propagandists to subvert American policy. "The price of this sort of labor is not . . . very high here," the British minister reported to his foreign office.[20] They exploited and fomented divisions in the President's cabinet by spreading contradictory rumors to its different members, intrigued against Secretaries of State in collusion with opposition legislators, and had no scruples about intimidating the President himself by tactics verging on personal blackmail.[21]

Arrogance in society matched their arrogance in politics. Diplomats asserted that all cabinet members except the Secretary of State were beneath them in rank, and refused to yield precedence at state dinners. When the President's wife refused to pay the first courtesy call upon them they boycotted social functions at the White House.[22] Sparing no expense to outdo the Americans, they imported magnificent equipages, bought two adjoining houses and merged them when American executives could scarcely afford one, furnished them with Europe's finest, and staged lavish balls, likening the Americans' imitation thereof to a "three-shilling ticket ball at a second-rate tavern." [23] In a society where most executive employees lived in poverty or on the brink of it, they strutted in ruffled shirts and silver spurs, or tiaras and ropes of diamonds, and sent fifty miles to Baltimore for table delicacies.

Such flamboyance invited precisely the response it received from the Americans. Proclaiming himself an enemy to all form and ceremony, Jefferson abolished rights to precedence among diplomats and established the rule of "equality, or of 'pêle-mêle.' " [24] He left the British minister and his lady, speechless with indignation, to find seats where they could at a White House dinner; publicly remarked that the French minister would have to get out of gold lace unless he wanted boys running after him; snubbed diplomats while lavishing attention upon Indian chiefs at a presidential reception; and received the credentials of a resplendent British minister in a state of undress.[25] Following suit, lesser politicians made a point of coming to diplomatic entertainments with muddy boots and wild hair, and affected to chew tobacco in salons unequipped with spitoons. "And then the spitting! O the spitting!" commented a house guest of the British envoy.[26] A delegation of executive wives told Napoleon's sister-in-law that "she must promise to have more clothes on" at their parties; and a congressman inspired a local drinking song entitled "The Extinction of the British Fire" by putting the British minister's fireplace to an unorthodox personal use during the Queen's birthday ball on the eve of the War of 1812.[27]

To such types of warfare there was no parallel in the community on Capitol Hill. With all the cultural antipathies contained in it, none were so deep or irreconcilable as those between the Old World and the New, thrown into intimate confrontation in the executive community.

If the conflicting interests and the cultural disparities of its international membership gave the executive community frictions of a kind unknown on Capitol Hill, the departmental subdivisions of the executive branch gave it structural sources of cleavage fully as acute as any to be found on the Hill. In the departments of State, Treasury, War, and Navy the executive community harbored separate and rival interests even less likely to converge in common purpose or viewpoint than the "little legislatures" or the different regional blocs of the congressional community.

Institutionalized divergences among the fiscal point of view, the naval point of view, the organized army interest, and the organized foreign policy interest sufficed to create enduring sources of policy conflict and "persevering oppositions" [28] within the executive branch, as they did in Congress among committees specializing in the same policy jurisdictions. More than this, answerability to different mandates in the form of their respective statutory authorities, and supervision by different sets of outsiders—their superintending committees—added further divisive elements among departments that did not exist among the different regional blocs or the different sublegislatures of the congressional community. And executive departments lacked even the stimulus to collaboration and compromise that was present, however weakly felt, in a decision-making body proceeding on the principle of majority rule. Departments were far more highly organized, too, and far more cohesive within themselves than their counterpart committees on the Hill. Each was an organizational empire unto itself, with its own field forces, its own independent system of communication with the outside world, its own sources of information, its own considerable resources of patronage. Within each department at Washington, a chain of command and a politically weak officialdom below the department chief facilitated internal cohesion. Each department was, moreover, a continuing group entity with virtually the same personnel year in and year out. None experienced the constant infusions of new blood and the annual dispersals to the constituencies, as on the Hill, to impede the development of group solidarity and bureaucratic parochialism.

Here were causes galore for intraparty rivalry and dissension on the executive side, as President Jefferson noted: "ill-defined limits of their departments" to generate jurisdictional disputes among cabinet members; "jealousies, trifling at first, but nourished and strengthened" by different proprietary interests, to generate disagreement for disagreement's sake among departmental chiefs; opportunities for "intrigues . . . of designing persons to build an importance to themselves on the divisions" in the cabinet.[29] Small wonder it is, then, that in the eyes of one officeholder with experience on both sides of the Tiber the power struggles at the highest levels of the executive community surpassed in intensity those on the Hill: "a play of passions, opinions, and characters," wrote Secretary Adams, "different . . . from those in which I have been accustomed heretofore to move." [30] Small wonder, either, that the first major conflict to erupt within the government of the new nation originated not in Congress but in the executive branch, between a Secretary of State and a Secretary of the Treasury: the Jefferson-Hamilton feud in George Washington's administration.[31] Here, in short, were "inherent forces of disintegration" in the executive community no less persistent than those in the congressional establishment, and no more likely to be overcome without assiduous leadership effort.[32]

No amassing of illustrative incidents is needed to make, for the Jeffersonian period, a point which is familiar and accepted by students of bureaucracy: that departmental segmentation locks conflict into the system of executive government, no less than committee segmentation and divergent constituencies lock conflict into the system of congressional government.[33] There were, however, circumstances and developments in the Jeffersonian era which aggravated these institutional sources of conflict in the executive branch—perhaps more so than today—and these do need pointing out.

As in modern times, appointments to the cabinet positions were distributed on a geographic or sectional basis, within the limits of personnel availability and political feasibility. The effort was made, furthermore, to get a balanced representation at the cabinet level of the various wings or factions comprising the President's party.[34] Unlike the modern practice, however, high-level executive appointees were then drawn in large proportion from the membership of the party on Capitol Hill.[35] Appointment practices in the Jeffersonian era thus tended to have the consequence of importing into the highest levels of the executive branch not only sectional cleavages but also the factional cleavages existing in the congressional establishment. Here was a quadruple threat to political and social cohesion among the Secretaries: different sectional affiliations outside Washington; different factional affiliations in Congress; accountability to different congressional committees; and different institutional affiliations within the executive establishment.

Nor were these the only sources of cleavage among them. As the Jeffersonian era advanced, cabinet members came to confront each other not only as protagonists with different sectional, factional, and institutional interests but also as competitors for the Presidency. In 1816 the two leading contestants for the caucus nomination were Secretary of State Monroe and Secretary of War Crawford. Presidential fever began to sweep Monroe's cabinet within two years of his victory over Crawford. In 1818 his erstwhile competitor, who had been rewarded with the Treasury portfolio, was again in pursuit of the presidential nomination, soon followed by Secretary of War Calhoun, and then by Secretary of State Adams. By 1821 the executive community was witnessing three full-scale presidential campaigns conducted in its midst. Department heads acquired newspapers, showered each other with invective, made an affair of state over quarrels about precedence at the President's dinner table, and cut short their workdays to lobby for caucus votes on Capitol Hill.[36] Calhoun managed to get a congressional delegation to come across the Tiber and draft him on his own doorstep; Adams spent until late at night making good-will tours of the boardinghouses on the Hill; and the candidates' wives interrupted executive sessions of the Senate to round up recruits for rival theater parties.[37] "This

Government is, indeed, assuming more and more a character of cabal," Adams commented, "—that is, working and counterworking, with many of the worst features of elective monarchies." [38]

The only possible chance for a head of Department to attain the Presidency is by ingratiating himself personally with the members of Congress; and, as many of them have objects of their own to obtain, the temptation is immense to corrupt coalitions. . . . [This is] one of the numerous evils consequent upon the practice which has grown up under this Constitution, but contrary to its spirit, by which the members of Congress meet in caucus and determine . . . upon the candidate for the Presidency . . . —a practice which . . . leads to a thousand corrupt cabals between the members of Congress and the heads of the Departments, who are thus almost necessarily made rival pretenders to the succession.[39]

Both reflecting and aggravating all the other sources of cleavage among cabinet members, finally, was the emergence of rival social formations, in extraofficial life, around each cabinet position. In the second half of the Jeffersonian era, these groupings received institutional expression with the development of the secretarial salon, variously called "drawing-room," "assembly," or "circle."

The salon defined an executive's intimate or close acquaintances, as distinguished from the much larger number with whom his family maintained relationships of courtesy. It signified those who, in the quaint and instructive phrase of one executive wife, became "domesticated with us": attached to the executive's household without being domiciled there.[40] At an early stage in the development of this social form, being a member of an executive's "social circle" meant little more than frequenting his parlor, where at least one member of the family appears to have been always "at home" to visitors. By 1815, however, executives began to set aside special salon evenings for increasing numbers of domesticated friends.[41] Rivalry among them led to ever more elaborate and costly formats for attracting and holding salon followings as the Jeffersonian era advanced. Games were provided, and sideboards were heaped high with extravagant foods. Wives and daughters were conscripted for poetry readings. Secretary Adams instituted chamber music at his salons, and other Secretaries competed for the services of an ensemble from the Marine Band and a Philadelphia lady who entertained with a tambourine. A presumably reformed opium eater who had wandered to Washington built up a brisk business giving recitations in a Roman toga, and visiting notables—Baron Humboldt, Fenimore Cooper, Robert Owen of Lanark, Washington Irving—were lionized to provide centers of attraction at one or another salon.[42] The salon became fully institutionalized by the 1820s when rival coteries were recruited early each fall to remain with the salon of their choice for the rest of the social season. Secretary of State Clay, for example, sent out his autumn bids in this form:

Mr. and Mrs. Clay, request the favour of Dr. C_____'s company, on Wednesday evening, the 30th inst, and on every alternate Wednesday, till the 20th of March.[43]

"Society is now divided in separate batallions as it were," a veteran member of the executive community noted.[44] Chieftains of separate departmental empires had now acquired separate loyal followings as well.

A twofold political significance is to be seen in the development of the secretarial salon.

First, the emergence of salon society afforded the President's subordinates continuing extraofficial liaison with legislators and continuing opportunities for cultivating congressional good will which had earlier been available to the President alone. During Jefferson's two terms in the White House, legislators rarely appeared west of the Tiber except as guests at presidential dinners, and extraofficial interaction of any sort between department heads and members of Congress was at a minimum:

The Heads of Departments visit few members of either House [commented a legislator in 1806]. Mr. Madison [Secretary of State], for two or three years past, has entirely omitted even the ceremony of leaving cards at their lodgings. He invites very few to dine with him. Mr. Gallatin [Secretary of the Treasury] leaves no cards, makes no visits, scarcely ever invites a member to dine, or even has a tea party. General Dearborn and Robert Smith, Secretaries of War and Navy, leave cards with all the members, but invite few to tea, and scarcely any to dine.[45]

With the emergence of salons during Madison's administration, and especially after the War of 1812, legislative guests appeared on the executive side with increasing numbers, and not a single report of secretarial social functions in the 1820s has been encountered which fails to mention the conspicuous presence of legislators. Something of a record appears to have been established by Secretary Adams in 1824, who claimed sixty-eight congressional members for his salon.[46] The advent of secretarial salons was contemporaneous, therefore, with the advent of congressional supervision of executive departments through the committee system and the rise of secretarial competition for the congressional caucus nomination. Desire for the presidential nomination and vulnerability to congressional committees may well explain why department heads bestirred themselves to cultivate congressional good will, making it impossible for the President ever again to monopolize the social lobbying of legislators. Salons served, in any case, precisely the same purposes and offered precisely the same political advantages for cabinet members that Jefferson's legislative dinners had once afforded for the White House.

Second, the development of the secretarial salon suggests that the executive community, behind the façade of its social and political hierarchy, came to acquire more and more the segmented characteristics of the congressional community as the Jeffersonian era advanced. That is to say, executive society came to be subdivided into separate group conclaves, each with its own after-hours meeting place, each defined by a distinctive membership. No less than boardinghouse fraternities, each salon was a primary group bound together in mutual partisanship. To be a member of Mr. Clay's "dinner company" was thus to acknowledge oneself as a "Clay man," and to frequent Secretary Calhoun's house was to be known as a man of "Mr. C's politics." To attend Secretary Crawford's salon was to join the Crawford partisans, or friends of the Treasury. In fact, when Crawford fell ill during the 1824 campaign for the caucus nomination, it was his salon members who carried on the work of organizing his intracommunity support; and it was his assembled salon coterie whom the defeated candidate consulted about his deci-

sion not to accept reappointment to the Treasury under Adams—
the very letter declining the appointment being the product of a
joint effort by the Secretary and his parlor partisans.[47] As with
members of different fraternities on Capitol Hill, social distance between Secretaries increased as they became more heavily involved in
salon life, and executive families became "estranged by different and
conflicting politics." [48] Executives competing for the Presidency
rarely appeared at the same social gathering, and extraofficial mingling declined to the mere perfunctory performance of social obligations.[49] By the 1820s one hostess found it worthy of remark that
several Secretaries had appeared at a social function without incident, and that there still remained one secretarial family that was on
amicable visiting terms with the rest. For "you have no idea, neither
can I in a letter give you an idea of the embittered and violent spirit
engendered" by political and social rivalry among department
heads.[50]

Increased frequency and range of interaction between executives
and legislators was thus associated with fragmentation of executive
society into partisan groupings not unlike the congeries of groups
comprising the congressional community. "Separate battalions" in
1824 described executive society experiencing the full impact of social and political interaction with the long-established "separate battalions" of the companion community atop Capitol Hill.

A stable and nonelective membership and a formally hierarchical
structure notwithstanding, then, the executive establishment of
Jeffersonian times was no more a coherent entity than the representative community on Capitol Hill. Separate bureaucracies, their respective cabinet spokesmen further divided by divergent sectional
and factional affiliations, each with his own partisan following in
Congress and furnished with the necessary tools for keeping it, each
locked in battle for the succession—here were "separated institutions sharing powers" even less likely to cohere politically, without
the intervention of some unifying influence, than those on the Hill.

Here, as with the community on Capitol Hill, the Presidency
offered the only hope of supplying that unifying influence. Here,
too, the only hope for Presidents in accomplishing that objective lay

not in removing the sources of cleavage—for these were beyond any individual's power to remove—but in remedying their effects.

What resources, then, were available to Jeffersonian Presidents for exercising leadership over their own executive branch? How did they use these resources? With what effect?

CHAPTER 11

THE PRESIDENCY AND THE EXECUTIVE ESTABLISHMENT

There is a waning but still ubiquitous viewpoint about bureaucratic formations which holds that power in the executive arena is a function of authority. The *capacity* to get things done—to elicit affirmative action responses from one's subordinates—is thought to follow, more or less automatically, from the *right* to give orders. By this view, whatever limitations there are upon presidential power in the sphere of executive relations stem from the Constitution and laws which define the scope of the President's authority; and the task of presidential leadership becomes merely the vigorous utilization of the chain of command. Building consensus and acquiescence among one's subordinates becomes unnecessary.

Modern thinking on the subject places consensus-building at the center of the process of presidential leadership in the executive establishment, because it recognizes what common sense ought to have indicated long ago, namely, that anything which lessens policy agreement between the President and those who command the machinery for implementing policy lessens the probability that the President's policy decisions will get translated into action. Modern analysis recognizes, in other words, the distinction between a President's authority and a President's power in his executive dealings, and the insufficiency of a President's authority alone to sustain a role of leadership. By this view the chief limitations upon the President's power in the executive branch stem not so much from legal prescriptions as from the problems of achieving compliance from his bureaucracy; and a major task of presidential leadership becomes the building of consensus among subordinate executives around the policy objectives of the President, with a view to getting that compliance. Consensus-building thus is no less an essential ingredient of leadership in the executive branch than it is clearly recognized to be in Congress.

The cabinet becomes, therefore, a key institution for any exploration of presidential leadership in the Jeffersonian era. A committee of department heads and the Attorney General, convened and chaired by the Chief Executive, it was the only institution in the executive community which brought spokesmen for different sections, political factions, and bureaucratic interests together in a work group affording the President a leadership role.

The cabinet was not new to the Jeffersonian period, having already become established in practice during the administrations of Washington and Adams.[1] Without constitutional status, it had originally been devised to serve as a policy-making organ which would substitute for the Chief Executive when he was absent from the seat of government.[2] By 1793, however, department heads were being convened in the presence of the President to deliberate crisis questions, particularly those relating to foreign policy. It is apparently under precedent of this usage that the committee acquired the designation of "cabinet," and that the device originally intended as a substitute for an absent President became a regularly employed device of the President for discussing a wide range of policy issues with his subordinate officers.

Such use of the cabinet was continued throughout the Jeffersonian era, Monroe most frequently convening the group with roughly ten meetings monthly.[3] Meetings were not devoted to purely intradepartmental or administrative matters having little political significance, and only rarely did they serve as briefing sessions for informational purposes or to announce presidential policy decisions. Rather they were used as policy forums, to discuss matters on which presidential action was contemplated or required and which would involve the President in a political commitment. The usual procedure, in so far as it is known from detailed reports of cabinet meetings from 1817 to 1828, was for the President to open the ses-

sion by stating the matter presented to him for decision, indicating
or not his own inclinations, discussion being confined to topics designated by the President in advance of the meeting.[4] Usually the
President reserved decision after having heard the members' views;
President Jefferson, with an unusually cohesive cabinet, asserted
that he put the final decision to a vote.[5] Foreign policy questions
were perhaps the most frequent subject of cabinet business. Presidential nominations were occasionally discussed. White House communications to Congress were a major item on the cabinet agenda
throughout the Jeffersonian era, and the most important of these
was the President's annual State of the Union message. What the
President said in these messages, including recommendations for legislation, was, in every administration, largely the product of joint
effort by the cabinet. Discussions on the annual message typically
required a number of meetings and furnished, as Leonard White has
put it, "an invaluable annual occasion for a review of events and for
welding the Cabinet, if possible, into a single composite body." [6]

In the Jeffersonian era it seems clear, therefore, that the cabinet
was a political device "in both the partisan and policy meanings of
the term." [7] No other rationale for continued use of this Federalist
device is discernible. Given the small number of departments and
the diminutive size of the Washington bureaucracy, the need for
administrative coordination was clearly not such as to necessitate
group consultations with the President. Conserving the President's
time was surely not the reason for group sessions at a period in history when Presidents could regularly afford three months' annual
vacation. Certainly the President's conceded need for information
and policy guidance from his department heads did not require their
convocation as a group. A persuasive argument can be made, on the
contrary, that the advice a Chief Executive receives from department heads in a group is apt to be less candid than that he is likely to
get through individual consultations with them. And, while Jeffersonian Presidents neither brought all major policy issues before the
cabinet nor acknowledged any obligation to follow majority rule
within the cabinet, there were obvious threats to the President's
preeminence in opening matters to committee discussion which con-

stitutionally were the President's alone to decide. Falling captive to his department heads was an inherent risk the President ran in an institution which tended to make his business the business of all his department chiefs.

But these risks evidently seemed less important than the opportunities offered by the cabinet for building a consensus upon which to govern and upon which to lead. Jeffersonian Presidents must have recognized the importance of consensus among Secretaries whose support they needed to carry their programs both on the Hill and into the lower levels of the administrative structure. Having no personal staff and depending largely upon their cabinet members for political liaison with Congress, they must have been aware that their chances for rallying congressional support depended largely on their ability to rally their department heads in support of their policy objectives. Especially after Secretaries had preempted tools once monopolized by the Presidency for influencing Congress, they must have known that schisms among department heads would inevitably have a divisive impact upon Congress as well. More than this, cabinet consultations provided insurance against unwitting commitments to policies which might aggravate cleavages within the congressional party. To the extent that a cabinet reflected in its own composition the range of factions in Congress, cabinet consultations provided a testing ground for congressional reaction in advance of actual presentation of presidential policy requests to Congress. The President gained a general political advantage, too, in implicating his department heads as a group in decisions for which the President alone would have to take responsibility. A presidential decision known to have been sanctioned by the cabinet would not only be likely to carry greater weight in Congress and with foreign sovereigns but would also offer the President greater security from political attack if the policy later proved ill-advised.

The Jeffersonian cabinet thus appears to have been a device employed by Chief Executives in recognition of the independent political power wielded by their Secretaries; in recognition of the political risks to themselves of failing to achieve a working consensus among them; and in recognition of forces always working to destroy a sense of common purpose among executives with widely divergent interests. The cabinet, in other words, was the executive equivalent of a legislative caucus, intended to preconcert the policy views of party members representing different political interests.

As such, it achieved notable success under Thomas Jefferson. "In truth all measures were the measures of all," Jefferson recalled the year he retired from the Presidency.[8] "The third administration, which was of eight years," he wrote again in 1811,

presented an example of harmony in a cabinet of six persons, to which perhaps history has furnished no parallel. There never arose, during the whole time, an instance of an unpleasant thought or word between the members. We sometimes met under differences of opinion, but scarcely ever failed, by conversing and reasoning, so to modify each other's ideas, as to produce an unanimous result.[9]

Yet Jefferson added significantly:

Able and amicable as these members were, I am not certain this would have been the case, had each possessed equal and independent powers . . . the power of decision in the President left no object for internal dissension, and external intrigue was stifled in embryo by the knowledge which incendiaries possessed, that no division they could foment would change the course of the executive power.[10]

Madison's accession to the Presidency brought a dramatic and disastrous change. "Our Cabinet presents a novel spectacle in the political world," wrote a congressman in 1811; "divided against itself, and the most deadly animosity raging between its principal members, what can come of it but confusion, mischief, and ruin?" [11] Personal vendettas between department heads, their active involvement in legislative intrigues, and insubordination to the President which not even a grave national emergency served to suspend became the order of the day.

As in Washington's administration during a time of international tension, a major feud developed between the Secretary of the Treasury (Gallatin) and the Secretary of State (Smith). Although both men had served in Jefferson's cabinet, all vestiges of Jeffersonian harmony vanished as Smith took the feud to the newspapers, accusing Gallatin of speculating for private profit with public funds, of treachery to the nation, and of maligning the President's character. Their wives indulged in name-calling, and the families broke off all social relations.[12] When the President refused to side with Smith, the Secretary of State leaked confidential cabinet discussions to his partisans in Congress and worked actively against the President's legislative recommendations, which he had supported in cabinet.[13] A mistrustful President required the Secretary of State to conduct all diplomatic communications in writing and composed diplomatic notes himself over the Secretary's signature. Smith boycotted the White House and vowed to ruin the Chief Executive: "The course I have taken I am confident will lead to the injury of Mr. Madison and to my advantage. . . . I will make no compromise with him. His overthrow is my object and most assuredly will I effect it." [14] Gallatin forced the President to dismiss Smith by offering his own resignation. Smith partisans in the Senate retaliated by maneuvering Gallatin out of the cabinet as well.

Troubles with other cabinet members also plagued Madison. One Secretary of War, in collusion with an economy-minded group in Congress, opposed preparations for the War of 1812; another failed to comply with a presidential directive to make ready for a British assault upon the capital.[15] Madison's first Secretary of the Navy joined forces with a congressional clique to present the President with a swollen naval appropriation Madison did not want and the Secretary of the Treasury could not raise the revenues to provide. His successor in the Navy overspent his budget in anticipation of an appropriation that failed to materialize, and saddled the President with an unauthorized debt that was owing for two months before the Chief Executive learned anything about it.[16]

Presidential efforts to enlist the aid of cabinet members in rallying Congress were evaded or rebuffed. Mending their own fences on the Hill took priority over helping the President, and Madison was obliged to ferret out legislators individually and to ask them secretly to introduce bills that his Secretaries would not press on his behalf.[17] Department heads sent facts and reports to Congress of which they did not apprise the President, with the result of undercutting presidential policy requests already submitted to the legislature.[18] His administration "aground at the pitch of high tide," nothing remained to Madison "but to lighten the ship," and he resorted to removals from the cabinet.[19] He had two Secretaries of State, three Attorneys General, four Secretaries of the Treasury, four Secretaries of War, and four Secretaries of the Navy during his eight years in the White House. But resignations and dismissals were a poor substitute for consensus; on the contrary, they merely made it more difficult to achieve. Madison simply could not hold a cabinet together.

So it went, too, with Monroe's cabinet. Animosities of the sort that generated resignations and dismissals in Madison's cabinet led to intensified infighting among Monroe's department heads, most of whom remained in office from beginning to end of the Monroe administration. Hardly had they settled into office when a feud developed, once again, between the Secretary of the Treasury and the Secretary of State. Within four years the two had become competitors to succeed their chief, joined by the Secretary of War as a third presidential candidate. Mutual vituperation and character assassination reached a new low in newspapers each of the three Secretaries used to promote his candidacy. Secretary Adams was accused of everything from appearing in church tieless and barefooted to forging changes in the language of the Constitution, the original copy of which was entrusted to his department for safekeeping.[20] Secretary Crawford was accused of corruption, mental incompetence, espionage against cabinet colleagues, and using his prerogatives as Secretary of the Treasury to pry into their personal finances.[21] "A state of irritation prevails which greatly exceeds anything which has occurred in the history of this government," wrote Secretary Crawford in 1822.[22] "It is time to be prepared for any event," mused the Secretary of State; for the administration "is at war with itself, both in the Executive, and between the Executive and the Legislature." [23]

Cabinet unity could not possibly be maintained against the doubly divisive impact of different congressional committees "now set as watch over the heads of departments" [24] and of competition for the Presidency among the Secretaries, whose "partisans in Congress are making a handle of [policy issues] to help or hurt those for or against whom they are." [25] Deadlock followed deadlock in cabinet meetings, no matter how large or how trivial the issue—from military and diplomatic policy on the Florida question to uniform rules on etiquette and protocol, from the still unresolved question of British impressment of seamen to a choice of location for a new executive office building. "After two hours of discussion this day, the subject was dismissed, leaving it precisely where it was, nothing determined, and nothing practicable proposed"; "the President . . . was very apparently affected by the conflict of sentiment among his advisers. . . . We parted, leaving the question yet undetermined"; "the President ultimately found a middle term, upon which he concluded, after expressing his regret that he was obliged to decide between us, equally divided in opinion as we were": such reports of cabinet meetings are legion throughout Monroe's eight years in the Presidency.[26] Monroe took cabinet members aside and made special pleas for unity, reminding them that no favorable action could be expected from Congress without it: "A difference of opinion in the Administration immediately got abroad," he pointed out; "advantage was instantly taken of it by its enemies; other objects and other views immediately connected themselves with it, and embarrassments multiplied upon the Administration." [27] He kept deadlocked sessions closeted until late hours. He tried the tactic of recommending nothing to Congress when the cabinet would not agree. "So harassed that he scarcely knew where to set his foot," he proposed distinctive uniforms for cabinet members to encourage a sense of group identity.[28] All efforts were unavailing.

Utter loss of presidential control over department heads went hand in hand with disintegration of the cabinet. Egged on by calls for legislative recommendations from strategically placed partisans in Congress, Monroe's Secretary of War used his position in the cabinet of a President publicly committed against internal improvements to urge legislation on internal improvements and to wage a presidential campaign on that platform.[29] Monroe's Secretary of State arranged with partisans in Congress to compel the release of an executive report the President had directed to be withheld.[30] His Secretary of the Treasury concealed a budgetary deficit from the President while transmitting the knowledge to Congress, and was driven from the White House by the President, armed with fire tongs, for insulting language to his chief. Monroe ended his administration not on speaking terms with the head of the Treasury, with whom he communicated through an intermediary.[31]

By contrast with the regimes of Madison and Monroe, the single term of John Quincy Adams' administration witnessed a period of relative calm within the executive establishment. Because detailed reports of all but a few cabinet meetings are lacking for this period, and because Adams apparently convened the cabinet rather less regularly and less frequently than his predecessor, harmony among the department heads may have been more apparent than real. Nevertheless, the final four years of the Jeffersonian era did not exhibit the intense internal warfare within the executive establishment that had raged for sixteen years prior to Adams' election.

Doubtless one factor was the demise of the congressional nominating caucus in 1824, which served to remove one prime source of contention among the Secretaries for the favor of congressmen. Probably more important in serving to reduce contention was the fact that Adams did not give a place in his cabinet to all the major factions comprising the shattered remnants of the Republican party in 1825. Omitted were the Calhoun faction and the faction attached to Andrew Jackson.[32] The result was a cabinet which, unlike those of Madison and Monroe, failed to reflect the factional composition of the Republican party on the Hill. While exclusion of the Calhoun and Jackson factions may have served to lessen tensions within the executive establishment, however, the political cost of their exclusion was fatal to Adams. For the excluded factions between them came to dominate Congress at the mid-term elections—Calhoun's the Senate, Jackson's the House. Unable to work their influence upon the executive establishment from within the cabinet, they mounted an assault on the executive from their respective bastions on Capitol Hill. With anti-Adams men dominating every Senate and House committee, Congress "spent its energy in a grand inquest into the conduct of the Executive," [33] in a campaign to discredit the

President that has rarely been equaled in scurrility or in success. The electorate rejected him for a second term.

If indeed Adams had considered bringing a Calhoun and a Jackson partisan into the cabinet, his choice would have been no better than Hobson's: to bring rival factions into the executive establishment, thus creating what in all likelihood would have been an unmanageable warfare within the executive establishment; or, as happened, to exclude rival factions, thus creating an unmanageable war between himself and Congress and foreclosing any practical possibility of achieving his legislative goals. Either alternative presented prospects ruinous to presidential power.

And even with a more cohesive cabinet than his two predecessors enjoyed, Adams failed to rally cabinet members in support of his major policy program. The draft of his first message to Congress calling for a broad program of internal improvements was greeted with two adverse responses, one favorable response, and one conditionally favorable response, while the remaining cabinet member was noncommittal. Additional cabinet meetings were called; numerous excisions and alterations were suggested; new disagreements arose over these. "I told them," wrote Adams, "I was like the man with his two wives—one plucking out his black hairs, and the other the white, till none were left." [34] Adams finally resolved to present the message without the support and with only the reluctant acquiescence of his cabinet. What small chance he had of getting favorable action from a hostile Congress was thus removed by the noncooperation of the only executive helpers he might have recruited to work for it.

Even this degree of implication in the President's program proved too much for the cabinet. When the next annual message was ready for cabinet presentation, President Adams noted in his diary a request by Secretaries Clay and Barbour that "the draft of the message . . . might be sent to the members of the Administration, to be considered by them without my being present; that the discussion might be more free than would be respectful in my presence." Despite private misgivings, Adams consented. The message was returned gutted of its significant and controversial proposals, and the

President himself deleted the one paragraph still in dispute among the Secretaries.[35] What went to Capitol Hill as the President's legislative recommendations were in fact not his at all but the recommendations of his cabinet.

By the time for presentation of the draft of his third annual message to the cabinet, Adams' morale was broken. "I am ashamed of it," he noted in his journal, "and almost afraid to read it to my confidential advisers." [36] Any degree of implication in the legislative proposals of a politically doomed President was precluded in Adams' last year, when every Secretary developed allegedly incapacitating illnesses—blisters, "vertigo," spells of blindness—which prevented attendance at cabinet meetings.[37]

The cabinet had thus come full circle: first convened in 1791 to substitute for the President, it had become, by the end of the Jeffersonian era, a decision-making body to supplant the President. From a device intended to rally support for the President, it had become an engine to thwart the President. Hamilton's worst fears, expressed in *The Federalist*, No. 70, had become political reality: a total loss of executive energy "by vesting [power] ostensibly in one man, subject in whole or in part, to the control and cooperation of others, in the capacity of counsellors to him."

The history of presidential-executive relations during the Jeffersonian era thus duplicates the history of presidential-congressional relations: impressive leadership exercised for a brief period by the first President; a sudden and drastic loss of leadership beginning with Madison and continuing for the remainder of the Jeffersonian era.

Why should this have been the case? The loss of presidential leadership of the executive establishment was far less in conformity with the intentions of the constitutional framers than loss of presidential leadership over Congress. Surely the framers did not intend the executive establishment to become the scene of factional contention, as they did the legislative establishment. "In the legislature," Hamilton commented in *The Federalist*, No. 70, "differences of opinion, and the jarrings of parties . . . must necessarily be submitted to . . . though they may sometimes obstruct salutary plans, yet often

[they] promote deliberation and circumspection, and serve to check excesses." But "no favorable circumstances palliate or atone for the disadvantages of dissension in the executive department," Hamilton noted in defense of a single executive:

> Here, they are pure and unmixed. There is no point at which they cease to operate. . . . they might impede or frustrate the most important measures of the government, in the most critical emergencies of the state. And what is still worse, they might split the community into the most violent and irreconcilable factions, adhering to the different individuals who composed the magistracy. . . . They constantly counteract those qualities in the Executive which are the most necessary ingredients in its composition,—vigor and expedition, and this without any counterbalancing good.

Why then were Chief Executives, topmost in the chain of command and having chairmanship of an executive "caucus" besides, unable to sustain leadership over their own subordinates? A key explanation lies in the nature of the leadership resources available to the men in the White House—in the carrots and sticks available for coaxing the department heads to see things the President's way and to lend their own influence to the accomplishment of his objectives. For the Jeffersonian experience, like modern experience with presidential management of the executive branch, leaves no doubt about the insufficiency of a President's authority alone to confer leadership. In Jeffersonian times no less than currently, presidential power in "the sphere of executive relations . . . resembles power in all others. . . . here as elsewhere [presidential] influence derives from bargaining advantages; power is a give-and-take." [38] The Jeffersonian Presidency must therefore be assayed as a bargaining position vis-à-vis the department heads, repeating the approach used earlier to explain the drastic decline in presidential leadership vis-à-vis Congress.

Here again what impresses is the weakness of the Jeffersonian Presidency.

Legislators might speak to department heads with the authority of *vox populi*, but not Presidents in the days before a plebiscitary Presidency. No Jeffersonian President could come to cabinet meetings claiming public support or electoral mandates for *his* policy aims and views. And no cabinet member of Jeffersonian times had anything to lose or to gain in the way of publicity from Presidents who had not the means to command a mass audience.

No Secretary of Jeffersonian times—unlike Jackson's cabinet members—need fear infiltration of his department by loyalists of the President.[39] None need fear watchfulness by a President lacking the eyes and ears of a personal staff and excluded by etiquette from social circulation within the community.[40] Indeed, Jeffersonian Presidents had to depend almost exclusively upon the Secretaries for knowledge of what was going on in their administrations and very largely, after Jefferson, for knowledge of what was going on at the Capitol. With the development of cabinet-committee relationships and secretarial salons, department heads had probably better sources of intelligence about goings-on at the Capitol than Presidents did. It may or may not have been innocent error when Secretary Clay misinformed President Adams about a congressional resolution requiring the President to transmit certain papers to Congress; in any case, the President was not aware of his own noncompliance with the resolution until a legislator was dispatched to the White House to ask an explanation for it.[41]

No Jeffersonian Secretary had to worry about clearance of either his legislative or his budgetary requests by the President; none had cause for indebtedness to the President for endorsement or expedition of these requests; and none had to worry about presidential impounding of funds appropriated for his department. For the President then had no statutory authority and no institutional machinery —no Bureau of the Budget—for performing such functions. There was no "President's budget," the prime instrumentality today by which a President impresses his policy objectives upon departmental programs. Nothing except a sense of courtesy to the President required department heads to bring any of their legislative business to the President's attention. Thus, it was from a legislator, not from his own Secretary of the Treasury, that President Monroe first learned that his administration had run up a deficit. The Secretary had communicated his annual report directly to Congress without even apprising the President of its contents. Secretary Gallatin had earlier done the same, with the result of torpedoing key aspects of President Madison's legislative requests already laid before Congress.[42]

Secretarial dependence upon the President for veto or endorsement of departmental patronage choices was limited both by statutes conferring authority to make such choices on the Secretaries or service chiefs [43] and by an informal "secretarial courtesy" which sanctioned presidential deference to the department head's recommendations.[44] It was President Monroe's breach of this custom—he objected to some of Secretary Crawford's personnel choices as unqualified—which caused Crawford to call him "you damned infernal old scoundrel!" and all personal communication between the two to cease.[45] President Adams ran no such risk. He permitted his Postmaster General to infiltrate the postal service with partisans of Calhoun.[46]

No Jeffersonian Secretary had to fear presidential reorganization of his department; Jeffersonian Presidents had no such statutory authority.

Only in part did high-level executives owe their jobs to the President. Almost one third of the top executives (cabinet members and Postmasters General) serving during the Jeffersonian era were holdovers from previous administrations, and were not in this sense indebted for their jobs to the Presidents under whom they last served.[47] Nor, as the previous chapter has pointed out, were these men chosen exclusively or even primarily for their loyalty to the Chief Executive. And while the President was understood to have the right to dismiss them, the threat of removal must have hung very lightly over department chiefs backed by partisans on the Hill whose support Presidents needed to keep. Throughout a period of foreign crisis, as we have seen, Madison tolerated an incompetent Secretary of State, backed by a powerful Senate faction, and dismissed him only when his continuation in office would have caused the President to lose another cabinet member through resignation. And Monroe swallowed the grossest personal insult from a Secretary of the Treasury with a large congressional following, whom Monroe would surely have alienated had he fired Crawford. By Adams' ad-

ministration, we witness the President, far from utilizing his authority to fire Secretaries, pleading with his own former enemy, now
the Secretary of State, not to withdraw from the cabinet. As an in-
ducement, the Chief Executive suggested a long vacation for Clay
and offered to spend the summer in Washington himself in order to
perform the Secretary's duties in Clay's absence.[48]

It is difficult to avoid the conclusion that the Jeffersonian Presidency was an even weaker bargaining position for purposes of executive leadership than it was for purposes of leading Congress.

Note, in contrast, the bargaining advantages Congress possessed
over the Secretaries. Legislators held the exclusive authority and the
power to grant or withhold departmental funds. To legislators, not
to the President, department heads looked for endorsement and authorization of their policy desires. Legislators shared, equally with
the President, the power to "require opinions, in writing," of the
department heads respecting the work of their bureaucracies. Calls
for reports and advice by Congress directly to cabinet members
caused more than one President considerable vexation, inasmuch as
"substantially all major legislation and much minor legislation were
based on administrative reports, giving facts and opinions for the
guidance of Congress." [49] Monroe struggled with little success to
get cabinet members to clear such reports with him. He warned his
cabinet that "the call of the House directly upon the Secretary of
War for this report [calling for legislative recommendations] was
itself irregular, and not conformable to the spirit of the Constitution
of the United States, the principle of which was a single Executive.
. . . And as heads of Departments were executive officers under the
President, it was to be considered whether the President himself was
not responsible for the substance of their reports." The cabinet
greeted these remarks with general silence, except for one Secretary
who merely noted that the practice had "existed ever since the establishment of the Government"—and presumably would continue,
presidential objections to the contrary notwithstanding.[50] When
Monroe tried to suppress a report from Secretary of State Adams to
Congress which would have involved the Chief Executive in an unwanted controversy, Adams claimed the privilege of getting "my

report" to the Hill. " '*Your* report!' said the President in a tone of sharp anger. ' 'Tis *my* report. It is no report at all until I have accepted it.' " [51] But Monroe capitulated. He might as well have, since Adams arranged with friends on the Hill to compel delivery of the report by means of a House resolution, the very day after Monroe had decided to suppress it.

Legislators shared with the President the capacity to issue instructions to department heads, both through resolutions and through regular legislation. Their instructions, morover, carried the authority of citizen spokesmanship, as the President's did not, and their capacity to instruct was not inhibited, as the President's was, by prevailing statutes. With the development of the standing committees, furthermore, Congress acquired the power and the means to exercise continuous watch over the work performance of the Secretaries and over their finances. The day-to-day scrutiny thus afforded and the threat of applying the "inquisitorial screw," as Secretary Adams called committee investigation,[52] effectively conferred upon legislators the capacity to harass, worry, and tease the President's subordinates into compliance with congressional desires. Presidents, on the other hand, had no comparable means or personnel for keeping their fingers on the bureaucratic pulse or for threatening a Secretary's peace of mind. Necessarily, then, keeping in the good graces of their superintending congressional committees tended to take priority among the Secretaries over keeping in the good graces of the President, as witness this report, by Secretary Adams, of a conversation with President Monroe:

It had always been considered as a practical rule that the Committee of Foreign Relations should be the confidential medium of communication between the Administration and Congress [Adams told the President]. The Speaker had now appointed a committee entirely new, of members chiefly known to be hostile to the Administration, with a Chairman generally understood to be at personal variance with me. To this committee all the papers relating to a complicated and delicate pending negotiation with France are confidentially committed, and the next day one of the members of the committee offers a resolution calling for them all. . . . I could solemnly declare that all my views hitherto had been exclusively confined to the support of his Administration. . . . I should continue to act on the same principles as long as it would be possible;

but, in the way things were now working, I knew not how long this might be.[53]

The annals of executive government probably contain no more candid forewarning, by the minister himself, of disloyalty to his chief. And what could President Monroe do about it? He could only reply that he had been in the same "predicament" when he was serving as Secretary of State under Madison.

Finally, legislators guarded the gateways to the Presidency. Until the collapse of the congressional nominating caucus in 1824, legislators had it within their power to fulfill or to deny the Secretaries' ambition to succeed their own Chief Executive. Leaving all other incentives aside, here alone was sufficient reason for the Secretaries, as Adams said, to "ingratiate themselves personally with the members of Congress."[54] Here indeed was incentive positively to dissociate themselves from any presidential policy objectives likely to meet with substantial opposition in Congress, for what aspiring candidate would knowingly attach himself to a cause that would antagonize those who did the nominating? Here was even political incentive for a Secretary to work actively *against* the Chief Executive, or to lay snares and traps for him if that might advance his own chances of replacing the man in the White House.

Crawford was more wary than candid in his remarks [in cabinet]. . . . [He] flattered the President with the hope that there might be a majority of Congress agreeing in opinion with [the President]. . . . Crawford knows better. But "dans les malheurs de nos meilleurs amis nous trouvons toujours quelque chose qui ne nous déplait pas." Crawford is not unwilling to see this disagreement between the President and Congress fester and inflame. It will all turn to his account.[55]

The conclusion to be drawn from the very great superiority of congressional over presidential bargaining advantages with department heads is this: the capacity of Jeffersonian Presidents to exercise leadership over their own top executives was crucially conditioned upon their ability to exercise leadership over Congress. To the extent that a President commanded influence in Congress, he acquired those indispensable ingredients of leadership in a system of separated institutions sharing powers: a currency with which to bargain; tools with which to persuade; sanctions and services to make it worth the while of the Secretaries to go along with the President. With influence over enough legislators, a President's recognized authority to dismiss heads of departments became more than an empty threat. With leadership over Congress, a President's support or denial of support might mean the difference between fulfillment or frustration of a Secretary's aims for policy and appropriations for his department. To the extent that a President commanded influence on the Hill, his willingness or refusal to intercede with legislators became a matter of vital importance to Secretaries striving to satisfy manifold and often conflicting legislative demands. The consequences to a Secretary of resisting the policy aims of a President who commanded influence on the Hill, of failing to cooperate in the furtherance of those aims, of committing sabotage upon his policy objectives, were enormously amplified. Keeping in the good graces of a President having partisans of his own on the Hill would become politically prudent for a Secretary aspiring to the congressional caucus nomination.

Leadership of Congress was indispensable not only to leadership over the executive branch but also to consensus and cohesion in the executive establishment. A cohesive congressional party amenable to the President would leave the President considerably freer to select cabinet members for their loyalty to himself and would obviate the need for importing spokesmen for rival factions into his cabinet. A cohesive congressional party under presidential leadership would not exacerbate "inherent forces of disintegration" within the executive community by projecting intralegislative rivalries over policy and patronage across the Tiber; and a cohesive congressional party would offer far fewer opportunities for the internal rivalries of the executive branch to buttress themselves with factional followings on the Hill. By the same token, the cohesive cabinet thus afforded would reinforce and facilitate the President's efforts to keep the congressional party cohesive under his leadership, depending as the Jeffersonian Presidents did upon the help of Secretaries for carrying their programs forward on Capitol Hill.

Lacking any but the most meager bargaining tools of their own, then, Chief Executives in Jeffersonian times needed to enlist the aid of Congress in maintaining the allegiance and cohesion of their own department heads. Leadership over Congress was the *sine qua non* for the President's mastery over his own house.

Dependence of presidential leadership west of the Tiber upon presidential leadership east of the Tiber provides the best answer to the question of why the decline of presidential power followed similar arcs on both the congressional and the executive side. Jefferson's Presidency was the only one to operate under the conditions prerequisite for leadership of the executive branch. Because he was the only President who succeeded in maintaining harmony and leadership on Capitol Hill he was the only one who succeeded in maintaining harmony and leadership in the executive establishment.

Then, as swiftly as Congress deserted Jefferson on the embargo in 1808-9, just so swiftly did Jefferson lose the support of his cabinet on that policy.[56] Madison could not lead Congress, and his cabinet was a failure from the outset. A Congress split into warring factions produced a cabinet split into warring factions; and a Congress which would not follow the President's lead produced a cabinet both insubordinate and disloyal. As quickly as Congress perfected the means, through its committee system, for challenging presidential dominance of the executive bureaucracies, just so quickly did the spokesmen for those bureaucracies move out of the President's orbit of influence. Desertion of the President then became such a political necessity that Monroe's most loyal Secretary felt free to notify the President that his bond of allegiance to the Chief Executive was at an end; accountability to a congressional committee hostile to the President was his excuse. Congress having already displaced the President as master in his own house, it remained only for the cabinet to master the President. After one hopeless try at recouping leadership, the last Jeffersonian President obliged. Unwillingly and with inexpressible inner anguish, but with as much grace as possible, he served as caretaker of the White House and received instructions from his cabinet.

Prisoner in a public mansion house, Adams likened himself to another and more famous prisoner, and cried

> O Richard! O mon roi!
> L'univers t'abandonne.[57]

It was a fitting epitaph for the Jeffersonian experiment in party government under presidential leadership. For such was the estate to which the Presidency had fallen: powerless on the Hill; powerless west of the Tiber; reigning, not ruling, and deserted by all.

It remains to note, in conclusion, the consequences of the political destruction of the Presidency. They may be stated quite simply. Loss of presidential leadership over Congress put an end to any possibility that a legislative establishment fractured into sociopolitical blocs and incapable of developing leadership within itself could perform the necessary functions of governing. Loss of presidential leadership over the executive branch ended any possibility that an executive establishment fractured into sociopolitical blocs could perform those functions in Congress' stead.

For nowhere did leadership arise to supplant that of the Presidency under Jefferson. Quite the contrary. As the Presidency became powerless, the forces of fission proceeded apace. Factions multiplied on the Hill and extended their divisive influence across the Tiber. Contending politicians of the executive bureaucracies reached out to the Hill for partisans. The last vestiges of an originally vital ruling party disappeared, the victim of a governmental establishment which would not, could not, govern. Contention mounted into conflict, and conflict grew into anarchy.

It is a striking irony that Madison's words in *The Federalist*, No. 10, describing the evils government was instituted to remedy, describe the governmental establishment itself at the terminal phase of the Jeffersonian era:

A zeal for different opinions concerning religion, concerning government, and many other points . . . an attachment to different leaders ambitiously contending for pre-eminence and power; or to persons of other descriptions whose fortunes have been interesting to the human passions, have . . . divided mankind into parties, inflamed them with mutual animosity, and rendered them much more disposed to vex and oppress each other than to co-operate for their common good. So strong is this propensity . . . to fall into mutual animosities, that where no substantial occasion presents itself, the most frivolous and fanciful distinctions have been sufficient to kindle their unfriendly passions and excite their most violent conflicts.

The Jeffersonian era thus ends in a crisis of power at the center of power: a crisis directly and specifically resulting from a failure to solve the constitutional problem of government by "separate and rival interests."

Such an establishment could not long substitute for a government. New solutions would have to be devised. Two, perhaps, were foreshadowed in the 1820s when two frustrated politicians—two factional leaders—abandoned Washington for home.

One was John Calhoun, bound for Carolina and armed with the doctrine of nullification. He went to prepare the legislatures of the South to take power away from Washington, where power he had lost.

The other was Andrew Jackson, bound for Tennessee. He went to arouse a sleeping giant of a people, and ride their fervor back to Washington, where he too had once lost.

Both their solutions were to be tried, and both for a while would succeed. But the constructive solution was the first to be tried, and the first to succeed. Victory went first to the Jacksonians: they who sought to solve the problem of government by separate and rival interests by solving the problem of government at a distance and out of sight. Victory went first to those who blazed new paths to Washington with the mighty sword of democracy.

It is well that the Jacksonians did succeed in 1828. For the nation could not have survived the ordeal of 1860 with a governmental community such as it had in the Jeffersonian era.

GOVERNING THE NEW NATION: THE JEFFERSONIAN EXPERIENCE

The first new nation of the modern age emerged from its dawn with a government thrice handicapped. A remote and indifferent citizenry failed to contribute that civic attachment which a representative government founded on the sovereignty of the people needs above all; and a new and isolated governmental establishment having only negligible engagement in the lives of the people failed to provide sufficient stimuli to overcome this indifference. A second handicap was the organization of the governmental establishment itself. The risk of crippling instability which inheres in a system of government by separate and rival interests was enormously amplified by a governing group which made much the same choices as to their informal organization at Washington that the constitutional framers had made for the formal organization of government. Separate social systems formed around separate branches of government; rival subsystems formed within each of these. There was no adequate social process for stabilizing inevitable conflict among these groups, and there was no adequate political process for producing a consensus upon which to govern. As a third handicap, negative attitudes toward power among the rulers themselves—attitudes deeply rooted in American culture—rationalized a governmental community which denied dominant power to any subgroup and enduring leadership to any position at Washington. Antipower attitudes justified artlessness in politics and stifled the impulse toward that statecraft which seems essential for the effective management of conflict in a government designed to ensure conflict.

Common membership in a victorious political party was the only web which might have bound disparate groups at Washington into an association capable of governing. But the party tie proved too fragile to hold a governing group together. Its membership deployed across a fragmented structure, the majority party was subjected to balkanizing forces which required the unifying influence of leadership to counteract. The only position in the Washington community which might have supplied that leadership was the Presidency. For a brief period the Presidency under Jefferson did so. But a Constitution which denied the Chief Executive any significant resources for leadership and community values which denied legitimacy to presidential leadership rendered the Presidency incapable of leading under any but the extraordinary circumstance of a party membership which had no pressing incentives for opposing the President. Opposition in Congress, triggered by transitory constituency opposition to injurious economic policies, brought presidential leadership to an abrupt end in 1808, and from that time forward the Presidency was reduced to the status of a figurehead. Without leadership, the majority party degenerated into warring factions—an accelerating process which neither the gravest of external threats to the nation, nor domestic issuelessness following war, nor rarely equaled votes of popular confidence in the regime served to brake.

Constitutional orthodoxy in the organization of power at Washington thus emerged triumphant over the Jeffersonian experiment in party government under presidential leadership. To the analyst of the early governmental community, that outcome seems to have been foreordained. For the Jeffersonian experiment, in both its objective (dominance of government by a single group) and in the means necessary to secure that objective (presidential leadership), ran counter not merely to constitutional mandate but also to the preferred organizational behavior and the deep-seated values of the rulers themselves.

The triumph of constitutional orthodoxy inspires new respect for the framers' gift for organizational planning, and it reveals the irreversibility of the American commitment to the form of government decided upon in 1787–88. The consequences of that triumph in the Jeffersonian era, however, are sobering to contemplate. For constitutional orthodoxy at Washington deprived the nation of the only security it had against an egregiously unstable government. The destruction of the majority party as a meaningful entity left the nation with a governmental establishment lacking the means either to check burgeoning forces of disintegration within itself or to resolve those conflicts which were bound, sooner or later, to irrupt into the Washington community from the outside. Constitutional principles had triumphed, but at the cost of viable government.

The failure of the Jeffersonian experiment in party government can only be interpreted, therefore, as a crisis of profound significance in the history of the republic. A crossroads had been reached, and a national destiny hung in the balance. Twenty-eight years had demonstrated both the futility of attempting any fundamental change in the constitutional scheme of power and, at the same time, the utter inadequacy of that scheme as a system of government. The only possible salvation for the nation lay in the development of a capacity for rulership within a constitutional framework deliberately designed to make rulership difficult. Keys were needed to unlock the American genius for politics. Keys were needed to liberate the governmental community from bondage to constitutional orthodoxy and give it freedom enough to rule.

The Jacksonian revolution seems to have provided those keys. An aroused and demanding citizenry would nudge the officeholders at Washington to develop the political skills and the political organization necessary to satisfy popular demands—and necessary also for a viable government. A disposition to negotiate differences, a willingness of disparate groups to collaborate, and a craft of consensus-building would ultimately ensue from the need to win the confidence and the votes of a politically attentive populace. Jacksonian democracy would provide both incentives and rationale for the development of organized parties—incentives and rationale which popular indifference withheld from the Jeffersonians. Serving the needs of an aroused and demanding citizenry would relieve power-seeking from the onus of self-seeking at Washington, and would provide incontestable justification for leadership initiatives in a governmental community deeply committed to the representative principle. Above all, Jacksonian democracy would retrieve a chance for leadership for the Presidency. Moving the nominating function from Washington to a popular forum would release incoming Presidents from bondage to kingmakers in Congress and would relieve the governmental community of the acute stresses of succession struggles which were deeply prejudicial to presidential leadership. Nomination and election by popular acclaim would give the Presidency the stature of popular spokesmanship and an independent electoral strength which was convertible, on occasion, to bargaining advantages over Congress. Party organization outside Washington, dependent in part upon presidential patronage, would begin to gird the Presidency for pressure politics. In a nation pervasively mistrustful of government, democracy, and democracy alone, could convert a figure of authority into a personage of national influence.

It would seem, then, that the problem of government by separate and rival interests was not to be solved but by solving also the problem of government at a distance and out of sight. A major lesson of the Jeffersonian experience seems to be that a viable governmental establishment could not be maintained as long as the governmental community confronted a remote and indifferent citizenry. The politicians at Philadelphia in 1787, but more significantly the politicians at Washington from 1800 to 1828, had created a government that could not work—could not survive—without democracy.

That Jacksonian democracy would not provide a final solution to the problem of government by separate and rival interests is evident from the events of 1860: an aroused citizenry would in time feed passionately felt conflicts into the Washington community which were beyond either reconciliation or avoidance by the rulers. But in 1828 Jacksonian democracy seems to have been the only alternative to the disintegration of the only institution which could hold the nation together: the Washington community. At the very least, Jacksonian democracy brought time enough—another three decades—for the polity to have a fair chance of surviving in the face of open insurrection.

This study must therefore close with a query. Given the functional value of the Jacksonian revolution, was it an accident of history?

If so, Americans have to thank a benevolent fate for the survival of the nation and the achievement of democracy.

If not, Americans have to thank their politicians for national survival and the creation of a democratic system.

If not, we have to thank that which we delight to scorn for that which we most cherish. We have to thank the thirst for power among ingenious politicians for the creation of American democracy.

NOTES

Abbreviations Used in the Notes

AC   *Annals of Congress*
ASP   *American State Papers*
CHS *Records*   Columbia Historical Society, *Records*

Prologue: The Community Plan

1. See Kite, *L'Enfant and Washington,* for a documentary record of L'Enfant's involvement in the planning and building of the capital.
2. The phrase is George Washington's, quoted *ibid.,* p. 159.
3. Quoted *ibid.,* p. 53.
4. Quoted in Varnum, *Seat of Government,* p. 38.
5. Quoted in Kite, *L'Enfant and Washington,* p. 78. Although a few congressmen complained that the President's house was not made adjunct and subordinate to the halls of Congress, L'Enfant's scheme was readily preferred over other modes of organizing the community. Jefferson's idea for the capital, though it differed in other respects, coincided with L'Enfant's plan in separating the presidential and the congressional centers. See *District of Columbia Sesquicentennial* [exhibition catalogue], plate no. 57.
6. Quoted in Varnum, *Seat of Government,* p. 38.
7. Quoted in Kite, *L'Enfant and Washington,* p. 57.
8. *Ibid.,* p. 47.
9. *Ibid.,* p. 37.

Chapter 1: "Government at a Distance and Out of Sight"

1. New York *Advertiser,* January 27, 1791.
2. Quoted in Tindall, *Origin and Government,* p. 34.

3. Nash, " '. . . and Distinguished Guests,' " *Princeton Alumni Weekly,* LXIV, No. 1 (September 24, 1963), 37.

4. *Centennial History,* p. 69.

5. While the Constitution (Article I, Section 8) gives Congress exclusive authority over the District of Columbia, the residents of the District in fact enjoyed the franchise, as though citizens of Maryland or Virginia, for a decade after the area was ceded to the national government by these states. The status quo was changed only when Congress chose in 1801 to assume actual jurisdiction over the District and to refuse local requests to stipulate in the statute that the local population could continue to vote. Disfranchisement was known beforehand, and acknowledged in Congress, to be the effect of this refusal. The language of the Constitution would not appear to have prevented Congress from making an accommodation to the local citizenry similar to that which permits residents of other federally owned and controlled land—military reservations, for example—to vote. See Green, *Washington,* pp. 11–12, 24–27, 29–31.

6. Quoted in Bryan, I, 12.

7. The clause, in the same wording, originated in the Pinckney draft of the Constitution and was adopted by the convention without debate. In only four of the state ratifying conventions was the provision discussed, opposition being voiced by some members of the North Carolina and Virginia conventions. *Ibid.,* pp. 20–21.

8. The legislative history of attempts to fix a site for the capital is summarized in Tindall, *Origin and Government,* pp. 30–74. On the same subject, see also Bryan, *History,* I, 4–7; *Centennial History,* pp. 70, 76–77; Maclay, *Journal,* pp. 260–61.

9. Hopkinson, *Miscellaneous Essays,* I, 188.

10. See Busey, *Pictures of Washington,* p. 23.

11. 1 Stats. 130; Busey, *Pictures of Washington,* p. 23.

12. Quoted in *Centennial History,* p. 80.

13. Tindall, *Origin and Government,* pp. 72–75.

14. Quoted in Varnum, *Seat of Government,* pp. 17–18. (Italics in the original.)

15. See *ibid.,* p. 12.

16. 1 Stats. 130; *Centennial History,* p. 84.

17. Bryan, *History,* I, 123 ff.

18. Whether or not from the same motive, the same purpose was served when Washington asked Congress for authority to acquire additional land south of the Anacostia. *Ibid.,* pp. 120, 127–29.

19. *Ibid.,* pp. 134, 173.

20. *Ibid.,* pp. 159–60; Kite, *L'Enfant and Washington,* p. 78. It seems that the President and his advisers never considered holding the sale at

some commercial or financial center where men of means congregated or, alternatively, making lots purchasable across the country at the offices of port collectors and postmasters.

21. Bryan, *History*, I, 204–5; Busey, *Pictures of Washington*, p. 50.

22. Bryan, *History*, I, 213–14; Varnum, *Seat of Government*, pp. 31–32; Ellis, *Sights and Secrets*, pp. 56–58.

23. Busey, *Pictures of Washington*, p. 50.

24. *Ibid.;* Green, *Washington*, p. 17.

25. Bryan, *History*, I, 219, note 3.

26. Busey, *Pictures of Washington*, p. 50.

27. Bryan, *History*, I, 218–20, 298.

28. *Ibid.*, pp. 187, 264–70; *ASP*, Misc. Ser., I, 133.

29. Major L'Enfant, who was dismissed for his failure to cooperate in the efforts to sell lots to the public, had forewarned President Washington of failure: "To look upon the property . . . as a source of supply and to use it to defray the first expenses," he wrote in 1791, "would be to destroy the capital from the very beginning." L'Enfant predicted to the President that the first sale "will fail through lack of numbers. It will be confined to a few individual speculators who will not be interested to improve the lots; besides the low sale in the first instance may prove injurious to subsequent ones by serving as a precedent. Moreover I apprehend the underselling of lots . . . will rather disgrace the whole business." Kite, *L'Enfant and Washington*, pp. 68–71.

30. Bryan, *History*, I, 271–72.

31. *Ibid.*, pp. 231–32, 323; Busey, *Pictures of Washington*, pp. 51–53; Twining, *Travels in America*, pp. 100–104.

32. Bryan, *History*, I, 245, 287.

33. *Ibid.*, pp. 162–63, 217, 278, 362; Nicolay, *Our Capital*, p. 68.

34. *ASP*, Misc. Ser., I, 256–67; Gibbs, *Memoirs*, II, 377; Busey, *Pictures of Washington*, pp. 142–47.

35. La Rochefoucauld-Liancourt, *Travels*, II, 652.

36. Bryan, *History*, I, 291, 415, 434.

37. Quoted in Green, *Washington*, p. 23.

38. Bryan, *History*, I, 162–63, 217, 278, 284, 289, 362.

39. Gibbs, *Memoirs*, II, 378.

40. Henry Adams, *Gallatin*, p. 252.

41. Bryan, *History*, I, 190; Varnum, *Seat of Government*, p. 33, note.

42. Gibbs, *Memoirs*, II, 378.

43. Green, *Washington*, pp. 27–28.

44. Bryan, *History*, I, 553–54.

45. Green, *Washington*, pp. 28, 72, 83.

46. *Ibid.*, pp. 34–35.

47. *Ibid.*, pp. 59, 73–75, 83–85.
48. Tindall, *Origin and Government*, p. 80; *AC*, XXVIII (13th Congress, 3d sess.), 396.
49. Foster, *Jeffersonian America*, p. 7.
50. Hamilton, *Men and Manners*, II, 29.
51. Trollope, *Domestic Manners*, I, 310.
52. Cooley, *Etiquette*, p. 56.
53. Itemized population statistics for Washington and the other towns in the District, taken from *U.S. Census*, Second through Ninth, 1800–1870, are most conveniently available in Green, *Washington*, p. 21.

54.   *Percent of population increase*
                                  1810–30

District of Columbia	65.8
United States	77.9
Suffolk County (Boston)	181.1
New York County	210.2
Philadelphia County	328.8
Baltimore County	367.7

Source: *U.S. Census*, Third and Fifth.

55. Busey, *Pictures of Washington*, p. 353. The *Memoirs* of John Quincy Adams offers abundant documentation for the presence of such supplicants and sycophants, who plagued Adams no less as President than as Secretary of State.
56. Bryan, *History*, I, 541.
57. Gibbs, *Memoirs*, II, 377–78.
58. *ASP*, Misc. Ser., I, 256; Bryan, *History*, I, 355–56, 470–72.
59. *Centennial History*, pp. 408–9. Seven hundred forty-six Negroes, most of them slaves, comprised 23.2 percent of Washington's population in 1800; Negroes comprised 28.9 percent of its population in 1830. Green, *Washington*, p. 21.
60. Green, *Washington*, pp. 41–42, 88, 90–94, 101–2; Bryan, *History*, I, 540–53.
61. During the period from 1797 to 1829, when Congress ranged from about one-fourth to less than one-half its present size, there were, on the average, 16 resignations in each Congress, as compared with an average of 14 resignations per Congress in the modern legislative body (76th through 80th Congresses). Of these resigners, more than two thirds continued their office-holding careers elsewhere than in Washington. For details, see p. 263, note 70, below.
62. See White, *The Jeffersonians*, pp. 302–3.
63. Foster, *Jeffersonian America*, p. 3. Compare this assessment with Hamilton's prediction in *The Federalist*, No. 17: "It is a known fact in human nature, that its affections are commonly weak in proportion to

the distance or diffusiveness of the object. Upon the same principle that a man is more attached to his family than to his neighborhood, to his neighborhood than to the community at large, the people of each State would be apt to feel a stronger bias towards their local governments than towards the government of the Union. . . . There is one transcendent advantage belonging to the province of the State governments . . . the ordinary administration of criminal and civil justice. This, of all others, is the most powerful, most universal, and most attractive source of popular obedience and attachment. It is that which . . . regulating all those personal interests and familiar concerns to which the sensibility of individuals is more immediately awake, contributes, more than any other circumstance, to impressing upon the minds of the people, affection, esteem, and reverence towards the government. . . . The operations of the national government, on the other hand, falling less immediately under the observation of the mass of the citizens, the benefits derived from it will chiefly be perceived and attended to by speculative men. Relating to more general interests, they will be less apt to come home to the feelings of the people; and, in proportion, less likely to inspire an habitual sense of obligation, and an active sentiment of attachment."

64. *AC*, XLI (18th Congress, 1st sess.), 1304.

65. Gibbs, *Memoirs*, II, 377.

66. "In America the attempt [to ascertain national wealth] has never been made; for how would such an investigation be possible in a new country . . . where the national government is not assisted by a multitude of agents whose exertions it can command and direct to one end, and where statistics are not studied because no one is able to collect the necessary documents?" Tocqueville, *Democracy in America*, I, 228–29.

67. *"Private and confidential: if such a thing can be,"* the Secretary of the Treasury headed one of his letters. Henry Adams, *Gallatin*, p. 441.

68. Lubell, *The Future of American Politics*, p. 4.

Chapter 2: "The National Bantling"

1. Alfred J. Morrison, ed., *The District in the XVIIIth Century*, Section V, p. 45; Willson, *Friendly Relations*, p. 97.

2. Busey, *Pictures of Washington*, pp. 56–57.

3. Green, *Washington*, p. 66.

4. Howitt, *Letters*, p. 78.

5. John Quincy Adams, *Memoirs*, IV, 409.

6. Green, *Washington*, p. 94.

7. *Ibid.*; Henry Adams, *Gallatin*, p. 253.

8. Foster, *Jeffersonian America*, p. 17.

9. Howitt, *Letters*, p. 80.
10. Pope-Hennessy, ed., *Aristocratic Journey*, p. 165.
11. Mann, ed., *A Yankee Jeffersonian*, p. 202.
12. Story, ed., *Life*, I, 160, 162.
13. Bryan, *History*, I, 626–27.
14. Abigail Adams, *Letters*, p. 240.
15. Margaret B. Smith, *First Forty Years*, p. 10.
16. Nicolay, *Our Capital*, pp. 272–73.
17. Clark, "The Trollopes," CHS *Records*, XXXVII–XXXVIII, 91.
18. Quoted in Wharton, *Social Life*, p. 60.
19. John Quincy Adams, *Memoirs*, IV, 74.
20. Hamilton, *Men and Manners*, II, 30.
21. Margaret B. Smith, *First Forty Years*, pp. 27–28.
22. Henry Adams, *The Education of Henry Adams*, pp. 44, 99.
23. Bryan, *History*, I, 618.
24. *Ibid.*, p. 610.
25. Latrobe, *Capitol and Washington*, pp. 25 ff.
26. Coke, *Subaltern's Furlough*, I, 89.
27. Todd, *Washington*, p. 63.
28. Quincy, *Life*, p. 137.
29. Wilson, *Congressional Government*, pp. 86–87.
30. *AC*, XVII (10th Congress, 1st sess.), 1061.
31. Gibbs, *Memoirs*, II, 377.
32. Abigail Adams, *Letters*, p. 241.
33. Bryan, *History*, II, 236; Singleton, *White House*, I, 16; Margaret B. Smith, *First Forty Years*, p. 246.
34. "The cause of decay, both in this house and in the Capitol is to be found . . . in the green state of the timber when first used, in its original bad quality, and its long exposure to the weather, before the buildings could be roofed." Quoted in Singleton, *White House*, I, 16.
35. *Ibid.*, pp. xxiii, 16; Nicolay, *Our Capital*, pp. 67–68; Bryan, *History*, I, 377; Janson, *The Stranger*, p. 213.
36. Brant, *James Madison, the President*, p. 32.
37. Janson, *The Stranger*, p. 213.
38. Morris, ed., *Diary*, II, 394–95. "All we lack here are good houses, wine cellars, decent food, learned men, attractive women and other such trifles to make our city perfect . . . it is the best city in the world to live in—in the future."
39. Quoted in Green, *Washington*, p. 45.
40. Trollope, *Domestic Manners*, I, 333.
41. Hines, *Early Recollections of Washington City*, p. 75.
42. Mann, ed., *A Yankee Jeffersonian*, p. 207.
43. John Quincy Adams, *Memoirs*, VI, 478.

44. Hamilton, *Men and Manners*, II, 35.
45. Margaret B. Smith, *First Forty Years*, p. 213.
46. *Ibid.*, p. 137.
47. Foster, *Jeffersonian America*, p. 9.
48. Margaret B. Smith, *First Forty Years*, p. 273.

Chapter 3: Self-Image: "Splendid Torment"

1. Melish, *Travels*, I, 203.
2. Plumer, *Life*, p. 337; Bruce, *Randolph*, I, 559.
3. Nicolay, *Our Capital*, p. 67; Beveridge, *The Life of John Marshall*, III, 1.
4. Gibbs, *Memoirs*, II, 378; Henry Adams, *Randolph*, p. 293.
5. Mann, ed., *A Yankee Jeffersonian*, p. 196.
6. *AC*, XXX (14th Congress, 2d sess.), 503, remarks of Mr. Randolph of Virginia.
7. Mann, ed., *A Yankee Jeffersonian*, p. 215; Gibbs, *Memoirs*, II, 378; Story, ed., *Life*, I, 311.
8. Nicolay, *Our Capital*, p. 63.
9. Quincy, *Life*, p. 306.
10. Henry Adams, *Randolph*, p. 293.
11. John Quincy Adams, *Diary*, p. 186, note.
12. Green, *Washington*, p. 89. The figure of $15,000 excludes amounts appropriated for the public buildings and small contributions toward road maintenance.
13. *Ibid.*, pp. 87, 90.
14. *AC*, XXVIII (13th Congress, 3d sess.), 396.
15. Green, *Washington*, p. 65.
16. Kennedy, *Wirt*, II, 172.
17. Margaret B. Smith, *First Forty Years*, p. 45.
18. *Ibid.*, p. 80, quoting Jefferson.
19. Kennedy, *Wirt*, II, 172.
20. Quincy, *Life*, pp. 186–88, 137.
21. Foster, *Jeffersonian America*, p. 9.
22. Gibbs, *Memoirs*, II, 498–99.
23. Margaret B. Smith, *First Forty Years*, p. 78.
24. John Quincy Adams, *Diary*, p. 287.
25. Kennedy, *Wirt*, II, 135–36, 172.
26. *AC*, XXX (14th Congress, 2d sess.), 551, remarks of Mr. Randolph of Virginia.
27. *Ibid.*, p. 607, remarks of Mr. Wilde of Georgia.
28. Kennedy, *Wirt*, II, 172–73, 242.

29. Margaret B. Smith, *First Forty Years*, p. 77, quoting Jefferson.
30. *AC*, XXX (14th Congress, 2d sess.), 670, remarks of Mr. Wendover of New York.
31. Margaret B. Smith, *First Forty Years*, pp. 165, 204.
32. *Ibid.*, pp. 94, 204.
33. Maclay, *Journal*, p. 19. Senator Maclay's observations predate the move to Washington, but they are so consistent with the observations made by members of the Washington community as to warrant their use here.
34. Plumer, *Life*, p. 245.
35. Quincy, *Life*, pp. 186–87.
36. *AC*, XXX (14th Congress, 2d sess.), 598, remarks of Mr. Wilde of Georgia.
37. *Ibid.*, p. 601, remarks of Mr. Wilde of Georgia.
38. *Ibid.*, p. 504, remarks of Mr. King of Massachusetts.
39. Margaret B. Smith, *First Forty Years*, p. 77.
40. *AC*, XXX (14th Congress, 2d sess.), 602, remarks of Mr. Wilde of Georgia.
41. Quoted in Ford, "Jefferson and the Newspaper," CHS *Records*, VIII, 87.
42. *AC*, XXX (14th Congress, 2d sess.), 642, remarks of Mr. Woodward of South Carolina.
43. *Ibid.*, p. 500, remarks of Mr. Randolph of Virginia.
44. *Ibid.*, p. 576, remarks of Mr. Calhoun of South Carolina.
45. *Ibid.*, p. 555, remarks of Mr. Hulbert of Massachusetts.
46. Quoted in Bruce, *Randolph*, I, 551.
47. Margaret B. Smith, *First Forty Years*, p. 349.
48. Kennedy, *Wirt*, II, 242.
49. Margaret B. Smith, *First Forty Years*, p. 77, quoting Jefferson.
50. Kennedy, *Wirt*, II, 242.
51. *AC*, XXX (14th Congress, 2d sess.), 637, remarks of Mr. Grosvenor of New York.
52. John Quincy Adams, *Memoirs*, IV, 242.
53. *AC*, XXX (14th Congress, 2d sess.), 645, remarks of Mr. Edwards of North Carolina.
54. *Ibid.*, p. 637, remarks of Mr. Grosvenor of New York.
55. John Quincy Adams, *Memoirs*, IV, 71.
56. Kennedy, *Wirt*, II, 243.
57. *AC*, XXX (14th Congress, 2d sess.), 514, remarks of Mr. Johnson of Kentucky.
58. Margaret B. Smith, *First Forty Years*, p. 280.
59. *Ibid.*, p. 310.

60. *AC,* XXX (14th Congress, 2d sess.), 510, remarks of Mr. Johnson of Kentucky.

61. Plumer, *Life,* p. 336.

62. Quoted in Margaret B. Smith, *First Forty Years,* p. 190.

63. *Ibid.,* pp. 77, 190.

64. John Quincy Adams, *Memoirs,* VI, 98.

65. George Clinton to Pierre Van Cortlandt, Jr., February 20, 1807, MS, Van Cortlandt Letters, New York Public Library.

66. Kennedy, *Wirt,* II, 172.

67. John Quincy Adams, *Memoirs,* IV, 242.

68. *AC,* XXX (14th Congress, 2d sess.), 330, remarks of Mr. Randolph of Virginia.

69. These figures are based on a study of the *Biographical Directory of the American Congress, 1774–1961.* Comparisons with resignations in the modern Senate and House are based on the number of resignations occurring in the 76th through the 80th Congresses.

70. Career information on these 229 resigners was obtained largely from the biographical sketches appearing in the *Biographical Directory of the American Congress.* One hundred fifty-nine of them (69.0 percent) held other public jobs not in Washington after they resigned. One hundred and five (45.9 percent) took other public jobs not in Washington within a year of their resignations. Of these 105, 58 (55.2 percent) took jobs immediately in state government; 44 (41.9 percent) went into jobs in the executive branch or judiciary of the federal government outside Washington; and 3 (2.9 percent) took jobs in local or county government.

71. It is likely that many other members "resigned" from Congress by choosing not to seek reelection, and that this helps explain the very high turnover in the early Congresses at each biennial election. (For turnover rates, see Table 4.) The extent to which other public jobs may have been preferred over congressional service, even among members who did not terminate their congressional service by resignation, is suggested by the fact that, of the 210 members of the 13th Congress on whom adequate biographical data are available, 123 (58.6 percent) held other public jobs after their service in Congress was terminated.

72. The President received an annual salary of $25,000; Supreme Court justices, $3,500; department heads, $6,000 (by 1828); members of Congress, $8 per day (after 1818) while Congress was in session, plus traveling expenses. Among the civil staff, the large majority earned between $800 and $1,400 annually. See White, *The Jeffersonians,* Chapter 27.

73. John Quincy Adams, *Diary,* pp. 420–21.

74. John Quincy Adams, *Memoirs,* VII, 120.

75. Margaret B. Smith, *First Forty Years,* pp. 382–83.

76. *AC,* XXX (14th Congress, 2d sess.), 515, remarks of Mr. Ross of Pennsylvania.

77. "There has never been an instant before of so unanimous an opinion of the people, and that through every State in the Union," commented Jefferson; "almost the entire mass [of Representatives] will go out, not only those who supported the law or voted for it, or skulked from the vote, but those who voted against it or opposed it actively, if they took the money." Jefferson, *Works,* XII, 35–36. The percentage of the membership of the 14th Congress who failed to return to the 15th Congress was 63.1, higher by 11.1 percentage points than any other biennial turnover from the beginning of national government to at least 1833. See Table 4 for complete figures.

78. *AC,* XXX (14th Congress, 2d sess.), 330, 500, remarks of Mr. Randolph of Virginia.

79. From the Kentucky Resolution of 1798. See Commager, ed., *Documents of American History,* p. 181.

80. *AC,* XXX (14th Congress, 2d sess.), 517, remarks of Mr. Barbour of Virginia.

81. How to reconcile the values of individual self-reliance and autonomy with the practical need for accommodating to constituency pressures was a problem that did not often have to be faced by the members of the early governmental community. The problem was foreshadowed in Jeffersonian times, however, and on at least one occasion was explicitly confronted. This was during a broad-ranging House debate in 1817, in which one of the issues was the duty of Representatives to obey constituency "instructions" and "mandates." See *AC,* XXX (14th Congress, 2d sess.), 483–84, 574–610, 700–715.

82. Neustadt, *Presidential Power,* p. 33.

*Chapter 4: Organization: Separate Societies
for Separate Branches*

1. Pope-Hennessy, ed., *Aristocratic Journey,* p. 175.
2. Hamilton, *Men and Manners,* II, 30.
3. D'Arusmont, *Views of Society,* p. 372.
4. Cooper, *Notions,* II, 11.
5. See, for example, Leech, *Reveille in Washington,* pp. 10–11. Between the townspeople of these subcommunities, and especially between those residing on Capitol Hill and residents of the White House vicinity, there was rivalry and bad feeling dating from the earliest years of the capital. See Bryan, *History,* I, 273; La Rochefoucauld-Liancourt, *Travels,* II, 628–32. In Jacksonian times, a covert culture of combat developed be-

tween them with the formation of "rival crowds of young men or Hood-
lums" bearings such names as the " 'Gum-balls,' 'Round Tops,' and 'Never
Sweats' of the First Ward [White House area] . . . and the 'Rams' of
Capitol Hill. It was dangerous then for a stranger to go outside of his
neighborhood into the territory controlled by a rival band." Busey, *Pictures of Washington*, p. 222.

6. Nicolay, *Our Capital*, p. 68.

7. Cooper, *Notions*, II, 15–16, 18; Nicolay, *Our Capital*, p. 90; Green,
Washington, p. 46.

8. Henry Adams, *Gallatin*, p. 252.

9. Janson, *The Stranger*, p. 215.

10. Cooper, *Notions*, II, 15. The Navy Yard settlement in 1860 was
still a "village community . . . rural and self-contained, although it was
connected with the rest of the city by an omnibus line," populated mostly
by "the mechanics, laborers, carpenters and office workers who were employed at the yard." Leech, *Reveille in Washington*, p. 10.

11. Bryan, *History*, I, 449–50, 527, 609; Trollope, *Domestic Manners*, I,
319.

12. Henry Adams, *Gallatin*, p. 252.

13. *Ibid.*, p. 253.

14. Crowninshield, ed., *Letters*, p. xiii.

15. Henry Adams, *Gallatin*, p. 252.

16. *National Intelligencer*, selected issues from 1801 to 1804.

17. Cooper, *Notions*, II, 20.

18. Margaret B. Smith, *First Forty Years*, pp. 13–17.

19. Bryan, *History*, I, 292.

20. Margaret B. Smith, *First Forty Years*, p. 95.

21. *Ibid.*, pp. 146–47.

22. Cooper, *Notions*, II, 20.

23. Basil Hall, *Travels*, III, 30–32.

24. Osborne, "Removal of the Government to Washington," CHS
Records, III, 149; Busey, *Pictures of Washington*, pp. 74–75; Bryan, *History*, I, 350–51, 409.

25. Bryan, *History*, I, 419–20.

26. *Ibid.*, p. 409. Churches were soon built in the executive sector
which made these arrangements unnecessary.

27. *National Intelligencer*, January 9, 1802.

28. Green, *Washington*, p. 45.

29. Bryan, *History*, I, 381; Busey, *Pictures of Washington*, p. 360.

30. Bryan, *History*, I, 335, 607–9.

31. John C. Smith, *Correspondence*, p. 208.

32. Quoted in the *National Intelligencer*, December 8, 1801.

33. Sunderland, *Sketch*, p. 15.

266 Notes to Pages 75-89

34. Henry Adams, *Randolph*, p. 217.
35. John C. Smith, *Correspondence*, pp. 204–5.
36. Singleton, *White House*, I, 17, 187–88.
37. Sunderland, *Sketch*, p. 15; Busey, *Pictures of Washington*, p. 235.
38. Bryan, *History*, I, 261.
39. Latrobe, *Capitol and Washington*, pp. 25–26; Bryan, *History*, I, 363–64; Busey, *Pictures of Washington*, p. 311.
40. Hamilton, *Men and Manners*, II, 127.
41. Margaret B. Smith, *First Forty Years*, pp. 96–97.
42. Story, ed., *Life*, I, 215–17.
43. Busey, *Pictures of Washington*, p. 315.
44. Margaret B. Smith, *First Forty Years*, p. 406.
45. Story, ed., *Life*, I, 217, 310–11, 537.
46. *The Federalist*, No. 51.
47. "The constitutional convention of 1787 is supposed to have created a government of 'separated powers.' It did nothing of the sort. Rather, it created a government of separated institutions *sharing* powers." Neustadt, *Presidential Power*, p. 33.
48. *The Federalist*, No. 51.

Chapter 5: Community and Society

1. See Arensberg, "American Communities," *American Anthropologist*, LVII, No. 6, Part 1 (December, 1955), 1148–51.
2. Foster, *Jeffersonian America*, p. 83.
3. The 439 legislators whose careers were studied include 210 members of the 13th Congress and 229 other Senators and Representatives who resigned from Congress from the 5th through the 20th Congresses. Among the members of the 13th Congress, 58.6 percent held other public jobs after leaving Congress. Among the resigners the percentage was 76.9. Of all 439, 288 or 67.9 percent held public jobs subsequent to their congressional service.
4. Busey, *Pictures of Washington*, Chapter 8.
5. There was considerable variation among states in the rate of turnover in their delegations. Two of the largest state delegations, Pennsylvania and New York, were conspicuous for their massive turnover with each of most congressional elections. John Quincy Adams noted in his diary in 1821 that "the State of New York has got into a practice of changing almost the whole of her delegation at every Congress. . . . They come with little knowledge of the general affairs of the whole Union . . . and by the time they have acquired experience necessary for the discharge of their duties their two years of service expire, and they

are heard of no more." *Memoirs*, V, 457. A study of the *Biographical Directory of the American Congress* reveals that almost none of the one-term servers from New York ever returned to Congress at a later time. It would therefore seem that the high rate of turnover was due to factors other than an evenly balanced party competition in this populous state. See also McCormick, "New Perspectives in Jacksonian Politics," *American Historical Review*, LXV (January, 1960), 288–301.

6. Based on the membership of the 13th Congress, Representatives averaged 5.1 years' continuous service in the House, and Senators 6.3 years' service in the Senate.

7. Basil Hall, *Travels*, III, 29.

8. *AC*, XXX (14th Congress, 2d sess.), 503.

9. Quincy, *Life*, pp. 186–87.

10. Martineau, *Western Travel*, I, 238, 301.

11. Basil Hall, *Travels*, III, 27.

12. Senators in the 13th Congress averaged forty-seven years of age; Representatives, forty-six.

13. Martineau, *Western Travel*, I, 301.

14. On the cultural diversity of the early nation, see Arensberg, "American Communities," *American Anthropologist*, LVII, No. 6, Part 1 (December, 1955), 1143–62.

15. Quincy, *Life*, p. 187.

16. Foster, *Jeffersonian America*, p. 83.

17. *Ibid.*, p. 84.

18. Maclay, *Journal*, p. 5.

19. Quincy, *Life*, pp. 187–88.

20. Quoted in Basil Hall, *Travels*, III, 29.

21. Quincy, *Life*, p. 125.

22. *Ibid.*, pp. 187–88.

23. Henry Adams, *Randolph*, p. 275.

24. Quincy, *Life*, p. 158.

25. Bruce, *Randolph*, I, 362.

26. See John Quincy Adams, *Diary*, p. 53; Green, *Washington*, pp. 109–10, 216; Quincy, *Life*, pp. 168 ff.; Galloway, *History of the House*, p. 46.

27. Basil Hall, *Travels*, III, 26.

28. *Ibid.*, p. 25.

29. Hamilton, *Men and Manners*, II, 78.

30. Basil Hall, *Travels*, III, 25.

31. Hamilton, *Men and Manners*, II, 79.

32. Galloway, *History of the House*, p. 70.

33. Basil Hall, *Travels*, III, 32.

34. *AC*, XXX (14th Congress, 2d sess.), 510.

35. *Ibid.*, p. 519.
36. Basil Hall, *Travels*, III, 25–26.
37. Hamilton, *Men and Manners*, II, 90–91.
38. Basil Hall, *Travels*, III, 56–57.
39. Hamilton, *Men and Manners*, II, 82–83.
40. D'Arusmont, *Views of Society*, p. 377; Plumer, *Life*, p. 342; *AC*, XXX (14th Congress, 2d sess.), 520; Margaret B. Smith, *First Forty Years*, p. 148; Basil Hall, *Travels*, III, 6–7; Hamilton, *Men and Manners*, II, 82–83; Pope-Hennessy, ed., *Aristocratic Journey*, p. 175; Bruce, *Randolph*, I, 565–66, 568.
41. Bruce, *Randolph*, I, 559.
42. The sources for all descriptive statements hereafter concerning composition, size, location, and numbers of boardinghouse groups are, except where otherwise specified, the *Congressional Directories* for the years 1807, 1809, 1816, 1822, 1828, and 1829. (The *Directory* for 1807 is the earliest available.)
43. The number of members who shared living quarters with one or more legislators from their own state decreased steadily from 81.5 percent of the total membership in 1807 to 56.4 percent in 1828. The political implications of this change in associational preferences of the members will be referred to in Chapter 9.
44. Boardinghouse groups decreased in size but increased steadily in number as the Jeffersonian era progressed. Albert Gallatin identified the total number of boardinghouse groups in 1801 as eight or nine, with his own mess being "twenty-four to thirty . . . at table." Henry Adams, *Gallatin*, p. 253. In 1807, 50.5 percent of the members lived in boardinghouse groups of 10 or more members, as against 25.3 percent in 1828; and in the same period the number of groups had increased from 17 to 28. More detailed information on these changes is presented in Table 11.
45. "Our little [traveling] party," wrote a member of the Connecticut delegation upon arriving at Washington, "took lodgings with a Mr. Peacock in one of the houses on New Jersey Avenue, with the addition of Senators Tracy, of Connecticut, and Chipman and Paine, of Vermont; and Representatives Thomas, of Maryland, and Dana, Edmund, and Griswold, of Connecticut." Busey, *Pictures of Washington*, p. 293.
46. "I dined today at Mrs. Coyles," wrote Daniel Webster in 1824. "Her house is not yet full. She says she has never had so much difficulty in making up a mess." Webster, ed., *Correspondence*, I, 355.
47. Cooley, *Etiquette*, p. 59.
48. By the end of the Jeffersonian era, however, the *Congressional Directory* had changed format, listing the members by state delegation group and only individually by boardinghouse.
49. Quincy, *Life*, p. 320.

50. Busey, *Pictures of Washington*, p. 317.

51. Nicolay, *Our Capital*, p. 292.

52. Webster, ed., *Correspondence*, I, 234. Among the few who did bring their wives, however, boardinghouse life was preferred to the isolation of a private dwelling, the couples taking a room or a suite to themselves in the boardinghouse but eating at a common mess table.

53. Busey, *Pictures of Washington*, p. 321.

54. Gibbs, *Memoirs*, II, 377.

55. Margaret B. Smith, *First Forty Years*, p. 12.

56. Busey, *Pictures of Washington*, p. 321.

57. Quincy, *Life*, p. 187.

58. Cooper, *Notions*, II, 30.

59. Henry Adams, *Gallatin*, p. 253.

60. *Ibid.*

61. Nicolay, *Our Capital*, p. 294.

62. Quincy, *Life*, p. 142.

63. Nicolay, *Our Capital*, p. 296.

64. Busey, *Pictures of Washington*, p. 321.

65. *Ibid.*, p. 293; Plumer, *Life*, p. 352.

66. As indicated in Table 8, roll calls were selected from the following five Congresses: 10th, 1st session (1807); 11th, 1st session (1809); 14th, 2d session (1816); 20th, 2d session (1828); 21st, 1st session (1829). Selection of roll calls in the above Congresses was determined by the following criteria. (*a*) Roll calls on procedural questions involving no apparent substantive issues were not analyzed. (*b*) Where the same issue was consecutively voted on, only the final vote was analyzed. (*c*) Only two roll calls on private bills in each congressional session were included. (No patterned differences in group voting behavior on these motions were apparent.) (*d*) Only those roll calls were included on which there was a substantial division in the House (see Table 9, note *a*). (*e*) Roll calls on which absenteeism or nonvoting was unusually high—typically toward the beginning or the close of a session—were not included. (*f*) All roll calls qualifying under these criteria in the 10th Congress, 1st session, and the 11th Congress, 1st session, were included in the analysis. For the remaining Congresses, the analysis, taking roll calls in the sequence in which they occurred, was stopped when group voting performance on each became sufficiently repetitive to establish the pattern. (No roll calls prior to 1807 could be analyzed because no boardinghouse lists before 1807 could be located.)

On these criteria, 2,657 group-votes (number of boardinghouse groups multiplied by number of roll calls) were yielded as the basic data for analysis.

It should be noted that 116 House roll calls fall far short of a statistically representative sample of roll calls over a period of twenty-eight years. For this reason the findings presented here should be regarded as tentative for the Jeffersonian period as a whole, and conclusive only for the specific time-periods of the congressional sessions selected for analysis. It goes without saying that the use of a statistically representative sample of roll calls for the entire Jeffersonian era would require a separate study of a scope unprecedented in the analytic literature on congressional voting. The number of group-votes analyzed here approaches the maximum that can be handled practically, short of resorting to the kind of elaborate machine methods that would be warranted only by a separate study. Roughly eighteen thousand visual scannings of 116 House vote rosters, for example, were required in order to carry out the single mechanical operation of transposing these rosters into boardinghouse vote rosters, before analysis could begin.

67. Errors in the *Congressional Directories* may account for some cases of ostensible nonagreement. Thus, for example, one Representative in the 21st Congress is listed as having been a member of two mess groups, and two legislators in other Congresses were found to be listed in the *Directory* with groups of which they were not, by direct evidence, members. It is also probable that some of the groups showing a high incidence of nonagreement were not true "messes" but rather hotel "groups," associated merely by coresidence and having none of the communal life style of the messes. In the 21st Congress, for example, the eleven Representatives living in Gadsby's Hotel agreed on only three of the twenty roll calls analyzed for that Congress in Table 8. Because it is impossible on present evidence to make a reliable distinction between hotel groups and mess groups, all groups have been included in the analysis, even where the evidence strongly suggests that a particular group lived in the hotel style. It is known, however, that there were but a very few hotel-style groups in the Jeffersonian era. See Busey, *Pictures of Washington*, Chapter 8.

68. Exploration of the voting behavior of boardinghouse groups has been limited in this study mainly to the facts demonstrating that the groups regularly voted together (Table 8) independently of the size of the majority margin in the whole House (Table 9). Further investigation is in progress on the dynamics of group agreement, including its relationship to such variables as size of the group, composition of the group, and nature of the policy issue involved. Preliminary impressions from the data might be noted here. One is that the size of the group did not have any consistent relationship to the number of times the group agreed on policy issues. Another is that a high proportion of the disagreements occurred among a relatively few groups. In the 20th Congress, for example, a mere one fifth of the boardinghouse groups supplied two thirds of the cases of nonagreement. A third impression is that interregional groups tended to

vote more often in disagreement than regional groups. In the 20th Congress, for example, five of the six groups manifesting the highest incidence of internal disagreement were markedly interregional.

69. Margaret B. Smith, *First Forty Years*, pp. 191–92.

Chapter 6: Resolving Conflict

1. Ostrogorski, "The Rise and Fall of the Nominating Caucus, Legislative and Congressional," *American Historical Review*, V, No. 2 (December, 1899), 263–64.

2. Harlow, *Legislative Methods*, pp. 191–92.

3. The influence of Harlow's interpretation is evident, for example, in Binkley, *President and Congress* (Chapter III), White, *The Jeffersonians* (pp. 45–49), Galloway, *History of the House* (pp. 97–99, 128–31), and Burns, *The Deadlock of Democracy* (pp. 36–42).

4. Party affiliations of Representatives are identified for the first time in the official record of proceedings for the 28th Congress (1843); party affiliations of Senators for the first time in the *Congressional Globe* for the following Congress. The most likely sources of information about legislators' party affiliations in the Jeffersonian era are contemporary electioneering literature and local newspapers. The task of searching these staggers the imagination and offers no assurance of yielding complete party rosters for any one Congress. Such rosters are an essential precondition for statistical analysis of party performance on roll call votes.

5. Because authoritative party rosters are unavailable, the purportedly authoritative figures on party strength found in some texts on Congress are not wholly reliable for the Jeffersonian era. The original text from which these figures are apparently derived (Alexander, *History and Procedure of the House of Representatives*, pp. 411–12) does not itself cite sources for the figures. One suspects that they are the subjective estimates made by contemporary officeholders on the basis of Senate and House votes which they considered to be "tests" of party strength. Thus, for example, Jefferson wrote in 1798 that "the issue of the question on foreign intercourse has enabled us to count the strength of parties in the H. of Representatives. It is 51 and 55 if all members were present . . . but in this computation all wavering characters are given to the other side." (Quoted in Cunningham, *The Jeffersonian Republicans*, p. 122.)

6. Two cohesive congressional parties in the pre-Jeffersonian period have been postulated by Cunningham (*The Jeffersonian Republicans*), partially on the basis of roll call voting in the 2d and 3d Congresses. The method was to examine the frequency with which Representatives voted in agreement or disagreement with James Madison, then a leading Repub-

lican in the House. Republicans were identified as those who voted in agreement with Madison on at least two thirds of the roll calls examined; Federalists were identified as those who voted with the same frequency in disagreement with Madison. Representatives who fell into neither category—numbering slightly more than half the House membership—were classified as independents. Two cohesive parties may have been the reality, as Cunningham proposes. But they may also be the fictitious creatures of the method employed, inasmuch as the method ensures that two "parties"—no more nor less—will emerge from the data, and practically precludes a finding of noncohesive parties. Were the parties really cohesive, or do they merely appear so because their most conspicuous dissenters were classified as "independents"? Were they parties at all, or merely opposed voting blocs—a pro-Madison and an anti-Madison clique, perhaps? These are indicative of the bafflements that must plague any effort to investigate congressional party cohesion when the membership of the parties cannot be authoritatively identified.

    7. Quoted in Galloway, *History of the House,* p. 129.

    8. Quoted in Harlow, *Legislative Methods,* p. 170.

    9. Quoted *ibid.,* p. 204.

    10. Quoted in Galloway, *History of the House,* p. 130.

    11. Quoted in Harlow, *Legislative Methods,* p. 187, note.

    12. Quoted in Galloway, *History of the House,* p. 129.

    13. Note that all but one of the quotations cited, which are representative of the documentary record on this subject, fail to employ the term "party," using instead such terms as "phalanx," "Jacobins," "followers." Where the term is used, in the first quotation, it is used ambiguously.

    The small size and the markedly sectional composition of the voting groups called "parties" in Cunningham's *The Jeffersonian Republicans* suggest that they may have been boardinghouse groups. In the 2d Congress (1791–92) Cunningham identifies a Federalist party of thirteen House members, all except two of them from New England states (p. 22). Seventeen members are said to comprise the Republican party in the same Congress. All but five were from Virginia, North Carolina, and Maryland, and only two of the remaining five were from nonsouthern states (p. 22).

    14. Ames, *Works,* I, 212.

    15. Quoted in Harlow, *Legislative Methods,* p. 170.

    Harlow does not, however, fail to take cognizance of several commentaries which report confusion and lack of discipline in the Republican following. He does not see any inconsistency here, and explains these commentaries as symptomatic of transitional phases in the evolution of the party, in which control over the party following was shifting from one institutional position to another. One such phase, according to Harlow, occurred immediately after Jefferson's first inauguration as President, before the congressional party habituated itself to presidential direction. The other such phase is said to have occurred upon Madison's first inauguration, when control over the congressional party was in the process of recapture by congressional leaders, a process completed in "1814 [when] . . . the Clay contingent obtained such complete control . . . that . . . friction practically disappeared." *Legislative Methods*, p. 203.

In point of fact, commentaries reporting internal schism and lack of discipline within the party following are by no means limited to the periods Harlow treats as transitional phases in party development. For examples, see below, pp. 136–37.

16. In these charges, parties were commonly linked with corruption or subversion of the Constitution: "For party and corrupt purposes, you have broken down the barriers interposed by the Constitution . . . you have . . . altered it, changed it, and mangled it, to . . . perpetuate your power and misrule." Harlow, *Legislative Methods*, p. 204. Also worthy of note, in this connection, were the exotic, "un-American" metaphors used to characterize party activity by one's opponents, e.g., "Prussian" discipline, Roman "phalanxes," "Jacobin" practices (caucuses), "Romanist" orthodoxy.

17. Thompson, *Nominating Caucus*, p. 32.

18. On the caucus see Ostrogorski, "The Rise and Fall of the Nominating Caucus, Legislative and Congressional," *American Historical Review*, V, No. 2 (December, 1899), 253–83; Whitridge, "Caucus System," *Economic Tracts*, No. 8; Stanwood, *A History of the Presidency;* Dallinger, *Nominations*, pp. 13–21; Thompson, *Nominating Caucus*.

19. Federalist or opposition parties held no nominating caucuses at the capital.

20. John Quincy Adams, *Memoirs*, I, 506–7.

21. *Ibid.*

22. See Thompson, *Nominating Caucus*, p. 34; Brant, *James Madison, the President*, pp. 458–59; Galloway, *History of the House*, p. 295. A second caucus at which Gerry was nominated as the vice-presidential candidate was attended by a bare majority of Congress.

23. On the 1816 caucus, see *National Intelligencer*, March 14, 18, and 19, 1816; Thompson, *Nominating Caucus*, p. 36; Shipp, *Giant Days*, p. 144. The total vote cast in the caucus appears to have been 119. Absenteeism percentage is based on a purported Republican party membership of 122 in the House (see Galloway, *History of the House*, p. 295) and a conservative estimate of 28 in the Senate.

24. John Quincy Adams, *Memoirs*, V, 60–61.

25. Parton, *Jackson*, III, 26–28; Shipp, *Giant Days*, p. 175.

26. Inexplicably, Harlow's work does not mention the collapse of the

caucus in 1824, nor does it once refer to such published works containing information on votes in the caucus as Thompson's informative short study, written more than a decade before Harlow's book. Yet the nominating caucus is treated by Harlow as being evidence of the first importance in establishing the existence of Republican party discipline in Congress.

27. Knowing, in all probability, that Jackson could not win the caucus nomination in 1824, the Senator and his friends tried to prevent one from being held. Jackson appears to have perceived the vote-getting potential of an attack upon "King Caucus" at this time. "Virginia has taken a stand against the caucus," he noted in a letter from Washington, "and her State elections are canvassed on that ground. In London [?] a Mr. Osborn has been elected by a large majority on this avowed principle." Parton, *Jackson*, III, 26, 42–43.

28. While the party identification of all these candidates is unknown, partisan affiliations of enough candidates are known or are inferable from other contexts to allow confidence in asserting that the multiplicity of candidacies is not attributable to either the majority or the opposition party exclusively.

29. Even in this period, of course, when the voting strength of the two parties was nearly equal, a candidate polling an "insignificant" number of votes could deprive either party's candidate of the majority necessary to win the speakership. This happened, for example, in 1839, when four "insignificant" candidates, polling less than 10 percent of the vote among them (the votes were 11, 3, 5, and 1 respectively), denied a majority to either of the two leading candidates, polling 113 and 102 votes respectively.

30. In the election of 1853, for example, a total nonparty vote of 39 was split among 10 lesser candidates, with the two uppermost (third- and fourth-place candidates) polling a mere 47.4 percent of the whole nonparty vote.

31. One wonders whether there is a connection between the decline of the boardinghouse pattern and the decline of organized party dissidence. By 1850, only about half the members of Congress were affiliated with a boardinghouse group of three or more members, as compared with more than 90 percent in 1807. This erosion of the primary-group organizational base of the congressional community, especially to the extent that it had served as a source of political cues for the members, may have created an environment more permissive and more needful of parties.

One would like to know also whether the minority party's members contributed disproportionately to the increasing disorganization of party dissenters suggested in Figure 5, given the minority party's special susceptibility to splinter that has been observed in the modern Congress. For summary statements of his findings on this point, see Truman, *The Congressional Party*, pp. 90–93, 190–92. In at least two speakership elections before the Civil War (1839 and 1855), however, it was not the minority but the majority party that was conspicuously splintered—so much so that the minority party candidate was able to win the speakership.

32. The findings here tend to support Mary P. Follett's observation that party caucuses to choose speakership candidates were not known in the Jeffersonian era. See Follett, *The Speaker*, p. 40. Harlow's rejection of this view is based largely on the reasoning that, since caucuses were held to nominate presidential candidates, they must have been held to select speakership candidates, too. *Legislative Methods*, p. 249.

33. No region held a majority of seats in the House or the Senate. The largest percentage of House seats held by a single region during the Jeffersonian era was 35.2 percent held by the middle Atlantic states; of Senate seats, the southern states held 30.4 percent.

34. It is not intended to assert here what could not be known without elaborate analysis of roll call votes, and then only by hint: that in its internal dynamics on policy issues the party *behaved* like a coalition of boardinghouse blocs. Table 9 would suggest that this was the case. So also would pragmatic considerations: for it would seem that—assuming a one-party composition for the boardinghouse groups—the most efficient method for concerting the party membership would be by seeking cooperation among messes en bloc rather than between single individuals living in various boardinghouse blocs. The point in the text, however, is that irrespective of party behavior on roll calls the scattering of the party membership into boardinghouse fraternities gave the party the sociological, if not necessarily the political, characteristics of a coalition of blocs.

35. On the question of whether boardinghouse groups were one-party or two-party in composition, fragmentary evidence exists to indicate both. In 1809 Congress voted a large increase in naval expenditures against the wishes of the President and over the strong protest of Secretary of the Treasury Gallatin. Gallatin left in his personal papers a sardonic analysis of the vote, entitled "The Navy Coalition of 1809," in which he identified 40 Republicans who had defected from the party, classed by faction (e.g., "Smith Faction, or Ruling Party," "Quids," "New York Malcontents"). Matching Gallatin's roster of defectors with boardinghouse lists for that Congress reveals that an extraordinarily high incidence of disunity among messmates accompanied the disunity in the Republican party on this vote. The suggestion is, therefore, of a one-party composition for the boardinghouse groups. See Henry Adams, *Gallatin*, pp. 387–88.

On the other hand, Senator William Plumer's biographer notes that Plumer, a Federalist, "brought about [a] social union at the same boarding-house between members of the different parties; and . . . succeeded . . . in forming a mess . . . of liberal minded men from both parties." "I dislike," wrote Plumer in 1807, "this setting up of partition walls between Members of Congress, because some are Federalists and others Republicans. The more we associate together, the more favorably shall we think of each other. . . . This day Henry Clay, and Matthew Clay, his uncle, joined the party at our lodgings. They are Republicans, and I am glad they have come." Plumer, *Life*, p. 352. If such intermingling of the parties within the boardinghouses did not indicate a weak sense of party affiliation in the first place, the long-run effect of the practice must have been to weaken party identifications.

36. Cooper, *Notions*, II, 30.

37. Harlow, *Legislative Methods*, pp. 187, 191.

38. Binkley, *President and Congress*, p. 54.

39. Harlow's *Legislative Methods* is the most extensively documented work which asserts the existence of party caucuses on policy. Excluding references to nominating caucuses and statements too ambiguous to be counted as statements about caucuses on policy issues, a total of thirteen statements from three Federalist newspapers and five Federalist legislators comprises his cited evidence on the subject of party caucuses in the period 1801–25. Of these thirteen statements, nine go no further than general allegations that Republicans had concerted their views or arranged their legislative strategy in advance of floor votes. The remaining four statements purport to describe or identify specific Republican caucuses. One of these is a patently fictional account of a Republican caucus, amounting to caricature, which appeared in a Federalist newspaper. Another is a statement in the same newspaper to the effect that "it is said that a *Jeffersonian Caucus* met last Friday evening . . . with their Genevan Director [Gallatin] and his Subalterns" (p. 187, note). A third is an allusion to a caucus which aborted and "broke up in confusion" (p. 202). The remaining statement is a plausible newspaper account of caucusing on the question of the Embargo Act—which was held in public and was open to Federalists.

40. "On both occasions," Gallatin continues, "we were divided; and on both the members of the minority of each meeting were left at full liberty to vote as they pleased, without being on that account proscribed or considered as having abandoned the principles of the party." Quoted in Cunningham, *The Jeffersonian Republicans*, p. 82. One of the aforementioned caucuses was on the issue of appropriations to implement the treaty with Britain; the other was on the issue of a policy toward France, then in the midst of revolution.

41. See Harlow, *Legislative Methods*, pp. 189, 195.

42. Nicolay, *Our Capital*, p. 163.

43. On the emergence of formal party organization in Congress, see Truman, "The Presidency and Congressional Leadership: Some Notes on Our Changing Constitution," *Proceedings of the American Philosophical Society*, CIII, No. 5 (October, 1959), 687–92.

44. Truman, *The Governmental Process*, pp. 510–11.

45. Harlow, *Legislative Methods*, pp. 175–77, 192.

46. *Ibid.*, p. 207. None of the prerogatives of the modern party leadership—scheduling of bills, assignment of speakers, committee assigments, sitting on conference committees, and miscellaneous patronage—were available to the presidential spokesmen in the Jeffersonian era. The only instance of sanctions that has been found is the case of Speaker Varnum's removal of John Randolph from the Ways and Means Committee following Randolph's breach with Jefferson in 1806. Here, however, the purported leader was himself the victim of the sanction, and it is not even clear whether the removal was related to his breach with Jefferson. It was carried out over the explicit protest of Secretary Gallatin, who was then residing on Capitol Hill and who was regarded as Jefferson's principal spokesman on the Hill. See Henry Adams, *Gallatin*, p. 363.

47. Harlow, *Legislative Methods*, p. 207.

48. Representative Randolph, after his breach with Jefferson, felt constrained to confess to his erstwhile role as presidential spokesman in a speech before the House and to label such a role as being incompatible with an honest and independent character. *AC*, XV (9th Congress, 1st sess.), 984. A spokesman for President Monroe was subjected to such "sneering hints and innuendoes . . . as if he were a dependent tool of the Executive" that he felt constrained to oppose the President in order to demonstrate his independence to his colleagues. John Quincy Adams, *Memoirs*, IV, 65–66.

49. John Quincy Adams, *Memoirs*, I, 403–4. The other three "parts" of the Republican party which Adams identified were: the President's reluctant supporters; the waverers "now supporting one side . . . and now supporting the other"; and, finally, the party's steady dissenters.

50. Plumer, *Life*, p. 341.

51. The careful reader of Harlow's Chapter 10 will note several internal inconsistencies concerning his proposition that there was a single presidential "leader" in Congress. On page 167, for example, Harlow states that, following Gallatin's departure from Congress in 1801 to become Secretary of the Treasury, "the unenviable task of guiding the administration party in the House fell to William B. Giles" as floor leader. On pages 170–71 and 181, however, it is John Randolph whom he identifies as floor leader at this time. Evidence is cited on page 178, on

the other hand, indicating that Nicholson was presidential spokesman at the same time, and that he shared this role with Randolph. It should also be noted that Harlow's observations, while phrased in terms of party leadership in Congress, derive almost exclusively from evidence relevant only to the House of Representatives.

52. Quoted in Harlow, *Legislative Methods*, p. 178.

53. Quoted *ibid.*, p. 170.

54. *Ibid.*, pp. 177–78; Bowers, *Jefferson in Power*, pp. 223–25, 338 ff.; Henry Adams, *Gallatin*, pp. 338–44.

55. See Henry Adams, *Gallatin*, p. 302; John Quincy Adams, *Memoirs*, I, 343–44; Margaret B. Smith, *First Forty Years*, p. 93; Plumer, *Life*, pp. 244, 248, 340; Quincy, *Life*, pp. 116–17, 120–21, 173–74; Jefferson, *Works*, X, 211, note; Harlow, *Legislative Methods*, pp. 170, 178; *AC*, XI (7th Congress, 1st sess.), 666; Washington *Federalist*, February 17, March 25, 27, 1802; Bowers, *Jefferson in Power*, Chapter 5 and pp. 225, 338, 340, 436; Gallatin, *Writings*, I, 380.

56. A Washington newspaper in 1802 identified Giles as "the leader of the ministerial phalanx," a judgment echoed by a legislator who called him "the premier, or prime minister of the day." See Harlow, *Legislative Methods*, pp. 168–69. But the same newspaper later in 1802 named Giles and Stevens Mason as the outstanding leaders of the Republican party in Congress. Washington *Federalist*, March 27, 1802. Senator John Quincy Adams, on the other hand, named Giles, Logan, Eppes, and Nicholson as Jefferson's congressional leaders for roughly the same historical period. *Memoirs*, I, 343–44. But his colleague, Senator Plumer, identified John Randolph as the President's spokesman then. Plumer, *Life*, p. 340. These examples are cited to indicate the confusion even of the documentary record on the subject of congressional leadership.

57. Jefferson, *Works*, IX, 370–71.

58. Fuller, *The Speakers of the House*, p. 58.

59. Harlow, *Legislative Methods*, p. 208.

60. Follett, *The Speaker*, p. 79.

61. Schurz, *Clay*, I, 172–202, 214–22.

62. *Ibid.*, pp. 145, 208.

63. *AC*, XXX (14th Congress, 2d sess.), 495–98, 714–15.

64. Schurz, *Clay*, I, 164–65.

65. *Ibid.*, p. 147; *AC*, XXX (14th Congress, 2d sess.), 740–43, 770.

66. Schurz, *Clay*, I, 146–50, 165–67, 212.

67. *Ibid.*, pp. 151–59.

68. *Ibid.*, Vol. I, Chapter 10; Parton, *Jackson*, Vol. III, Chapter 6. John Quincy Adams contended that Clay had sought the congressional caucus nomination as Vice President in 1820. *Memoirs*, V, 58.

69. Wilfred E. Binkley has asserted an intraparty cleavage into "Na-

tional Republicans" and "Democratic Republicans," with Clay a leader of the former. *American Political Parties*, pp. 94–95, 101 ff.

70. Galloway, *History of the House*, Chapter 6; Harlow, *Legislative Methods*, Chapter 12.

71. The chairmen of the eleven top-ranking committees had, as a voting group, a mean cohesion index of 28.9 (range of indexes: 0.0 to 100.0). The chairmen of the select committees appointed to suggest action on the President's legislative requests received in the State of the Union message had, as a voting group, a mean cohesion index of 24.1 (range of indexes: 0.0 to 37.5). The Rice Index of Cohesion is used here: an index of 100.0 indicates unanimity; an index of 0.0 indicates an even division on each side of the issue. See explanatory note in Table 9. The roll calls on which the voting behavior of the chairmen was tested are the same as those included in Table 8.

72. Story, ed., *Life*, I, 311.

73. In so far as it avoids distribution of committee chairmanships on the basis of bloc membership, the modern system of distribution on the seniority principle would, by comparison, seem to reduce—not to increase—the problems of mobilizing the party for concerted action. This may help to explain the emergence of the seniority system later in history.

74. Webster, ed., *Correspondence*, I, 237.

75. See Galloway, *History of the House*, p. 295.

76. Plumer, *Life*, p. 248.

77. Donnan, ed., *Papers of James A. Bayard*, II, 165.

78. Quincy, *Life*, pp. 136–37.

79. Quoted in Harlow, *Legislative Methods*, p. 199, note 2.

80. Story, ed., *Life*, I, 311.

81. Basil Hall, *Travels*, III, 32. The picture of party leadership presented here, as shared and shifting between occasionally cooperative activists—"friendly rivals," Henry Adams has called them—resembles that drawn by Albert Gallatin for the pre-Jeffersonian Congress. "It is certainly a subject of self-gratulation," he wrote concerning his congressional service in the 1790s, "that I should have been allowed to take the lead with such coadjutors as Madison, Giles, Livingston, and Nicholas." Henry Adams, *Gallatin*, p. 156. The impression is, moreover, that the Republican party leadership was rather more closely knit during the 1790s, when their party was an opposition party in Congress, than it was after the Republicans acquired the status of majority party. See Cunningham, *The Jeffersonian Republicans, passim.*

82. Jefferson, *Works*, X, 55.

83. "In Congress we have nothing to do, and do nothing. We are tired of Jefferson and Jefferson of us. Intrigues for the Presidency are

the order of the day. . . . We meet and adjourn, do ordinary business, wrangle, and then the majority retire to intrigue for the Presidency." Quincy, *Life*, p. 136.

84. "When a Senator is making a set speech," observed a member, "there is seldom a quorum within the bar; the chairs are deserted; and the question is, in the meantime, settled in conversation at the fireside." Plumer, *Life*, p. 341. "I recollect distinctly," said a Representative, that "the argument at the fireside was unquestionably not in every case the argument of the floor." *AC*, XXX (14th Congress, 2d sess.), 520.

85. Quincy, *Life*, p. 178.

86. Quoted in Parton, *Jackson*, III, 46–47

87. While they probably occurred earlier, 1833 is the first year for which direct evidence has come to notice of state delegation caucuses on substantive policy issues (as distinguished from caucuses on questions involving executive or judicial appointments or presidential elections). See John Quincy Adams, *Diary*, pp. 434–35.

88. Hamilton, *Men and Manners*, II, 113.

Chapter 7: *The Congressional Establishment: A Community Perspective*

1. Exclusion of other stimuli to the development of organized congressional parties is by no means implied here—as, for example, growth in the size of Congress. See Truman, *The Congressional Party*, p. 195.

2. While approximately 43 percent more public acts were passed per Congress from 1814 to 1828 than from 1800 to 1814, the largest number passed in any Congress was 167, roughly one-quarter the volume of public acts passed in the modern Congress. The really dramatic upsurge in volume of legislative business came during the Civil War. See Galloway, *History of the House*, pp. 303–5.

Chapter 8: *Statecraft*

1. See John Quincy Adams, *Memoirs*, IV, 80–81; V, 118–19.

2. Previous service in Congress was not a peculiar attribute of Jeffersonian Presidents. Except for Zachary Taylor, all Chief Magistrates through Abraham Lincoln had seen previous service in Congress, if the Presidency of the Senate is counted as congressional service. In the four-year span of Monroe's second administration (1821–25) seven of the next ten Presidents were office-holders at Washington, all but one of the seven, Secretary Adams (a former Senator), being legislators. The com-

mon belief that Andrew Jackson was a "rank outsider," as Elmer E. Schatt-schneider calls him, is erroneous. (See his *Party Government*, p. 152.) He had served in both houses of Congress, resigning from the Senate in 1825, presidential ambitions thwarted, to return triumphant from Tennessee three years later, dressed conspicuously in the political garb of an "outsider."

3. Harlow, *Legislative Methods*, p. 177.

4. See Truman, *The Congressional Party*, Chapter 8, and "The Presidency and Congressional Leadership: Some Notes on Our Changing Constitution," *Proceedings of the American Philosophical Society*, CIII, No. 5 (October, 1959), 687–92.

5. Quincy, *Life*, p. 287.

6. John Quincy Adams, *Memoirs*, IV, 65–66.

7. *AC*, XV (9th Congress, 1st sess.), 984.

8. Only one individual besides the President comprised the President's office. This was his personal secretary, often a member of the President's family, paid out of general funds for the maintenance of the executive mansion. So far as can be told from the written record, the position was of no political significance.

9. Jefferson used other cabinet members also, though never so frequently or confidentially as Gallatin, it would appear. See White, *The Jeffersonians*, p. 51.

10. Careless reading of this passage in Henry Adams' *The Life of Albert Gallatin* (pp. 302–3) appears to be responsible for the widely held belief that Jefferson attended or presided over secret party meetings on the Hill.

11. Quoted in Brant, *James Madison, the President*, p. 298.

12. John Quincy Adams, *Memoirs*, IV, 217.

13. *Ibid.*, p. 65, and V, 474.

14. It was this "double-dealing" that provided the occasion for John Randolph's breach with Jefferson. See Bruce, *Randolph*, I, 222 ff.

15. Numerous firsthand accounts of these dinners are available. Descriptive material presented in the paragraphs following is drawn from these principal sources, *passim:* John Quincy Adams, *Memoirs*, Vol. I; Plumer, *Life;* Margaret B. Smith, *First Forty Years;* Morris, ed., *Diary*, Vol. II; Wharton, *Social Life;* Cutler and Perkins, *Life;* Mitchill, "Letters from Washington," *Harper's New Monthly Magazine*, LVIII, No. 347 (April, 1879), 740–55. Bowers' *Jefferson in Power* (pp. 46–49) gives an excellent description of the dinners.

16. Margaret B. Smith, *First Forty Years*, pp. 388–89.

17. Plumer, *Life*, pp. 245–46.

18. Margaret B. Smith, *First Forty Years*, p. 388.

19. Bowers, *Jefferson in Power*, p. 46; Cutler and Perkins, *Life*, II, 132–33.

20. Mitchill, "Letters from Washington," *Harper's New Monthly Magazine*, LVIII (April, 1879), 744.

21. John Quincy Adams, *Diary*, pp. 37–38.

22. White, *The Jeffersonians*, p. 33.

23. Margaret B. Smith, *First Forty Years*, p. 389.

24. John Quincy Adams, *Diary*, pp. 25–26, 28.

25. The dinners may well have outlived their usefulness even to Jefferson. His Washington wine expenditures declined as follows:

1801	$2,622.38	1805	546.41
1802	1,975.72	1806	659.38
1803	1,253.57	1807	553.97
1804	2,668.94	1808	75.58

See Singleton, *White House*, I, 42.

26. President Monroe regretted he had ever decided to continue the practice, and proposed to restrict the guests to invitees. He was, however, dissuaded by his Secretary of State. See John Quincy Adams, *Memoirs*, IV, 493–94.

27. Singleton, *White House*, I, 71.

28. Nicolay, *Our Capital*, p. 135.

29. Quoted in Singleton, *White House*, I, 71.

30. Margaret B. Smith, *First Forty Years*, p. 183.

31. John Quincy Adams, *Memoirs*, IV, 493–94.

32. Webster, ed., *Correspondence*, I, 234.

33. It seems that the Commissioner of Public Buildings had absconded with some of the appropriated funds. John Quincy Adams, *Memoirs*, VI, 287–88.

34. Singleton, *White House*, Vol. I, Chapter 8.

35. Margaret B. Smith, *First Forty Years*, p. 248.

36. Singleton, *White House*, I, xxii, 78.

37. Bryan, *History*, I, 365–66.

38. Emery, "Washington Newspapers," CHS *Records*, XXXVII–XXXVIII, 48–50.

39. *Ibid.* A cursory scanning of the *Intelligencer* indicates that Presidents did not dictate or control its content. There was that important difference with internal propaganda media utilized by the leadership in most organizations.

40. Witness the familiar charges against Jefferson for illicit liaison with a Negro servant, against Adams for white slavery, against Jackson for adultery—all widely circulated in the public press. Pseudonyms were characteristically used for such partisan accusations in the battle of the presses during Jeffersonian times.

41. Under a precedent established in George Washington's administration, Presidents did not appear at any social function outside the executive

mansion, nor did they pay visits at any residence. The rule was breached only thrice during the Jeffersonian era, on the evidence at hand, if we exclude presidential appearances at church. One occasion was Monroe's attendance at a banquet in honor of General Lafayette and another was a series of visits he paid to Mrs. John Calhoun when the Secretary of War's child was mortally ill. Cresson, *Monroe,* pp. 365, 460. The third was Monroe's attendance at a private party after Congress had adjourned in 1820. Kennedy, *Wirt,* II, 107.

42. Emery, "Washington Newspapers," CHS *Records,* XXXVII–XXXVIII, 49–50; John Quincy Adams, *Memoirs,* VI, 47, 56, 59; Bassett, *Jackson,* II, 378.

43. White, *The Jeffersonians,* p. 43. See Chapter 24 of White's work for an excellent account and analysis of staffing and personnel administration in the Republican era. Permission to quote from White's *The Jeffersonians* is gratefully acknowledged to The Macmillan Company.

44. Quoted *ibid.,* p. 351.

45. Quoted *ibid.,* p. 367.

46. *Ibid.,* p. 43.

47. *Ibid.,* p. 129.

48. This information is not given by White in his definitive work on the subject cited above.

49. Jefferson, *Works,* X, 393–94.

50. White, *The Jeffersonians,* p. 322.

51. *Ibid.,* pp. 151–52, 355.

52. Excluded here are appointments of uniformed officers. These were apportioned among the states in so far as practicable and candidates were required to pass written examinations. See *ibid.,* pp. 360–64.

53. John Quincy Adams, *Memoirs,* IV, 72. The President was Monroe, and the year 1818.

54. Service careers of cabinet members were reconstructed from the available biographical sources, principally the *Dictionary of American Biography.* The base figure of 49 confirmed cabinet appointees excludes chief clerks and others serving *ad interim* as department heads, and one confirmed appointee for whom sufficient biographical information is not available. The positions included are the Secretaries of State, Treasury, War, and Navy, and the Attorney General. The Postmaster General was not of cabinet rank, nor was the Post Office separated from the Treasury Department, until Jackson's administration. The administrations of Jackson and John Adams have been included to gain a more significant number of cases for analysis, and because these Presidents utilized the same principal source of recruitment for cabinet positions as the four Jeffersonian Presidents, Jackson drawing somewhat more heavily than they on members of the congressional community.

55. The average elapsed time from termination of congressional service to cabinet appointment was three years; from termination of service in state government to cabinet appointment, six and one-half years. The numerical incidence of cabinet members appointed from a last preceding service in state government may exaggerate the real importance of this secondary source of recruitment. Some of such appointees (James Madison and Martin Van Buren, for example) had achieved their most conspicuous service as legislators in the governmental community, and the state government posts from which they were appointed to the cabinet were but brief interludes between their congressional and their cabinet service. Unwillingness of some legislators to accept a cabinet post may have induced Presidents to turn to state officers as second choice; Jefferson, particularly, experienced difficulty in finding men to accept the less prestigious portfolios of War and Navy. See White, *The Jeffersonians*, p. 83.

56. See, for example, Jefferson, *Works*, X, 370–71.

57. John Quincy Adams, *Memoirs*, IV, 76.

58. Jefferson, *Works*, X, 342.

Chapter 9: Power Won and Power Lost

1. White, *The Jeffersonians*, pp. 51–52.

2. *Ibid.*

3. Harlow's *Legislative Methods* does not even mention the event. See White, *The Jeffersonians*, Chapters 29 and 30.

4. Henry Adams, *Gallatin*, pp. 85, 156–57; *ASP*, Misc. Ser., I, 724–921; White, *The Jeffersonians*, pp. 476–78. In thus signaling to Congress his doubts about the constitutionality of the proposal Jefferson would appear less committed to internal improvements than some portraits make him out to be. Note the contrast in his behavior on the Louisiana Purchase, when Jefferson sought to suppress the constitutional issue while privately conceding the purchase to be unconstitutional.

5. A detailed account may be found in White, *The Jeffersonians*, Chapters 29 and 30.

6. Henry Adams, *Gallatin*, p. 430.

7. White, *The Jeffersonians*, pp. 34–35.

8. Henry Adams, *Gallatin*, p. 355.

9. White, *The Jeffersonians*, p. 80, note 6.

10. Henry Adams, *Gallatin*, p. 376.

11. *Ibid.*, pp. 376–77.

12. *Ibid.*, p. 434.

13. *Ibid.*, pp. 429, 474–77.

14. White, *The Jeffersonians*, p. 266.
15. *Ibid.*, pp. 235–36.
16. Harris, *Advice and Consent*, pp. 48–50.
17. Brant, *James Madison, the President*, pp. 296–97.
18. Harris, *Advice and Consent*, pp. 48–50.
19. Madison, *Letters*, II, 472.
20. Jefferson, *Writings*, XII, 267.
21. Huntington, "Letters from the Samuel Huntington Correspondence, 1800–1812," *Tract No. 95, Annual Reports of the Western Reserve Historical Society*, Part II, p. 141.
22. Quoted in Mayo, *Clay*, I, 353, note 2.
23. Henry Adams, *History*, VIII, Chapter XI; Wiltse, *Calhoun*, I, 89; Carey, *The Olive Branch*, p. 83; Binkley, *American Political Parties*, p. 96.
24. Millis, *Arms and Men*, pp. 56–63; White, *The Jeffersonians*, pp. 235–36, 273.
25. Morison, *Otis*, II, 66–67; Henry Adams, *History*, VII, 389.
26. Wiltse, *Calhoun*, I, 95–96, 98–100.
27. Ingersoll, *Sketch of the Second War*, I, 126.
28. Green, *Washington*, p. 59.
29. Cresson, *Monroe*, p. 265.
30. *Ibid.*, pp. 266, 269.
31. White, *The Jeffersonians*, p. 37.
32. Green, *Washington*, p. 60; Margaret B. Smith, *First Forty Years*, pp. 101–3.
33. Nicolay, *Our Capital*, p. 110.
34. Cresson, *Monroe*, pp. 270–71; Goodwin, *Dolly Madison*, p. 177.
35. Fearon, *Sketches*, p. 285.
36. Henry Adams, *Gallatin*, p. 392.
37. Story, ed., *Life*, I, 311.
38. John Quincy Adams, *Memoirs*, IV, 457.
39. Monroe, *Writings*, VI, 286.
40. Binkley, *President and Congress*, pp. 60–61; White, *The Jeffersonians*, p. 481.
41. John Quincy Adams, *Diary*, pp. 249–52.
42. John Quincy Adams, *Memoirs*, IV, 70.
43. White, *The Jeffersonians*, p. 40.
44. Story, ed., *Life*, I, 311.
45. John Quincy Adams, *Memoirs*, V, 324.
46. Quoted in Binkley, *President and Congress*, p. 61.
47. Quoted in White, *The Jeffersonians*, p. 483.
48. White, *The Jeffersonians*, pp. 31, 42; John Quincy Adams, *Memoirs*, VII, 367.

49. John Quincy Adams, *Memoirs*, VII, 273.

50. *Ibid.*, p. 311.

51. *Ibid.*, pp. 374, 508 ff.

52. See, for example, White, *The Jeffersonians*, pp. 52–53.

53. Binkley, *President and Congress*, p. 63. See also Sydnor, "The One-Party Period of American History," *American Historical Review*, LI (April, 1946), 439 ff.

54. Leonard White suggests that it was not until 1803 that Jefferson sufficiently unburdened himself of his party's commitment to the principle of a weak executive to undertake active leadership of Congress. *The Jeffersonians*, pp. 31–32.

55. *Ibid.*, p. 38.

56. See Henry Adams' biography, *John Randolph of Roanoke*.

57. Plumer, *Life*, p. 342.

58. See, for example, White, *The Jeffersonians*, pp. 480–83.

59. The reasoning here follows one of the central themes in Neustadt's *Presidential Power*.

60. Webster, ed., *Correspondence*, I, 501.

61. White, *The Jeffersonians*, p. 44.

62. John Quincy Adams, *Memoirs*, I, 404.

63. Henry Adams, *Gallatin*, p. 253. Representative Gallatin's mess alone numbered more than thirty legislators—equivalent to 29 percent of the entire House. The number of Senators in the group is, however, unknown.

64. See McCormick, "New Perspectives in Jacksonian Politics," *American Historical Review*, LXV (January, 1960), 299–301. It appears that two-party states were still few at the close of the Jeffersonian era, however.

65. Information about the development of the single-member district system appears to be woefully lacking, and no work has been located which details the growth of this practice in elections for the national House. In 1842 Congress made election by single-member districts mandatory. Considering the major impact of a conversion from at-large election to election by district on the political fortunes of the incumbents, it is likely that the 1842 requirement merely gave official sanction to an evolution that had already been accomplished in the main. Galloway (*History of the House*, p. 27) states, without elaboration, that "the practice . . . had become well established" by 1842. In the Jeffersonian era it was believed that a constitutional amendment was necessary to require single-member districts, and one such was introduced in the House in 1817. Though failing of the necessary two-thirds majority, the measure was approved by the comfortable majority of 81 to 57, suggesting that

the change was well under way by that time. See *AC*, XXX (14th Congress, 2d sess.), 256–57, 301–11, 322–36, 338–55. Also suggestive of significant progress toward single-member districts is a statement made in 1828 by Secretary of War Barbour concerning the appointment of cadets to West Point: "I determined to appoint a cadet from every Congressional district, and two from each State." Quoted in White, *The Jeffersonians*, p. 256.

66. Analysis of roll call votes in this study is neither extensive nor intensive enough to demonstrate how such conflicts were principally resolved. Table 10 offers fragmentary evidence that, despite the growing irreconcilability of mess group and state delegation solidarity suggested in the text, the voting cohesion of both types of groups was at almost as high a level in 1828 as it was in 1807. The failure of the figures in Table 10 to show a decrease in state delegation solidarity could be explained by the increase in the number of legislators who failed to join a mess. Lacking fraternal group ties, members living alone or in pairs may have relied for guidance and consultation on colleagues from the same state; and state delegations may thus have gained in cohesion among the growing ranks of the nonaffiliated legislators what they might have lost in cohesion among legislators affiliated with different boardinghouse groups.

Preliminary exploration suggests, moreover, that the larger state delegations—the ones that would have been most useful to Presidents as blocs —were less successful than the smaller delegations in mobilizing their full voting strength, and that their capacity to do so declined with the passing years. On a total of 27 roll calls (the first nine roll calls analyzed in Table 8 in each of the 10th, 14th, and 20th Congresses), the voting cohesion of each state delegation having three or more members was figured, with the following results:

	1807	*1817*	*1828*
Mean of cohesion indexes:			
for the six largest delegations	56.1	44.1	45.2
for all other delegations	73.3	54.8	75.2

While they probably occurred earlier, state delegation caucuses on substantive policy issues (as distinguished from caucuses on questions involving executive or judicial appointments or presidential elections), first come to notice in 1833. See John Quincy Adams, *Diary*, p. 435.

67. Hamilton, *Men and Manners*, II, 68–69.

68. John Quincy Adams, *Memoirs*, VII, 377. Two years earlier Adams' own Vice President had put half of the Senate committees—including Foreign Relations and Finance—under the control of members of the President's opposition. Before and after that time, Senate committees were

staffed by the voting membership of the Senate rather than by the Vice President as presiding officer. Wiltse, *Calhoun*, I, 322–23; Haynes, *The Senate of the United States*, I, 273–77.
69. Harlow, *Legislative Methods*, p. 237.

Chapter 10: Separate Battalions

1. See White, *The Jeffersonians*, pp. 360–61. Even as late as 1829—the first year of Jackson's administration—half (50.7 percent) of the civil employees at Washington below the rank of department head were native sons of the District of Columbia and Maryland and Virginia. An additional 14.4 percent had been born abroad. (*A Register of Officers and Agents, Civil, Military, and Naval, in the Service of the United States on the 30th of September, 1829*.) (Percentages exclude the 55 employees of the General Post Office at Washington, whose birthplaces are not given in the register.) It should be noted that the positions of Assistant and Under Secretary did not exist for most of the Jeffersonian era. The seconds-in-command of the departments were ordinarily their chief clerks.
2. White, *The Jeffersonians*, pp. 548, 555–56.
3. See, for example, Crowninshield, ed., *Letters*.
4. Margaret B. Smith, *First Forty Years*, pp. 336–37.
5. See White, *The Federalists*, pp. 295–98; *The Jeffersonians*, Chapter 27.
6. Presidents and Secretaries ordinarily departed Washington following the close of the social season on July 4, leaving the departments in charge of the chief clerks during their summer absence. Presidential vacations from Washington averaged more than three months per year from 1801 to 1828. For heads of departments the workday ended ordinarily at three in the afternoon, while clerks remained in attendance, in some departments at least, until five or six o'clock. See White, *The Jeffersonians*, p. 407; Singleton, *White House*, I, xv.
7. See Mann, ed., *A Yankee Jeffersonian, passim*. One of the exceptions to the rule of political distance between civil staff and their superiors was the case of Colonel McKenney, head of the Indian Bureau in the War Department, who served as editor of Secretary John Calhoun's political newspaper. See Margaret B. Smith, *First Forty Years*, p. 160.
8. White, *The Jeffersonians*, pp. 383–85, 416–19, and Chapter 27.
9. Busey, *Pictures of Washington*, pp. 242–44.
10. Padover, *The Complete Jefferson*, p. 309.
11. Crowninshield, ed., *Letters*, p. 21; Henry Adams, *Gallatin*, p. 253; John Quincy Adams, *Memoirs*, V, 239.

12. Exclusive of "dissipation . . . dinners, evening parties, and balls," Adams reported that "about one-fourth part of my time is absorbed in the round of receiving and returning visits." *Memoirs*, IV, 279–80, 509.

13. Margaret B. Smith, *First Forty Years*, p. 213.

14. *Ibid.*, pp. 93–94.

15. *Ibid.*, p. 164.

16. John Quincy Adams, *Memoirs*, VII, 453.

17. Hamilton, *Men and Manners*, II, 35.

18. Donnan, ed., *Papers of James A. Bayard*, II, 189–90; Busey, *Pictures of Washington*, p. 344.

19. Henry Adams, *Gallatin*, p. 573; Foster, *Jeffersonian America*, pp. 86–87; Brant, *James Madison, the President*, pp. 442, 477–79, 487–88.

20. Brant, *James Madison, the President*, p. 94.

21. *Ibid.*, p. 99.

22. Singleton, *White House*, I, 139 ff.

23. Pope-Hennessy, ed., *Aristocratic Journey*, pp. 170, 173–74, 180; Singleton, *White House*, I, 71–72, 150; Foster, *Jeffersonian America*, pp. 9, 10, 17; Busey, *Pictures of Washington*, pp. 241–42, 351.

24. Padover, *The Complete Jefferson*, p. 309.

25. Foster, *Jeffersonian America*, p. 52; John Quincy Adams, *Diary*, pp. 24–25; Singleton, *White House*, I, 33; Quincy, *Life*, pp. 92–93.

26. Pope-Hennessy, ed., *Aristocratic Journey*, p. 189; Foster, *Jeffersonian America*, pp. 21, 55.

27. Margaret B. Smith, *First Forty Years*, pp. 46–47; Foster, *Jeffersonian America*, pp. 55–56.

28. Jefferson, *Works*, XI, 185.

29. *Ibid.*

30. John Quincy Adams, *Memoirs*, IV, 37.

31. See White, *The Federalists*, Chapter 19.

32. White, *The Jeffersonians*, p. 82.

33. See, on this point, Neustadt, *Presidential Power*, pp. 37–43; Truman, *The Governmental Process*, Chapter 14.

34. White, *The Jeffersonians*, p. 83. Madison described the practice thus: "An eye must be had to [a prospective appointee's] political principles and connexions, his personal temper and habits, his relations of feelings toward those with whom he is to be associated; and the quarter of the Union to which he belongs." President Monroe emphasized the need for a variety of sectional affiliations in the cabinet: "A head of a Department (there being four) should be taken from the four sections of the Union." Both quotations from White, *The Jeffersonians*, p. 83, note 17.

35. See above, pp. 176–77.

36. John Quincy Adams, *Memoirs*, IV, 295–97; VI, 63, 66, 95–96, 415.

37. *Ibid.*, V, 468–69, 471; VI, 448; Margaret B. Smith, *First Forty Years*, p. 170.
38. John Quincy Adams, *Memoirs*, IV, 193.
39. *Ibid.*, p. 242.
40. Margaret B. Smith, *First Forty Years*, p. 238.
41. See Crowninshield, ed., *Letters*, pp. 32–33.
42. Margaret B. Smith, *First Forty Years*, pp. 47, 179, 198, 200–201, 244, 395 ff.; John Quincy Adams, *Memoirs*, IV, 515; Foster, *Jeffersonian America*, pp. 84–85; Nicolay, *Our Capital*, p. 82; Pope-Hennessy, ed., *Aristocratic Journey*, p. 82; Singleton, *White House*, I, 64, 144.
43. Cooley, *Etiquette*, p. 26.
44. Margaret B. Smith, *First Forty Years*, pp. 165, 170.
45. Plumer, *Life*, pp. 353–54.
46. John Quincy Adams, *Memoirs*, VI, 443.
47. Margaret B. Smith, *First Forty Years*, pp. 193 ff.
48. *Ibid.*, p. 165.
49. *Ibid.*, p. 274.
50. *Ibid.*, pp. 165, 170.

*Chapter 11: The Presidency and
the Executive Establishment*

1. Information on the development of the cabinet before 1800 is drawn largely from White, *The Federalists*, pp. 38–49.
2. White, *The Jeffersonians*, p. 39.
3. *Ibid.*, Chapter 6; Learned, "Some Aspects of the Cabinet Meeting," CHS *Records*, XVIII, 109.
4. John Quincy Adams' memoirs for the period 1817–28 provide the principal source for detailed information about cabinet meetings in the Jeffersonian era.
5. Jefferson, *Works*, IX, 69, 273.
6. White, *The Jeffersonians*, p. 84.
7. *Ibid.*, p. 88.
8. Quoted *ibid.*, p. 80.
9. Jefferson, *Works*, XI, 185. White (*The Jeffersonians*, p. 80) feels that Jefferson was here minimizing the frictions between Secretary Gallatin and Navy Secretary Robert Smith; "and on the embargo Jefferson secured acquiescence rather than agreement" in his cabinet.
10. Jefferson, *Works*, XI, 185.
11. Henry Adams, *Gallatin*, pp. 430–31.
12. Brant, *James Madison, the President*, pp. 113, 131, 163.
13. *Ibid.*, pp. 296–97.

14. *Ibid.*, p. 289.
15. White, *The Jeffersonians*, pp. 217, 220.
16. Brant, *James Madison, the President*, p. 132.
17. *Ibid.*, pp. 298, 293.
18. John Quincy Adams, *Memoirs*, IV, 501.
19. Brant, *James Madison, the President*, pp. 277–78.
20. John Quincy Adams, *Memoirs*, IV, 54–55, 124–27.
21. *Ibid.*, pp. 57, 59, 63.
22. Henry Adams, *Gallatin*, p. 580.
23. John Quincy Adams, *Memoirs*, V, 490.
24. *Ibid.*, p. 226.
25. Henry Adams, *Gallatin*, p. 591.
26. See, for examples, John Quincy Adams, *Memoirs*, Vols. IV, V, VI. Quoted statements are from IV, 36–37 and 149, and VI, 173.
27. John Quincy Adams, *Memoirs*, IV, 451.
28. *Ibid.*, VI, 367; Nicolay, *Our Capital*, p. 134.
29. John Quincy Adams, *Memoirs*, IV, 217–18.
30. *Ibid.*, p. 508.
31. *Ibid.*, VII, 80–81.
32. The leader of the Clay faction, which had given Adams the vote necessary to win the Presidency in the House election, was of course appointed Secretary of State. Secretary Crawford declined reappointment, but a Crawford man was appointed Secretary of War. Richard Rush, a neo-Federalist, was given the Treasury portfolio. Southard and Wirt, respectively Secretary of the Navy and Attorney General, were retained from the Monroe administration. As the price of their support for the administration, the Calhounites had demanded two South Carolinians—Cheves and Poinsett—as Secretary of State and Secretary of the Treasury. Adams rejected this impossible demand. John Quincy Adams, *Memoirs*, VI, 506–7.
33. Binkley, *The Powers of the President*, p. 68; see also White, *The Jeffersonians*, Chapter 7.
34. John Quincy Adams, *Memoirs*, VII, 59–65.
35. *Ibid.*, pp. 178, 189–90.
36. *Ibid.*, p. 362.
37. Margaret B. Smith, *First Forty Years*, p. 257.
38. Neustadt, *Presidential Power*, pp. 38–39.
39. Jackson's "spoils system" had perhaps an additional purpose besides rewarding the party workers: achieving a bureaucratic structure, beneath the Secretaries, that was loyal to the President. It will be recalled that some members of his "kitchen cabinet" held executive offices of secondary rank.
40. Monroe took to the practice of paying surprise visits to the offices

of his department heads, ostensibly to deliver papers or for casual conversation. See, e.g., John Quincy Adams, *Memoirs*, IV, 473, 496.

41. "I had spoken of this resolution several times to Mr. Clay," Adams noted in his diary, "who had given assurance that no such resolution had been adopted. I had relied upon this information." *Ibid.*, VII, 85.

42. *Ibid.*, IV, 500–501.

43. See above, pp. 175–76.

44. Diplomatic appointments—going largely to members of Congress—were a conspicuous exception to the custom of secretarial courtesy.

45. John Quincy Adams, *Memoirs*, VII, 80–81.

46. "He plays his game with so much cunning and duplicity that I can fix upon no positive act that would justify the removal of him," Adams commented. *Diary*, pp. 382–83.

47. Nine of the thirty executives serving in the Jeffersonian era were in this category, excluding those who remained less than a year in office under a new administration, and excluding officers not confirmed by the Senate, serving *ad interim*.

48. John Quincy Adams, *Memoirs*, VII, 520.

49. White, *The Jeffersonians*, p. 93.

50. John Quincy Adams, *Memoirs*, IV, 217–18.

51. *Ibid.*, p. 508.

52. *Ibid.*, VI, 127.

53. *Ibid.*, V, 474–75.

54. *Ibid.*, IV, 242.

55. *Ibid.*, p. 163.

56. White, *The Jeffersonians*, p. 80.

57. John Quincy Adams, *Diary*, p. 406. The verse is sung to the imprisoned king by the minstrel Blondel in *Richard Coeur-de-Lion*.

BIBLIOGRAPHY

Adams, Abigail. Letters of Mrs. Adams. Vol. II. Edited by Charles F. Adams. 3d ed. Boston: Little and Brown, 1841.

Adams, Henry. The Education of Henry Adams. Modern Library Edition. New York: Random House, 1931.

—— History of the United States of America during the Administrations of Thomas Jefferson and James Madison. 9 vols. New York: Charles Scribner's Sons, 1889–91.

—— John Randolph. Boston and New York: Houghton Mifflin Company, 1898.

—— The Life of Albert Gallatin. New York: Peter Smith, 1943.

—— The United States in 1800. Great Seal Books. Ithaca: Cornell University Press, 1955.

Adams, John Quincy. The Diary of John Quincy Adams. Edited by Allan Nevins. New York: Longmans, Green and Company, 1928.

—— Memoirs. Edited by Charles F. Adams. Vols. I, IV, V, VI, VII. Philadelphia: J. B. Lippincott, 1874–75.

Alexander, De Alva S. The History and Procedure of the House of Representatives. Boston and New York: Houghton Mifflin Company, 1916.

American State Papers: Documents, Legislative and Executive, of the Congress of the United States. 38 vols. in 10 classes. Washington, D.C.: Gales and Seaton, 1832–61.

Ames, Fisher. Works. Boston: T. B. Wait and Company, 1809.

Anderson, Dice Robins. William Branch Giles: A study in the Politics of Virginia and the Nation from 1790 to 1830. Menasha, Wis.: George Banta, 1914.

Anthony, Katherine. Dolly Madison: Her Life and Times. Garden City, N.Y.: Doubleday & Company, 1949.

Arensberg, Conrad M. "American Communities," American Anthropologist, LVII, No. 6, Part 1 (December, 1955), 1143–62.

—— "The Community as Object and Sample," American Anthropologist, LXIII, No. 2, Part 1 (April, 1961), 241–64.

Arensberg, Conrad M. "The Community Study Method," *American Journal of Sociology*, LX (September, 1954), 109–25.

Aronson, Sidney. Status and Kinship in the Higher Civil Service: The Administrations of John Adams, Thomas Jefferson, and Andrew Jackson. Cambridge, Mass.: Harvard University Press, 1964.

Atwater, Caleb. Remarks Made on a Tour to Prairie du Chien; Thence to Washington City, in 1829. Columbus: Jenkins and Glover, 1831.

Bassett, John S. The Life of Andrew Jackson. Vol. II. Garden City, N.Y.: Doubleday, Page and Company, 1911.

Benton, Thomas H. Abridgement of the Debates of Congress. Vol. II. New York: D. Appleton and Company, 1857.

Beveridge, Albert J. The Life of John Marshall. Vol. III. Boston and New York: Houghton Mifflin Company, 1919.

Binkley, Wilfred E. American Political Parties: Their Natural History. 1st ed. New York: Alfred A. Knopf, 1943.

—— The Powers of the President. Garden City, N.Y.: Doubleday, Doran and Company, 1937.

—— President and Congress. New York: Alfred A. Knopf, 1947.

Biographical Directory of the American Congress, 1774–1961. Washington, D.C.: Government Printing Office, 1961.

Bowers, Claude G. Jefferson in Power. Boston: Houghton Mifflin Company, 1936.

Brant, Irving. James Madison, the President, 1809–1812. Indianapolis and New York: Bobbs-Merrill, 1956.

—— James Madison, Secretary of State. Indianapolis and New York: Bobbs-Merrill, 1956.

Bruce, William Cabell. John Randolph of Roanoke. Vol. I. New York and London: G. P. Putnam's Sons, 1922.

Bryan, Wilhemus Bogart. Bibliography of the District of Columbia. Senate Document No. 62, 56th Congress, 1st sess., pp. 3–15. Washington, D.C.: Government Printing Office, 1900.

—— A History of the National Capital. 2 vols. New York: The Macmillan Company, 1914, 1916.

Buckingham, J. S. America: Historical, Statistic, and Descriptive. Vol. I. London: Fisher, Son and Company, 1841.

Burns, James MacGregor. The Deadlock of Democracy: Four-Party Politics in America. Englewood Cliffs, N.J.: Prentice-Hall, 1963.

Busey, Samuel C. Pictures of the City of Washington in the Past. Washington, D.C.: Wm. Ballantyne and Sons, 1898.

Carey, Mathew. The Olive Branch. 6th ed. Philadelphia: Carey, 1815.

Centennial History of the City of Washington, D.C. Dayton: Published for H. W. Crew by the United Brethren Publishing House, 1892.

Clark, Allen C. Greenleaf and Law in the Federal City. Washington, D.C.: W. F. Roberts, 1901.

—— "The Trollopes," Columbia Historical Society Records, XXXVII-XXXVIII, 79–100. Washington, 1937.

Coke, E. T. A Subaltern's Furlough. Vol. I. New York: J. and J. Harper, 1833.

Commager, Henry Steele, ed. Documents of American History. 5th ed. New York: Appleton-Century-Crofts, 1949.

Congressional Globe. 23d through 35th Congresses, 1833–59. 28 vols. Washington, D.C.: Blair and Rives (or John C. Rives), 1837–60.

Cooley, E. A Description of the Etiquette at Washington City. Philadelphia: E. B. Clarke, 1829.

Cooper, James Fenimore. Notions of the Americans: Picked Up by a Travelling Bachelor. Vol. II. Philadelphia: Carey, Lea and Carey, 1828.

Cresson, W. P. James Monroe. Chapel Hill: University of North Carolina Press, 1946.

Crowinshield, Francis B., ed. Letters of Mary Boardman Crowninshield. Cambridge, Mass.: Riverside Press, 1905.

Cunningham, Noble E. The Jeffersonian Republicans, 1789–1801. Chapel Hill: University of North Carolina Press, 1957.

Cutler, William Parker, and Julia Perkins. Life, Journals and Correspondence of Rev. Manasseh Cutler. Vol. II. Cincinnati: Robert Clarke, 1888.

Dallinger, Frederick W. Nominations for Elective Office in the United States. New York, London, and Bombay: Longmans, Green and Company, 1897.

Dangerfield, George. The Era of Good Feelings. New York: Harcourt, Brace and Company, 1952.

D'Arusmont, Frances. Views of Society and Manners in America. London: Longman, Hurst, Rees, Orme, and Brown, 1822.

Davis, Richard Beale. The Abbé Correa in America, 1812–1820. American Philosophical Society Transactions, n.s., Vol. XLV, Part 2. Philadelphia, 1955.

De Roos, F. Fitzgerald. Personal Narrative of Travels in the United States and Canada in 1826. 3d ed. London: William Harrison Ainsworth, 1827.

Dictionary of American Biography. 20 vols. New York: Charles Scribner's Sons, 1928–37.

District of Columbia Sesquicentennial of the Establishment of the Permanent Seat of the Government [catalogue of exhibits in the Library of Congress, April 24, 1950, to April 24, 1951]. Washington, D.C.: Government Printing Office, 1950.

Donnan, Elizabeth, ed. Papers of James A. Bayard. Annual Report of the American Historical Association for the Year 1913. Vol. II. Washington, D.C.: Government Printing Office, 1915.

Ellis, John B. The Sights and Secrets of the National Capital. New York: United States Publishing Company, 1869.

Emery, Fred A. "Washington Newspapers," Columbia Historical Society Records, XXXVII–XXXVIII, 41–72. Washington, 1937.

Fearon, Henry Bradshaw. Sketches of America. 3d ed. London: Longman, Hurst, Rees, Orme, and Brown, 1819.

The Federalist. Modern Library Edition. New York: Random House, 1937.

Fergusson, Adam. Practical Notes Made during a Tour in Canada, and a Portion of the United States, in MDCCCXXXI. Edinburgh: William Blackwood; London: T. Cadell, 1834.

Follett, Mary P. The Speaker of the House of Representatives. New York: Longmans, Green and Company, 1896.

Ford, Worthington C. "Jefferson and the Newspaper," Columbia Historical Society Records, VIII, 79–111. Washington, 1905.

Foster, Augustus J. Jeffersonian America. San Marino, Calif.: The Huntington Library, 1954.

Fuller, Hubert B. The Speakers of the House. Boston: Little, Brown and Company, 1909.

Gallatin, Albert. Writings. Vol. I. Edited by Henry Adams, Philadelphia: J. B. Lippincott, 1879.

Galloway, George B. History of the House of Representatives. New York: Thomas Y. Crowell, 1961.

Gibbs, George. Memoirs of the Administrations of Washington and John Adams. Vol. II. New York: William van Norden, 1846.

Goodwin, Maud Wilder. Dolly Madison. New York: Charles Scribner's Sons, 1897.

Green, Constance McLaughlin. Washington: Village and Capital, 1800–1878. Princeton: Princeton University Press, 1962.

Grund, Francis J. Die Aristokratie in Amerika aus dem Tagebuch eines Deutschen Edelmanns. Vol II. Stuttgart: J. G. Cotta, 1839.

Hall, Captain Basil. Travels in North America in the Years 1827 and 1828. Vol. III. Edinburgh: Cadell and Company, 1829.

Hall, Francis. Travels in Canada and the United States in 1816 and 1817. London: Longman, Hurst, Rees, Orme, and Brown, 1818.

Hamilton, Thomas. Men and Manners in America. Vol. II. Edinburgh: William Blackwood; London: T. Cadell, 1833.

Harlow, Ralph V. The History of Legislative Methods in the Period before 1825. New Haven: Yale University Press, 1917.

Harriott, John. Struggles through Life. Vol. III. 3d ed. London: Longman, Hurst, Rees, Orme, and Browne, 1815.

Harris, Joseph P. The Advice and Consent of the Senate. Berkeley and Los Angeles: University of California Press, 1953.

Haynes, George H. The Senate of the United States. Vol. I. Boston: Houghton Mifflin Company, 1938.

Hines, Christian. Early Recollections of Washington City. Washington, D.C.: Chronicle Book and Job Print., 1866.

Hopkinson, Francis. The Miscellaneous Essays and Occasional Writings of Francis Hopkinson, Esq. Vol. I. Philadelphia: T. Dobson, 1792.

Howitt, E. Selections from Letters Written during a Tour through the United States in the Summer and Autumn of 1819. Nottingham: J. Dunn, [1820?].

Hunt, Gaillard. The Department of State of the United States. New Haven: Yale University Press, 1914.

—— Life in America One Hundred Years Ago. New York and London: Harper and Brothers, 1914.

Huntington, Samuel. "Letters from the Samuel Huntington Correspondence, 1800–1812," Tract No. 95, Annual Reports of the Western Reserve Historical Society, Part II, pp. 57–151. Cleveland, 1915.

Ingersoll, Charles J. Historical Sketch of the Second War between the United States of America and Great Britain. 2 vols. Philadelphia: Lea and Blanchard, 1845–49.

Jackson, Richard P. The Chronicles of Georgetown, D.C. Washington, D.C.: R. C. Polkinhorn, 1878.

Janson, Charles William. The Stranger in America, 1793–1806. New York: The Press of the Pioneers, 1935. Reprinted from the London edition of 1807.

Jefferson, Thomas. The Works of Thomas Jefferson. Vols. IX, X, XI, XII. Edited by Paul Leicester Ford. Federal Edition. New York: G. P. Putnam's Sons, 1905.

—— The Writings of Thomas Jefferson. Vols. VIII, IX. Edited by Andrew A. Lipscomb and Albert E. Bergh. Washington, D.C.: Thomas Jefferson Memorial Association, 1905.

Kennedy, John P. Memoirs of the Life of William Wirt, Attorney General of the United States. Vol. II. Philadelphia: Lea and Blanchard, 1849.

Kite, Elizabeth S. L'Enfant and Washington. Baltimore: The Johns Hopkins Press, 1929.

Kurtz, Stephen G. The Presidency of John Adams. Philadelphia: University of Pennsylvania Press, 1957.

La Rochefoucauld-Liancourt, François Alexandre Frédéric, duc de. Travels through the United States and Upper Canada in the Years 1795–1797. Vol. II. London: R. Phillips, 1799.

Latimer, Louise Payson. Your Washington and Mine. New York: Charles Scribner's Sons, 1924.

Latrobe, John H. B. The Capitol and Washington at the Beginning of the Present Century. Baltimore: W. K. Boyle, 1881 [?].

Learned, Henry Barrett. "Some Aspects of the Cabinet Meeting," Columbia Historical Society Records, XVIII, 95–143. Washington, 1915.

Leech, Margaret. Reveille in Washington. New York: Harper and Brothers, 1941.

Lubell, Samuel. The Future of American Politics, 2d ed., rev. Anchor Books. New York: Doubleday and Company, 1956.

McCormick, Richard P. "New Perspectives in Jacksonian Politics," *American Historical Review*, LXV (January, 1960), 288–301.

Mackall, Sally Somervell. Early Days of Washington. Washington, D.C.: Neale, 1899.

McKenney, Thomas L. Memoirs, Official and Personal. Vol. I. 2d ed. New York: Paine and Burgess, 1846.

Maclay, William. The Journal of William Maclay. New York: Albert and Charles Boni, 1927.

McMaster, John B. A History of the People of the United States. Vol. I. New York: D. Appleton and Company, 1938.

Madison, James. Letters and Other Writings, Published by Order of Congress. 4 vols. Philadelphia, 1865.

Mann, Mary Lee, ed. A Yankee Jeffersonian. Cambridge, Mass.: Harvard University Press, 1958.

Marryat, Captain Frederick. Diary in America. Vol. II. London: Longman, Orme, Brown, Green, and Longmans, 1839.

Martineau, Harriet. Retrospect of Western Travel. Vol. I. London: Saunders and Otley, 1838.

Mayo, Bernard. Henry Clay. Vol. I. Boston: Houghton Mifflin Company, 1937.

Melish, John. Travels in the United States of America. Vol. I. Philadelphia: T. and G. Palmer, 1812.

Millis, Walter. Arms and Men: A Study of American Military History. New York: Mentor Books, 1958.

Mitchill, Samuel L. "Letters from Washington," *Harper's New Monthly Magazine*, LVIII, No. 347 (April, 1879), 740–55.

Monroe, James. The Writings of James Monroe. Stanislaus Murray Hamilton, ed. 7 vols. New York: G. P. Putnam's Sons, 1898–1903.

Morison, Samuel E., ed. The Life and Letters of Harrison Gray Otis. Boston and New York: Houghton Mifflin Company, 1913.

Morris, Anne Carey, ed. The Diary and Letters of Gouverneur Morris. Vol. II. New York: Charles Scribner's Sons, 1888.

Morrison, Alfred J., ed. The District in the XVIIIth Century. [Washington, D.C.]: Judd and Detweiler, 1909.

Morrison, William M. Morrison's Stranger's Guide to the City of Washington. Washington, D.C.: William M. Morrison, 1842.

Nash, Gary B. " '. . . and Distinguished Guests,' " *Princeton Alumni Weekly*, LXIV, No. 1 (September 24, 1963), 37–42.

Neustadt, Richard E. Presidential Power: The Politics of Leadership. New York and London: John Wiley and Sons, 1960.

Nicolay, Helen. Our Capital on the Potomac. New York and London: Century Company, 1924.

Osborne, John B. "Removal of the Government to Washington," Columbia Historical Society Records, III, 136–60. Washington, 1900.

Ostrogorski, M. "The Rise and Fall of the Nominating Caucus, Legislative and Congressional," *American Historical Review*, V, No. 2 (December, 1899), 253–83.

Padover, Saul K. The Complete Jefferson. New York: Tudor Books, 1943.

Palmer, John. Journal of Travels in the United States of America and in Lower Canada. London: Sherwood, Neely, and Jones, 1818.

Parton, James. Life of Andrew Jackson. Vol. III. New York: Mason Brothers, 1860.

Phillips, P. Lee. The Beginnings of Washington. Washington, D.C.: W. F. Roberts, 1917.

Plumer, William, Jr. Life of William Plumer. Boston: Phillips, Sampson, and Company, 1857.

Pope-Hennessy, Una, ed. The Aristocratic Journey, Being the Outspoken Letters of Mrs. Basil Hall Written during a Fourteen Months' Sojourn in America, 1827–1828. New York and London: G. P. Putnam's Sons, 1931.

Quincy, Edmund. Life of Josiah Quincy. Boston: Ticknor and Fields, 1868.

A Register of Officers and Agents, Civil, Military, and Naval, in the Service of the United States on the 30th of September, 1829. Washington, D.C.: William A. Davis, 1830.

Rice, Stuart A. Quantitative Methods in Politics. New York: Alfred A. Knopf, 1928.

Riley, J. F. The History of Old Washington. New York: J. F. Riley, 1902.

Schachner, Nathan. The Founding Fathers. New York: G. P. Putnam's Sons, 1954.

—— Thomas Jefferson. Vol. II. New York: Appleton-Century-Crofts, 1951.

Schattschneider, Elmer E. Party Government. New York: Farrar and Rinehart, 1942.

Schurz, Carl. Henry Clay. Vol. I. Boston and New York: Houghton Mifflin Company, 1887.

Shipp, J. E. D. Giant Days, or The Life and Times of William H. Crawford. Americus, Ga.: Southern Printers, 1909.

Singleton, Esther. The Story of the White House. Vol. I. New York: S. S. McClure, 1907.

Smith, John Cotton. The Correspondence and Miscellanies of the Hon. John Cotton Smith. New York: Harper and Brothers, 1847.

Smith, Margaret Bayard. The First Forty Years of Washington Society. New York: Charles Scribner's Sons, 1906.

Spofford, Ainsworth R. The Founding of Washington City. Baltimore: J. Murphy and Co., 1881.

Stanwood, Edward. A History of the Presidency. Boston and New York: Houghton Mifflin Company, 1903.

Story, William W., ed. Life and Letters of Joseph Story. Vol. I. Boston: C. C. Little and J. Brown, 1851.

Stuart, James. Three Years in North America. 2d ed. rev. 2 vols. Edinburgh: Robert Cadell; London: Whittaker and Company, 1833.

Sunderland, Byron. A Sketch of the Life of William Gunton. Washington, D.C.: J. L. Pearson, 1878.

Sydnor, Charles S. "The One-Party Period of American History," *American Historical Review*, LI (April, 1946), 439–51.

Thompson, Charles S. The Rise and Fall of the Nominating Caucus. [New Haven, 1902?]

Thornton, Mrs. William. "Diary," Columbia Historical Society Records, X, 88–226. Washington. 1907.

Thwaites, Reuben Gold, ed. Early Western Travels, 1748–1846. Vols. XI, XII. Cleveland: Arthur H. Clark, 1905.

Tindall, William. Origin and Goverment of the District of Columbia. Washington, D.C.: Government Printing Office, 1907.

Tocqueville, Alexis de. Democracy in America. 2 vols. New York: Vintage Books, 1954.

Todd, Charles Burr. The Story of Washington. New York and London: G. P. Putnam's Sons, 1889.

Trollope, Frances M. Domestic Manners of the Americans. 2 vols. London: Whittaker, Treacher and Company, 1832.

Truman, David B. The Congressional Party. New York and London: John Wiley and Sons, 1959.

—— The Governmental Process. New York: Alfred A. Knopf, 1960.

—— "The Presidency and Congressional Leadership: Some Notes on Our Changing Constitution," *Proceedings of the American Philosophical Society*, CIII, No. 5 (October, 1959), 687–92.

Tudor, Henry. Narrative of a Tour in North America. 2 vols. London: James Duncan, 1834.

Twining, Thomas. Travels in America 100 Years Ago. New York: Harper and Brothers, 1894.

United States Census Office. Second through Ninth Census, 1800–1870. Washington, D.C., 1801–71.

United States Congress. Annals of the Congress of the United States. 1st through 18th Congresses, 1789–1824. 42 vols. Washington, D.C.: Gales and Seaton, 1832–61.

—— The Congressional Directory. 10th through 21st Congresses, 1807–29. Washington, D.C., 1807–29.

—— Register of Debates in Congress. 18th through 25th Congresses, 1825–37. Washington, D.C.: Gales and Seaton, 1825–37.

Van Cortlandt, Pierre. Letters. MS, New York Public Library.

Varnum, Joseph B., Jr. The Seat of Government of the United States. 2d ed. Washington, D.C.: R. Farnham, 1854.

Vedder, Mrs. Sarah E. Reminiscences of the District of Columbia. St. Louis: A. R. Fleming, 1909.

Vigne, Godfrey T. Six Months in America. Vol. I. London: Whittaker, Treacher and Company, 1832.

Wagstaff, Henry M., ed. The Papers of John Steele. Vol. I. Raleigh, N.C.: Edwards and Broughton, 1924.

Wakefield, Priscilla. Excursions in North America. 3d ed. London: Darton, Harvey, and Darton, 1819.

Walters, Raymond, Jr. Albert Gallatin. New York: The Macmillan Company, 1957.

Wandell, Samuel, and Meade Minnigerode. Aaron Burr. Vol. I. New York and London: G. P. Putnam's Sons, 1927.

Warden, D. B. A Statistical, Political, and Historical Account of the United States of North America. Vol. III. Edinburgh: Archibald Constable and Company, 1819.

Wayland, Francis Fry. Andrew Stevenson, Democrat and Diplomat, 1785–1857. Philadelphia: University of Pennsylvania Press, 1949.

Webster, Fletcher, ed. The Private Correspondence of Daniel Webster. Vol. I. Boston: Little, Brown and Company, 1957.

Weld, Isaac, Jr. Travels through the States of North America. Vol. I. 2d ed. London: John Stockdale, 1799.

Wharton, Anne Hollingsworth. Salons Colonial and Republican. Philadelphia and London: J. B. Lippincott, 1900.

—— Social Life in the Early Republic. Philadelphia and London: J. B. Lippincott, 1902.

White, Leonard D. The Federalists. New York: The Macmillan Company, 1948.

—— The Jacksonians. New York: The Macmillan Company, 1954.

—— The Jeffersonians. New York: The Macmillan Company, 1951.

Whitridge, Frederick W. Caucus System. Economic Tracts, No. 8. New York: The Society for Political Education, 1883.

Bibliography

Willson, Beckles. Friendly Relations: A Narrative of Britain's Ministers and Ambassadors to America. Boston: Little, Brown and Company, 1934.

Wilson, Woodrow. Congressional Government. 13th ed. Boston and New York: Houghton Mifflin Company, 1898.

Wiltse, Charles E. John C. Calhoun, Nationalist, 1782–1828. Indianapolis and New York: Bobbs-Merrill, 1944.

Wright, Frances. *See* D'Arusmont, Frances.

INDEX

Adams, John, 5, 52, 74, 230
Adams, John Quincy, 58, 114, 116; as President, 162, 188-90, 237-39, 247; as Secretary of State, 192, 217, 222, 223, 224-25, 226, 243-44, 244-45
Alexandria, Va., 17, 24, 184
Apathy, *see* Indifference
Appointment policy and practice: House Speaker, 132-35; presidential, 159, 174-78; Senate confirmation, 176, 183; cabinet members, 222-23, 242-43

Bloc voting, *see* Voting blocs
Boardinghouse groups: of legislators on Capitol Hill, 98-106; composition of (1807-28), 98-100, 99 (*table*); bloc voting, 101-5, 103 (*table*), 269-71*n*66-68; roll calls, agreement on, 1807-29, 104, 106 (*table*), 270-71*n*67, 68; party solidarity and 123-24, 133-34, 274*n*31; representation in House committee chairmanships, 132-33; attempts to unite different, 138-40; cohesion in voting on 24 roll calls, 139-40, 141 (*table*); changes in, 198-201, 199 (*table*)

Cabinet: political function and business of, 230-33; under Monroe, 230, 235-37, 242, 243, 247; under Jefferson, 231, 233; under Madison, 233-35; under J. Q. Adams, 237-39, 241, 242, 243, 245, 247, 290*n*4, 291*n*32, 292*n*41; reasons for failure in its political functions, 239-47
Cabinet members: as spokesmen for

President, 166-67; Senate confirmation, 176; appointment of, 176, 222-23, 242-43, 284*n*55, 292*n*47; past experience of, 176-77, 283*n*54, 284*n*55; social status of, 216; competition for Presidency, 223-24, 226, 227; development of secretarial salons, 224-27
Cabinet-presidential relations, 229-49
Calhoun, John C., 116, 223, 226, 237, 249, 292*n*46
Capital, *see* Governmental community
Capitol, 44-45, 75; as center of life of legislators, 87
Capitol Hill, 68, 71, 87-153; social groupings on, 98-107; *see also* Legislators
Careers: attitudes toward, by members of government, 51-57
Caucuses: congressional nominating, 113-17, 138, 147, 148, 161-62, 187, 223, 237, 245, 273-74*nn*26, 27; policy, infrequent use of, 125-27, 276*nn*39, 40; of state delegations, 139-40, 280*n*87
Civil staff: housing of, 22; presidential appointment of, 175; local origins of, 213, 288*n*1; low social status of, 215-16
Clay, Henry, 116, 128; as Speaker of House, 131-35, 203; as Secretary of State, 218, 225, 226, 241, 243
Cohesion and solidarity, party: boardinghouse blocs as obstacles to, 123-24, 133-34 (*see also* Voting blocs); lack of, on policy issues, 123-25, 133-34, 279*n*71; voting on 24 roll calls, by state delegations and boardinghouse groups, 139-40, 141 (*table*), 287*n*66; *see also* Conflict; Voting

304 *Index*